Acting and Being

Elizabeth Hess

Acting and Being

Explorations in Embodied Performance

Elizabeth Hess
Independent scholar
New York, New York, USA

ISBN 978-1-349-95729-3   ISBN 978-1-349-95106-2   (eBook)
DOI 10.1057/978-1-349-95106-2

Cover image: © miljko / Getty Images

Printed on acid-free paper

This Palgrave Macmillan imprint is published by Springer Nature
The registered company is Macmillan Publishers Ltd. London
The registered company address is: The Campus, 4 Crinan Street, London, N1 9XW, United Kingdom

ACKNOWLEDGEMENTS

Many hearts, minds and souls have inspired my acting and being through their support and recognition as I've explored the extraordinary truth and beauty of embodied performance. Their artistry and integrity has encouraged me to embrace the unknown with compassion and curiosity as I continue to follow my path, wherever it may lead.

My heart-felt thanks to:

Marjorie Forman, who has handed me back to myself with love, freeing me to share my inner discoveries through my artistry;

Nafe Katter, at the University of Connecticut, who told me I was a born teacher, long before I recognized its transformative role in my life as a theater artist;

Helen Cook, at New York University's (NYU), Tish School of the Arts (TSOA), Playwrights Horizons Theater School (PHTS), who gave me the freedom to treat my acting classes like a joyous laboratory of creative experimentation;

Mary Bitel, Craig Foisey and Sarah Ryndack at NYU's TSOA, Open Arts, who generously provided the opportunity to lead a workshop in embodied performance for the NYU acting community at large;

Rachel Jett at Eugene O'Neill Theater Center, National Theater Institute, for her fierce grace and embrace of my ever-evolving performance practices, preceded by Jeff Janesheski, who encouraged my growing interest in heightened storytelling;

Larry Sacharow at Fordham University, for his inclusivity and interdisciplinary artistic initiatives, followed by Matthew Maguire, for providing invaluable time and space for collaborative creation;

v

Frank and Eliza Ventura at Collaborative Arts Project (CAP21), for broadening my understanding and incorporation of multi-disciplinary influences;

Mary Fleisher at Marymount Manhattan College, for her openness and encouragement of my embodied approach to text work;

All the international theater and festival directors, organizations, educators and artists who have invited me to perform, teach and collaborate in a multitude of ways;

Fellow NYU faculty members who planted seeds and supported my process in numerous ways: Jean Andzulis, Fritz Ertl, Victoria Flores, Maggie Low, Theresa McCarthy, Ruben Polendo, Mary Robinson;

Former colleagues who have invited me to share my work in the classroom, or in my writing: Christine Farrell (Sarah Lawrence College), Cecilia Rubino (The New School);

Seminal teachers and coaches who encouraged me to spread my wings early in my evolution as an artist: David Perry at the Royal Academy of Dramatic Art (RADA), Andrew Neil, Helena Kaut-Howson at the London Academy of Dramatic Art (LAMDA) and Harold Guskin (private coach);

All the retreat, class and workshop leaders and specialists who guided me on thrilling adventures into unchartered embodied and imaginative territory—Per Brahe (Sacred Mask), Ephia and Jeff Gburek (Djalma Primordial Science), Dawn Saito (Butoh), Christine Sang (Movement Mandalas), Pamela Prather (Fitzmaurice Voicework), Penny Kreizer (Extended Voice), Mahayana Landowne (Viewpoints) Lane Savadore (Contact Improvisation and Viewpoints), Dan Safer (Contact Improvisation), Lainey Tant, Betsy Long (Kundalini Yoga), Theodora Skipitares (Puppetry), Pauline Grove and the Huli Tribe of Papua New Guinea (Sacred Dance) and Alix Keast (Shiatsu) for fine-tuning my physical instrument and teaching me to listen to the body's wisdom;

The advanced acting students at NYU, the beginning acting students at Molloy College/CAP21 and the photographer Dylan Kenseth, along with the editing expertise of Lisa Sacks, whose brave and compelling explorations into various states of being were captured so beautifully on camera for this book: Dylan Arredondo, Chloe Chappa, Madeline Corcoran, Gabrielle Chun, John Guaragna, Sarah Kaufman, Nikky Martin, Claire Mercier, Alexander Might, Mickaila Perry, Mary Rising, Daniel Roberts, Frankie Rocco, Danielle Sacks, Sarah Sumner, Katelyn Shreiner, Angela Strauman, Taylor Windle;

All my students and collaborators over the years who have dived into explorations in embodied performance with such courage and commitment and taught me to trust my own impulses, experience and imagination through their fearless example;

Cheryl King, for reading an early draft of the book and offering invaluable insights and adjustments, followed by reflections and responses from Maggie Low, Noel Carmichael Mseze and Danielle Sacks, who, in addition, patiently gathered together all the permissions;

Antje Oegel, my literary agent, for her on-going belief in my artistry and her attention to all the details;

Finally, Jen McCall and Felicity Plester, my editors, for responding to my voice and vision and inviting me to join their book list at Palgrave Macmillan, and April James, their assistant, for her thoughtful and generous responses to all my questions and queries.

CONTENTS

LIST OF FIGURES

CHAPTER 1

Introduction

There is no right or wrong in acting: there is only alive or dead. It can be tempting for actors to establish a set "truth" rather than embrace a strong yet flexible practice that leads to an ever-evolving and animated one. This search for an immediate yet resonant truth plunges one into the unknown, where aliveness comes from an embodied experience of being, moment by moment. This "beingness" can be both exhilarating and terrifying as it calls forth complex inner vibrations and responds with compelling outer resonance.

In *The Open Door*, Peter Brook writes, "within us at every moment, like a giant instrument ready to be played, are strings whose tones and harmonies are our capacity to respond to vibrations from the invisible spiritual world which we often ignore, yet which we contact with every breath."[1]

I have created a safe framework—in which to play dangerously—that is based on interconnecting states of being: behavioral, physiological and psychological, which activate "notes" of living truth in imaginary circumstances. I have chosen to call this awakening of the artistic instrument *Acting and Being: Explorations in Embodied Performance*.

ORIGINS

This framework is a response to my own vibrations as an actor, educator, playwright and director: a journey into my interiority that began when I first became curious about acting while studying psychology as an undergradu-

© The Author(s) 2016
E. Hess, *Acting and Being*, DOI 10.1057/978-1-349-95106-2_1

ate. I was writing a paper on Sylvia Plath as viewed through a Freudian lens. As I read Plath's poetry aloud while conducting research, one poem in particular, "Two Sisters of Persephone,"[2] struck me with the most intimate and undiluted immediacy. It speaks of two girls, one of whom sits indoors, the other outside. All day long shade and light play between them like a duet. I had the sense that I was like the sister who sat without and wanted to venture within, so as to have an experience of both light and dark; to plumb the depths and bring their contents forth and thereby play both parts of that duet in an empathetic and inhabited way.

Hungry for a deeper understanding of artistic aliveness, I enrolled in the Shakespeare Summer School at The Royal Academy of Dramatic Art (RADA) and was introduced to vocal and physical training alongside in-depth text analysis and acting sessions. The course sparked my interest in the work of Constantin Stanislavski, whom I began to read at the suggestion of faculty members and fellow students. His teachings helped to further unlock an imaginative, as well as compassionate, response to the human condition—something as enlivening to the actor's craft at large as it is intrinsic to animating the world of Shakespeare. As Stanislavski writes, "a conscious, reasoned approach to the imagination often produces a bloodless, counterfeit presentment of life. This will not do for the theatre. Our art demands that an actor's whole nature be actively involved, that he give himself up, both mind and body, to his part."[3]

Because of this initial acting training my interest in the psyche transformed from an academic inquiry into a more personal search for authentic expression. As an actor I was asked to inhabit, rather than simply analyze, the inner and outer worlds of a character. This was both liberating and daunting as I began to discover the interplay between self and otherness—someone different and distinct from my own persona. My research into a play needed to move beyond understanding alone to encompass compassion for the character, and their resonance within myself, in order to create a complex and compelling portrayal.

This experience whetted my appetite and led to full-time study at The London Academy of Dramatic Art (LAMDA), where I was also introduced to the work of Jerzy Grotowski, whose psycho-physical actions were a natural evolution of Stanislavski's teachings. (Other outgrowths of Stanislavski's work are well known and include the "Method" of Lee Strasberg's studio, among others.)

Along with the investigation into emotional truth Grotowski focused on the encounter with the core self. "The man who makes an act of self-revelation is, so to speak, one who establishes contact with himself ... not merely a confrontation with his thoughts, but one involving his whole body from his instincts and his unconscious right up to his most lucid state."[4]

It was this desire for a "totality of beingness" that prompted me to further explore my own recesses and resources when I then moved to New York. I began to study privately with Harold Guskin, who instilled in me a healthy irreverence for self-imposed rules and restrictions that inhibited my instincts from igniting—whatever they may be! "Creativity occurs when things that don't seem to belong together make something new when joined. It's what I call the 'illogical conclusion'. That's what we want in our acting—characters who are not just recognizable but surprising, unexpected, stimulating."[5]

I learned that one's truth is uniquely one's own in all its complex layers. It was liberating to discover a genuine theatricality whereby I could embrace a character's truth and still go anywhere, physically, vocally and emotionally, as long as I returned to my core self again and again. My work was free to be spontaneous and grounded simultaneously.

At this time I also began to practice Kundalini yoga, with its emphasis on energy centers in the body. These centers are also referred to as "chakras," a Sanskrit word which means "wheels." Identifying these "wheels of energy" helped me develop a conscious relationship to the vibrations in my body, so that I could recognize areas that felt sluggish or serene, over-excited or grounded, dense or light. Unexpectedly, I discovered that I was now better able to detect the vibrations of a character moving within me as well. Thus I learned to house and adjust to their specific energy center as expressed within my artistic instrument. This embodied experience further encouraged me to marry my inner life with the imaginary circumstances of the character in an organic way.

Not surprisingly I felt the need for a strong emotional container to hold all the contents of an expanding sense of self. I was drawn to the teachings of Carl Jung and began to work with an analyst, with whom I uncovered a wealth of emotional riches in dream work. The unconscious is stirred during the rehearsal process, and this work also served to illuminate a character through allegorical identification and archetypal energy. Of course, all this material was being offered up from my own interiority, and at times there were epiphanies that were as unsettling as they were enlightening.

From my own inner search I know how important it is to remember the courage it takes for an artist to embrace the fullness of their truth. As Jung writes in "archetypal forms grounded on the instincts and giving expression to them, have a numinous quality that sometimes arouses fear."[6] Yet it is through this quest for artistic truth that we may also arrive at self-knowledge. Conversely, by tapping into our deepest selves and bringing those inner contents to light, we are able to transform those dark discoveries into artistic expression of great illumination and catharsis. Artistry can be an integral part of the soul's journey toward wholeness, just as the characters in Plath's "Two Sisters of Persephone," with their light and shade, are two sides of the self that create complex harmonies through the interplay of acting and being.

With this rich and varied background I eventually became a teacher myself—privately, in university courses, workshops and international master classes—and was humbled by the great task of encouraging courageous and compelling work that was as engrossing as it was illuminating. Initially I would ask an actor, "What is your impulse?" only to be met, more often than not, with a blank stare or the answer: "I don't know." As wonderful as it is to live in the unknown, it is quite another thing to be frozen with fear, or simply to sit with an "unplayed" instrument. I found it necessary to help actors find a way to first "break open" their artistic instrument, to take it out of its case, so to speak, and pick it up and play it with love, curiosity and wild inventiveness before moving on to more sophisticated and transformative storytelling involving the interplay of acting and being with others as well as within one's self.

I have sought to uncover yet another avenue for accessing one's artistic truth through explorations into various states of being, or conditions of existence, that underscore the continuing need for a spontaneous, uncensored aliveness. By identifying behavioral, physical and psychological states of being, I have also generated various entry points into exploring the world of a play—be it original, devised or established text. Likewise, this approach can serve as a template whereby the actor can consciously identify, recognize or unlock a specific instinct, experience or act of imagination that feels "off-key": blocked or static; or conversely, "on pitch": released and present. The more alive an actor is, the more resonant their work becomes, creating an interplay of acting and being that is dynamic and layered.

This framework is meant to complement Stanislavski's teachings and those of other acting methodologies that are often an outgrowth of his work. Stanislavski encouraged experimentation, and he himself broke new ground by, for example, investigating psychological as well as physical actions; emotional memory as well as the magic "as if"; subtext as well as super-objective; inner as well as outer technique. But as

Stanislavski says, "Create your own method. Don't depend slavishly on mine. Make up something that will work for you! But keep breaking traditions, I beg you."[7]

In the process of creating my own "method" I have discovered, through interaction with fellow theater practitioners, that I've also been influenced unconsciously by others in the field, or that my approach resonates with aspects of their own creative process. As Jung might say, I have tapped into the collective unconscious—shared memory and/ or experience—and expressed it in a way that is unique to my psyche. I am pleased to be part of a long line of artists who've also sought relevance through experimentation, adaptation and innovation. And, like Stanislavski, I encourage others to also follow their own path, knowing that there are those who have gone before and blazed the trail, leaving their mark (visibly or viscerally) and offering possible ways to move forward into the unknown.

My own subliminal influences go back as far as *commedia dell'arte* with its archetypal characters and use of invented language to relate subversive stories through oblique means, which required an expanded sense of self that was equally immediate and elastic. Another influence, Michael Chekhov, coined the phrase "psychological gesture" to "mean the Gesture together with the Feelings connected with it,"[8] by which a character's essence is manifested in the actor's body. By engaging thought (or images), feelings and will-impulses in each psychological moment, he created a fluid relationship between psyche, soma and sentience. A third influence, Jacques Lecoq, developed "seven levels of tension" (which have been adapted by the theater company Complicite and others), in which actors move from a state of sub-relaxation to one of maximum resistance in conjunction with a setting that moves from an expression of survival to something close to asphyxiation.[9] This framework allowed the actor to embody a character's specific level of activation and awareness while also exploring some form of an elemental, movement and/or psychic landscape.

This interplay of acquired practices and unconscious influences is part of the continuing journey of actors, educators, directors and playwrights who are curious about and committed to uncovering their own voices and visions. Artistic openness inspires the re-interpretation of the existing canon of plays. It encourages the re-framing of known tools for acquiring the fundamentals of craft. It embraces the re-animation of the human condition in original work. It is through the non-duality of acquiring reliable techniques, while embracing fresh perspectives, that one arrives at genuine originality. This originality reflects one's singular search for a living truth which emerges in a spirit of receptivity to instruction, influence and the unknown.

This search for authentic artistic expression is particular to every theater artist and so, in laying out my own journey, I am simply offering it as an example of one individual process so far. Again, this framework is meant to embrace, rather than exclude, existing acting techniques and methodologies in the ongoing quest for artistic truth which is a visible manifestation of a vital interiority. I have cited the origins of my inspiration to underline the ways in which this approach is not a prescription but a detailed description of a viable and variable path in the ever-unfolding search for inner truth and artistic expression.

Magic, Metaphor and Myth

In the ongoing quest for authentic expression the theater itself has once again broadened its scope, so that it not only reflects the world of naturalism and its investigation of the individual psyche, but also welcomes heightened realism and its investigation of the collective unconscious. In the theater's pursuit of relevance and revelation the "kitchen sink" is making room for the "symbolic stage." In this way artistic expression returns to its earliest roots by spiraling around and arriving there once again with a fresh orientation. Thus along with the search for artistic aliveness, I also wanted to explore this enlarged and ever-evolving theatrical landscape.

Magic (to pretend; as if), in its interplay between truth and illusion, offers the possibility of transformation on both an individual and a collective basis. The behavioral states invoke sympathetic magic as a means to animate the essence of a character while also enlivening the world of the play. In *Acrobat of the Heart* Stephen Wangh states, "We fill the world around us with meaning ... many ancient religions were based on the belief that every object had a spirit. Of course we modern, rational folks have banished the gods of heaven ... Yet every once in a while our magical, animistic tendencies evince themselves."[10]

Metaphor, (to compare; as like), by illuminating the relationship between self and otherness, offers dynamic inter-relatedness. The physiological states incorporate the metaphors of body language and conditions that can also express collective alignment, "dis-ease," or uncomfortable truths. Aristotle in his *Poetics* writes that "to make good metaphors implies an eye for resemblances."[11] In its indirection, metaphor also creates a safe environment in which to explore volatile and visceral responses.

Myth (to pattern after; as in), intertwines universal and personal themes, leading to an expanded sense of self through the larger lens of collective experience. The psychological states engage the transpersonal as a way of tapping into archetypes that illuminate our shared humanity. As Edith Hamilton states in *Mythology*, the miracle of a myth is its ability to foster "a humanized world, men freed from the paralyzing fear of an omnipotent Unknown."[12]

As we employ magic, metaphor and myth to re-animate and re-imagine inner truth we also address the extraordinary, the transformative and the metaphysical.

Conversely, when we look for tangible symbols and signs that are emblematic and allegorical we can excite the instincts without retreating into overtly analytical thinking.

It is necessary, too, that practitioners of theater continue to find salient ways of engaging the uncertainty and "otherness" of a changing world. Chaos and confusion are as much a part of multiculturalism as innovation and re-invention. Images and information often overwhelm sensual and somatic response. Convenience and commercialization compete with our inner resources and appetite for life.

Susan Sontag in *Against Interpretation* has another interesting take on the need to refocus our artistic attention.

> Ours is a culture based on excess, on overproduction; the result is a steady loss of the sharpness in our sensory experience. All the conditions of modern life—its material plenitude, its sheer crowdedness—conjoin to dull our sensory facilities ... What is important now is to recover our senses. We must learn to see more, to hear more, to feel more. Our task is not to find the maximum amount of content in a work of art, much less to squeeze more content out of the work than is already there. Our task is to cut back content so that we can see the thing at all.[13]

Perhaps clarity comes by addressing the complexity or, should I say, the complications of modern-day life, by cutting through our over-loaded "techno" mindset to speak directly from the heart in all its messy glory.

The poet Rumi offers a mystical orientation when he writes:

> Thinking gives off smoke to prove the existence of fire. A
> mystic sits in the burning.
> There are wonderful shapes in rising smoke that imagination
> loves to watch. But it's
> A mistake to leave the fire for that filmy sight. Stay
> here at the flame's core.[14]

It takes great courage to "stay here at the flame's core," to embrace the unknown again and again, rather than settle for "smoke and mirrors" and the safety of familiar, even if comfortable, habits. But if encouraged, such openness can be as exhilarating as it is humbling; as intoxicating as it is unnerving; as astonishing as it is unpremeditated.

This means that the questions themselves can be animating and enlivening. As Rainer Maria Rilke writes, "Do not hunt for the answers—they cannot be given to you because you cannot live them. What matter is that you live everything. And you must now *live* the questions."[15] As I am often reminded on stage and off: the struggle itself is interesting.

Yet the paradox remains: the actor's "soul" work needs to be crafted in order to be surprising; specific to be immediate; grounded to be dangerous. One needs to translate this "spontaneous combustion" into a coherent and workable practice.

* * *

This book is divided into three parts. Part 1, "States of Being," focuses on a *description* of the framework itself which addresses and expands the actor's artistic aliveness through interconnecting behavioral, physiological and psychological states of being. Behavioral states focus on sentience, soul and instinct; physiological states focus on soma, body and experience; psychological states focus on psyche, mind and imagination.

The seven behavioral states include: primal, organic, willful, humanoid, psychic, mythic and cosmic.
The seven physiological states include: root, sacral, navel, heart, throat, third eye and crown.
The seven psychological states include: survival, connection, power, love, communication, awareness and destiny.

These states of being evolve through the embodiment of an essence and level of consciousness, the activation of an energy center, body language and sense and the engagement of an archetype and universal theme. The progression from state to state generates increasingly layered character work that illuminates an expanding range of possible actions and objectives while fostering collaborative creation and dynamic storytelling.

Part 2, "Explorations in Embodied Performance," focuses on the *application* of states of being, which embrace impulses, experience and imagination from various entry points to generate transformative, empathetic and expansive artistic expression.

Behavioral explorations include: elemental landscapes, levels of consciousness and essences.

Physiological explorations include: movement landscapes, senses and energy centers.

Psychological explorations include: psychic landscapes, universal themes and archetypes.

Approach to the states of being is conducted with instructions for the implementation of explorations in embodied performance. These include orientation, collective and actor-generated explorations as well as side-coaching and prompts, feedback and journaling. The interplay of the explorations ignites dynamic exchange, deep listening and moment-to-moment discovery. Orientation, collective and actor-generated explorations combine to create a complex relationship to one's own, and others', artistic expression through work that is informed and unpremeditated, singular and collaborative.

Part 3, "The Interplay of Acting and Being," focuses on the *adaptation* of explorations in embodied performance into states of being to address character work, scene study and production of a theatrical event. Explorations in embodied performance now become an integral part of character, play and rehearsal research, including implementation in the production of established texts and the creation of original or devised work.

A framework that engages character and play elements based on Stanislavski's teachings, as well as story elements inspired by Jung's theory of Individuation and the hero/heroine's journey, becomes the foundation for research. This provides actors from different schools of thought with a common language to spring forth in divergent ways. It also provides a bridge between techniques that can be tailored or transfigured to suit any genre.

Character elements include: origins, drives, issues, relationships, age, ability and arc.

Play elements include: setting, actions, objectives, characters, time, activities and super-objective.

Story elements include: reality, search, rebellion, rupture, involution, evolution and return.

The interplay of states of being with the elements helps to elucidate the character's inner monologue while driving outer actions forward. This aids in the creation of a complex, layered journey of a play, performance piece, or theatrical event in an organic and original manner. In this way, explorations help create storytelling that is clear and credible while being equally visceral and surprising.

* * *

The framework itself has been built primarily through studio work with either university-level acting students who are beginning to acquire the tools of their craft, or more advanced students who incorporate explorations into scene study or into original and devised work while also excavating specific blocks or restrictions they still encounter along the way.

This approach has also been implemented in acting classes for non-majors from all levels of training and disciplines. It has often had a significant impact on their chosen fields, helping to access self-expression, communication and collaboration skills that they can implement "on the job," both directly and indirectly. In this way, self-awareness can be an unexpected gift that comes along with a growing range of emotional and artistic expression. One's formation of ideas, strategies and dreams is informed by the search for a revealing and resonant truth.

I also encourage the use of this framework as a source of reference for seasoned actors, teachers, directors and playwrights who are looking for ways to stimulate or re-invigorate their artistic voice and vision in an embodied way. The approach itself helps to identify areas in need of attention by breaking down states of being into recognizable energies, alignments and orientations as well as identifying inhibitions, blocks and area of resistance.

This approach can likewise be valuable as an entry point into physical theater, multi-media projects, performance art and cross-cultural collaborations, owing to the nature of its elastic approach. The framework is flexible yet durable; open yet focused; inclusive yet expansive.

NOTES

1. Peter Brook, *The Open Door, The Golden Fish*, New York: Theatre Communications Group, Inc., 1995, p. 98.
2. Sylvia Plath, "Two Sisters of Persephone" in *Crossing the Water: Transitional Poems*, New York: Harper Perennial, 1971, p. 46.
3. Constantin Stanislavski, *An Actor Prepares*, New York: Routledge, 1989, p. 70.
4. Jerzy Grotowski, *Towards a Poor Theater*, New York: Routledge, 2002, p. 57.
5. Harold Guskin, *How to Stop Acting*, New York: Faber & Faber, Inc., 2003, pp. 66–67.
6. Carl Jung, *The Undiscovered Self*, New York: Mentor, 1957, p. 61.
7. Constantin Stanislavski, *The Stanislavski System*, by Sonia Moore, foreword by Joshua Logan, 2nd revised ed., New York: Penguin Books, 1984, p. xvi.
8. Michael Chekhov, *On the Technique of Acting*, New York; Harper Collins, 1991, p. 60.
9. Jacques Lecoq, *Theater of Movement and Gesture*, ed. David Bradby, New York: Routledge, 2006, pp. 89–91.
10. Steven Wangh, *Acrobat of the Heart*, New York: Vintage Books, 2000, p. 217.
11. Aristotle, *Aristotle's Poetics*, trans. S. H. Butcher, New York: Hill and Wang, 1961, XXII, p. 104.
12. Edith Hamilton, *Mythology*, New York: Warner Books, 1999, p. 17.
13. Susan Sontag, *Against Interpretation: And Other Essays*, New York: Farrar, Straus and Giroux, 1966, Part 9, p. 13.
14. Rumi, "Thinking and the Heart's Mystical Way," in *The Soul of Rumi*, trans. Coleman Barks, San Francisco: HarperSanFrancisco, 2001, p. 75.
15. Rainer Maria Rilke, *Letters to a Young Poet*, trans. Mark Harman, Cambridge, Massachusetts: Harvard University Press, 2011, letter 4, p. 46.

PART 1

States of Being

I have identified interlocking behavioral, physiological and psychological states of being. There are seven states in each category: a total of twenty-one states altogether. These states of being explore who we are at any given moment and how that is affected by the activation of specific conditions of existence. One can further refine the parameters of these states in the following way:

Behavior: sentience, soul and instinct;
Physiology: soma, body and experience;
Psychology: psyche, mind and imagination.
The behavioral states are: primal, organic, willful, humanoid, psychic, mythic, cosmic.
The physiological states are: root, sacral, navel, heart, throat, third eye, crown.
The psychological states are: survival, connection, power, love, communication, awareness, destiny.

Originally the basis for these states of being arose from my investigation into energy centers (vibrations) in the body. I have expanded upon these energy centers to represent different aspects of behavior, physiology and psychology. These states are flexible and fluid, not fixed and frozen. Neither are they hierarchical, like notes of a scale. One state informs another.

They can be in harmony or discord; complementary or conflicting. All are open to expansion and integration which in turn leads to increased awareness and invention.

I have consciously avoided the creation of a theory but instead offer an approach which is based on a series of "scales of actable notes." These "notes" (states of being), are activated through explorations that encourage visceral response by allowing meaning to arise from matter (substance) itself. Behavioral states focus on the embodiment of essences and impulses. Physiological states focus on the animation of bodily sense and feeling. Psychological states focus on the expansion of the emotional and imaginative palette.

Rather than imposing an external result, explorations illuminate the actor's inner truth and its outer manifestation as it unfolds in the moment. Consequently, each actor's journey is uniquely their own: creative expression rising up from their essential natures in relation to issues and authenticity; habits and awareness; attitudes and openness. Therefore there is no "correct" way to engage these explorations, no set gestural language or vocal placement or emotional expression.

The more flexible and open the instrument becomes, the more the truth will reveal itself in the doing. As fear of the unknown is embraced and transformed into aliveness, the actor becomes increasingly free of over-analysis and self-censorship. The actor breathes into an expanded sense of self which allows presence to come into play in surprising and unmediated ways.

The explorations can also be adapted and incorporated into character work, scene study, creation of original or devised work, rehearsal process and production. They are available for ongoing reference and endless interpretation. Just as I have arrived at this framework by adapting and incorporating other acting methodologies and related disciplines, so too does this approach seek to be inclusive, rather than exclusive. There is no one way to uncover the mystery of a character or the magic of storytelling.

CHAPTER 2

Behavioral States

FOUNDATION

The word "behavior" comes from the root words "to be" and "to have."[1] The foundation of the behavioral states is based on the exploration of various essences (to be) through embodiment (to have). Sympathetic *magic*—to pretend, as if—is activated through explorations of sentient beings of differing levels of consciousness set in diverse elemental landscapes. Through emulation, the actor suspends "everyday" expectations, allowing the imagination to inform the instincts in a way that is unstudied and transformative. Because this work is impressionistic rather than imitative, the actor incorporates the essential behavior of an "other"—a novel yet recognizable sentient being—in order to expand their range of responses.

Orientation, collective and actor-generated explorations encompass all three aspects of the behavioral states: elemental landscapes, levels of consciousness and essences. Orientation explorations are conducted as a group in which all participants engage in similar activity as a way to establish a working language. Collective explorations still involve the group as a whole but the individual actor begins to more fully entertain the multi-dimensionality of the essence they inhabit. Through the orientation and collective explorations the actors begin to recognize how these states reverberate within their own being. Actor-generated explorations are an opportunity to further investigate this interface. Finally, for each exploration I have included an example from a play or novel to illustrate the incorporation of the exploration into specific character work.

© The Author(s) 2016
E. Hess, *Acting and Being*, DOI 10.1057/978-1-349-95106-2_2

Instructions for implementing the explorations can be found in Part 2, "Explorations in Embodied Performance."

The more comfortable the actor becomes in embodying these behavioral states, the more they are able to access their impulses by uncovering and exercising them through the various explorations. They can begin to incorporate a specific behavioral state into character work, knowing that they are free to arrive at a spontaneous embodiment culled from a wide range of inbuilt possibilities.

Given that a character spends a good deal of time in conflict with self and/or others during the course of a play, their actions and reactions can be charged, visceral and unreflective. They often reveal their essence, which may initially be masked by socially appropriate behavior. Their essence, in turn, may be modulated by their level of consciousness. This interplay of urges and awareness may then generate character secrets of delicate subtlety or gross magnitude. It may also ignite an inner monologue that propels the character forward as they fulfill their psycho-physical actions, their rhythms, reflexes and responses resonating with their fears, hopes and desires.

Elemental Landscapes, Levels of Consciousness and Essences

By entering an *elemental landscape*—earth, water, fire, air, sound, light and ether—the actors conjure up an environment that gives them a context in which to activate the specific characteristics of a chosen behavioral state.

The states also reflect different *levels of consciousness*: instinct, impulse, intent, affect, influence, alteration and actualization, and these color one's experience and perception of self and other.

The states, primal, organic, willful, humanoid, psychic, mythic and cosmic, in turn reflect an evolution of *essence* from animal to spirit. By embodying an unfamiliar essence it's possible to arrive at a more deeply felt understanding of one's own nature—one that is intrinsic and unfiltered and all too human. By stepping away from identification with our humanness we find a willingness to suspend judgment as we embrace inborn qualities that are neither socialized nor self-referential.

INFLUENCES FROM RELATED DISCIPLINES

Animal Work and Extended Voice technique have been woven into the fabric of these explorations for their unpremeditated ability to grasp instinctual and imaginative immediacy.

Animal Work

Early in my training at LAMDA we spent an afternoon at the London Zoo, each observing a specific animal, whose behavior we translated into our own bodies back at the Academy. I had chosen to observe an orangutan who was squabbling with her mate over a banana, which she proceeded to eat without sharing. Afterwards she suddenly kissed her mate and groomed him until he stopped sulking! Clearly she was the boss, or at least she made sure her needs took precedence over her mate's. This observation was an invaluable insight when I later began working on the role of Natasha from Chekhov's *Three Sisters*. I now understood the character's withholding nature, flirtatiousness and possessive "nit-picking" as reflections of her innate instinct for survival. In a non-judgmental way I was inspired—through emulation of the orangutan's sentience—to make bold choices that were deeply empathetic and connected while being no less self-serving. Rather than approximate animal behavior, by distilling its essence it was possible for me to arrive at an aliveness that was unmediated and revealing.

In this way, we may discover that our character is essentially piggish, bullish or catty. By employing an animal metaphor we may arrive at their essence without premeditation. It is simply the character's nature to be a snake in the grass, chicken-hearted or an old goat. Therefore they may also be naturally inclined to butt heads, strut like a peacock or weep crocodile tears.

Extended Voice

Extended Voice technique encourages the release of sounds that are equally unscripted and innate. I first encountered Roy Hart's teachings on extended voice while in rehearsal for an original piece which focused on a victim of trauma. I wanted the text to move beyond language to address the "unspeakable" truth of the character. Not only did I find a soundscape that revealed her naked self, but I did so in a way that preserved the integrity of the character, allowing her to release painful contents without concretizing them.

It was liberating to connect to the inner life without an intellectual filter that required the formalization of thought. Emotions could rush to the surface in vocal emanations that were immediate and unsculpted, meaning they were also free of "polite" speech and socially acceptable thought and behavior.

STATES OF BEING

Primal

The first three behavioral states represent *inherent* behaviors which are reflections of the soul and are closely aligned to *animal* nature. The first of these, the primal state, is the most raw and uncensored. See Fig. 5.1.

Elemental Landscape: Earth

Earth can be grounding and make one feel planted and secure. It is the natural habitat of sentient creatures that burrow beneath it, snake their way through it or wallow in it. But it can also be challenging, as when one is uprooted by an explosion, sucked down by a mudslide or destabilized by an earthquake. These challenges present obstacles that need to be overcome in order to survive and, in doing so, drive life forward. We meet these challenges without conscious thought. "Fight or flight" automatically informs our actions. Afterwards we seek to restore our "footing," to "rest and digest."

In "earth" explorations it is as if earth were an outer layer of skin that one rubs up against or relaxes into as one feels their way: drawn down into it, nestling under it, struggling up against it, bathing in it, scurrying through it, groveling in it. This struggle or settling-in is accompanied by sounds that erupt out of the body in essential yet inarticulate ways. Vocalizations are naked and raw: rumblings from deep down inside like a self-satisfied growl, a gut-wrenching groan or a heart-felt moan. Whether ecstatic or agonized, they are undigested in the immediacy of their release.

Consciousness: Instinct

Instincts are unmediated and involuntary. We cannot will them or wish them away. They are all feeling and no formulation. Just like breath, instincts are innate and housed in the body without rational thought or conscious control. Sentient creatures in the primal state are governed by reactions that are unquestioned and immediate, allowing them to adapt to and engage their earth-bound environment with urgency if need be. They are adept at playing with extremes of light and dark; presence and absence; solidity and instability. They act and react with an animal wisdom that is inborn and automatic. Worms eat dirt as they move. Rats scurry through sewers and subway tunnels. Hippos cool off in mud.

Essence: Primal
In the primal state one is at the mercy of one's instincts. One breathes, eats and evacuates without conscious control or consent. It may feel like being submerged in primordial ooze where suppressed feelings swirl around inside one's innards. Primitive responses may offer up inklings of deeper, more unsettled and irrepressible urges. In the primal state a daily commuter bursts into road rage. A socialite howls with uncontrollable laughter. A patient murmurs incoherent nonsense while still sluggish from anesthesia.

Gregor Samsa in Franz Kafka's *Metamorphosis* moves beyond a metaphoric understanding of the primal state to embody it firsthand when he "...found himself changed in his bed into a monstrous vermin. He was lying on his back as hard as armor plate, and when he lifted his head a little, he saw his vaulted brown belly, sectioned by arch-shaped ribs...His many legs pitifully thin compared with the size of the rest of him, were waving helplessly before his eyes."[2]

Organic

The second behavioral state is still very much aligned with animal nature but it is more fluid and changeable. See Fig. 5.2.

Elemental Landscape: Water
Water leaves no imprint and yet its impact upon us can be profound. It is frightening to be pulled under by a furious undercurrent, yet soothing and sensuous to luxuriate in a warm bath. The fluid nature of water means our engagement with it needs to be equally flexible as we negotiate with its changeability, moment by moment. There are no correct, fixed or predetermined responses.

In "water" explorations, to "go with the flow" may be to accommodate or acquiesce. To "fight the tide" or "ride the wave" may be something we do with ambivalence or urgency as conditions fluctuate. We may swallow our feelings in silence or spit them out. This variability is mirrored in our breathing patterns as inhalation and exhalation rise and fall like waves, or come in gulps, sighs and whooshes that bubble up to the surface. Sounds from the deep echo in an incantatory way; murmurings flow forth like a babbling brook; hushed exclamations fly out like the spray from a waterfall.

Consciousness: Impulse
Impulses are characterized by their sudden and unreasonable desire to be enacted. They may be accompanied by a momentary flash of consideration

while one is in their grip, but they are as compelling as a wave upon which feelings ride with little resistance. We may actually dismiss rational responses outright, owing to the seductive and sensual nature of an impulse. We may rush ahead with unpremeditated urgency, regardless of the attractiveness or repulsiveness of the perceived outcome of the experience. One is swept up in a momentum that is greater than one's will and against which one feels helpless to resist. Appearances may be deceiving as seemingly contradictory sides of one's nature are exposed. Salmon swim upstream to spawn, fighting against the current, even unto death. A school of fish travels as a unit until one is lured aside by bait. Ospreys fly over the ocean with ease and grace, then suddenly swoop down to pluck up unsuspecting prey with their talons.

Essence: Organic

Fluids move through the organs in the body, supplying them with essential juices that nourish and purify and excite and calm and generate and moisten and detoxify and eliminate. In the organic state one may also be moved by a gush of emotional "juices" that overwhelm in a sudden burst of intensity, or enliven in a well-spring of unbidden feeling. Immersion in this state can have a strong or subtle pull, but one rarely questions its persuasiveness, and one responds to its promptings with little reflection or premeditation. Emotions can run high and be as exhilarating as they are uninhibited. In the organic state a thief slips his sticky fingers inside a purse like octopus's tentacles. A barfly drinks like a fish to drown her sorrows. Lovers dive into each other's arms with sweaty abandon.

The actress Nina in Anton Chekhov's *The Seagull* embodies this sense of almost helpless compulsion. She is aware of the carelessness and cruel detachment of the writer Trigorin's attentions to her but cannot resist their pull.

Nina: "I'm the seagull ... No, that's not it ... A man comes along, sees her, and destroys her life because he has nothing better to do ... subject for a short story ... I love him, I love him, I love him to despair."[3]

Willful

The third behavioral state is the most evolved of the animal natures. Here one begins to exercise some conscious control, so that the dynamic exchange of wild and tamed energy comes into play in a way that is driven and deliberate.

Elemental Landscape: Fire
For this element we go inside the body to house fire in the belly. We all know that a fireplace is a safe space in which to warm up a room, whereas uncontained fire can burn down the whole house. Likewise relationships are more likely to endure when fiery passion is partnered with warmth and well-defined boundaries, yet we are often drawn to the dazzling fireworks of dangerous encounters or illicit liaisons that flare out of control. We may be "burned" but feel incredibly alive as we tap into our untamed animality. This tension between security and spontaneity creates its own kind of friction as we test the extremes of power and potency against submission and servility.

In "fire" explorations a dance between domesticity and wildness may prompt displays of physical posturing and prowess as one attempts to intimidate or dominate, to impact or impress. Or one may signal acquiescence and obedience as one bows or begs, whimpers and collapses. Vocalizations are equally vociferous or "fizzled." Roars and shouts and screeches may be employed to demonstrate the supremacy of one's needs through intimidation, just as sighs and shushes and whimpers may be attempts to meet one's needs through passive-aggressive means.

Consciousness: Intent
Intention demands not only focused energy but some degree of calculation in order to fulfill one's goals. In the willful state there is the exhibition, and not just the presence, of animal intelligence at work. One negotiates not only to survive but in order to be more fully satisfied or realized. In addition to concentrated effort there is consideration of the impact of one's actions on others, but only in so far as they serve the self. One regards others as independent entities that can assist or withhold, recognizing one's own potential to be an ally or enemy as well. Interactions may involve a manipulation of shared feelings, or a projection of one's wishes onto the other.

In *Our Inner Ape* Frans de Waal investigates the way in which large-brained animals are capable of empathy but are just as capable of cruelty because they can imagine what the other will feel.[4] Likewise in the willful state, intent is all-consuming, where actions are undertaken without tremendous regard for the outcome or effect on others. A pet dog performs tricks until one delivers up that biscuit. An ape roars and beats its chest until its primacy in the tribe is secure. A wild horse bucks and snorts as the wrangler tries to rope it in.

Essence: Willful
The notion of willfulness is often used interchangeably with that of spirit-edness. We are capable of both civilized and savage behavior just like that of pets, farm and circus animals. Their wildness is always present under-neath, even though they have been tamed and domesticated. Even if their fiery nature has been completely beaten out of them they may still revert to uncharacteristic outbursts: peeing on the carpet, chewing through a rope, stampeding a barrier. The willful state is thus as unpredictable as it is prescriptive. Even though strategies may be employed they are based more on reaction and reward than on reason and rationale. The will may be harnessed or broken, yet it may just as easily be rebellious and free. In the willful state a prisoner spends months plotting an escape from a high-security jail. A father kidnaps his child in response to being denied custody. An immigrant gives all her money to a trafficker in order to cross an illegal border.

In *The Goat*, Edward Albee addresses the power of the will to meet its goal regardless of the consequences. Martin, an architect, risks the dis-mantling of a carefully constructed family and professional life in order to fulfill what feels like a naked expression of love—a love that is a projection of his own unlived creature wants.

Martin: It was as if an alien came out of whatever it was, and it … took me with it, and it was … an ecstasy and a purity, and a … love of a … un-i-mag-in-able kind, and it relates to nothing whatever, to nothing that can be related to.[5]

Humanoid

The fourth behavioral state is one of transition between animal and spirit natures. The three earlier states represented inherent behavior. Now we introduce the dawning of awareness on *experience* as it appears in pre-consciousness, or in our projections onto replications of human-like forms that are, or appear to be, curious and innocent.

Elemental Landscape: Air
This is the realm of infants as they sculpt the air, so to speak, inventing language as a way of understanding or incorporating experience. They navigate reality as an extension of their identity while also discovering the unique capabilities of their bodies and voices without the tools of language and labeled behavior. Their need for an articulate utterance is an

expression of dawning consciousness. Investigation leads to refinement and/or variation based on growing awareness. Every moment is one of awe or frustration, of pain or pleasure. One has no opinion about the experience. It simply is. Nothing is predictable, everything is possible.

While we are speaking of air, this is a good time to be reminded of the role breath plays in shaping our experience. In *Voice and the Actor* Cicely Berry writes: "With the voice, you depend on the breath to start the sound—not too much for that would make the sound breathy, not too little for that would make the attack glottal and the tone hard, but right and clean and using all the breath to make sound."[6] Infants do not question the right to express their needs and therefore are generous, yet economic, with their breath. They are playful yet purposeful, their breathing unhampered by social norms that can muffle or magnify genuine response. To breathe freely is also "to be" freely.

In "air" explorations there are no defined boundaries between self and otherness, foreground and background, positive and negative space. One experiments with body parts without any compartmental or conceptual framework. Soundscapes are composed not only of open vowels, as in the first three states of being, but are now laced with consonants in an attempt to formulate meaningful self-expression. This burbling and babbling may be playful but also sets in motion a necessary call and response with others.

Consciousness: Affect
Affect—the need to move or impress another—is embedded within both the words "affection" and "affectation." Infants need to "touch" adults emotionally as much as they need to be touched physically themselves in order to survive and thrive. They will use any means to bond with their caregivers. To ensure this necessary attachment they may cultivate either affection or affectation, as long as it leads to the desired result. Snuggling and cooing may be easily rewarded, but being cute and playing "possum" may be more effective if the child encounters resistance or competition. Through experimentation babies become surprisingly sophisticated at reading adults and learn how to "push their buttons." But since they live in the present they are also capable of forgetting the "rules." They cannot suppress the joy of discovery or the frustration of defeat before their feelings are fully articulated and owned. Of course adults also seek praise, or solace, or assistance or reward. At times they too demonstrate a lack of control over their feelings, but babies do so with the innocence

of an unstudied response to their needs and wants. There is no sense of consequences, ethical consideration or judgment in their acts.

This pre-conscious state is akin to the archetype of the clown, who also suspends judgment and invests fully in the unfolding of the moment. Ann and Barry Ulanov state in *The Witch and the Clown* that the clown "takes us directly to what we feel without the intermediary of words or analysis or a rational sequence of events. The clown is ardent, and awakens in us our own intensity of emotion. He expands our feeling space."[7]

Humanoids—human-like replicas—may also expand, or at least mirror, our feeling space. Rodney Brooks, the author of "Flesh and Machines," discovered that robots, like babies, process the world more fully through embodied intelligence— that is, sensory input: seeing, touching and balancing—than through symbolic processing, in other words abstract reasoning. "No cognition," he wrote, "just sensing and action."[8] And yet, like infants, robots need to be monitored and/or engineered by others. Neither would survive without the supervision, assistance or intervention of another with a more highly evolved consciousness. They need to affect us and/or be affected by us in order to exist and function. A baby gains attention by sharing a story through invented language and gestures. A puppet comes to life when its master pulls its strings. A robot responds to its owner's commands once it is programmed.

Essence: Humanoid

Interdependence or symbiosis is an essential feature of the humanoid state of being. Infants and human-like replicas depend on adults for their existence, but their caretakers, handlers and owners also depend on them for developing inter-relational skills or self-enhancement. We may do our best not to project our needs onto other human beings, but we do acquire humanoids such as a puppet, doll, action figure or robot specifically to endow their "otherness" with personal meaning, assumptions and expectations. Once they are animated they may appear to have singular personas, but in fact, they are solely a reflection of our own basic drives and desires. In the humanoid state a teenager is infatuated with an avatar. A mother whispers baby talk to her newborn. A marriage conducted over Skype replaces physical intimacy with its simulation.

Bernard Shaw took his inspiration for the play *Pygmalion* from a story of the same name in which a sculpture creates his ideal woman, who then comes to life. She is the projection of his inner opposite, his unlived feminine side, who takes on her own complex identity once she becomes conscious. In the play, Liza declares her independence by taking off the ring that Higgins gave her, ending the "unspoken" agreement to remain his student and surrogate. Higgins then reveals the untutored side of his own nature by reacting with unchecked emotion. It is a shock to both of them to recognize the other within the self.

Higgins: Hit you? You infamous creature, how dare you accuse me of such a thing? It is you who have hit me. You have wounded me to the heart.[9]

Psychic

The fifth, sixth and seventh states entertain the *imagination* as expressed in the behavior of the *spirit* realm. However, behavior in the fifth state still takes on human form even though it is inhabited in an alternate universe where these sentient beings have no qualms about being seductive and ingenious.

Elemental Landscape: Sound

Sighs and groans and whispers that seem to come from the "beyond" are often a projection of our own fears and desires onto the unseen "other." When we sense the presence of a ghost or a deceased ancestor, we are afforded a glimpse into this alternate universe—which is often referred to as the "real" world that resides alongside this "unreal" one. We may also anthropomorphize the natural world, translating sounds and movements into paranormal manifestations. We hear the gossip of fairies in the rustling of leaves; a ghoul falling to its death in the snap of a branch; an ecstatic witch's laugh in a bird call.

In "sound" explorations vocalization now includes invented language, known as gibberish: non-linguistic speech composed of a mad jumble of vowels and consonants. This sounds like a foreign language or glossolalia, commonly known as "speaking in tongues." One intimidates, ingratiates, excites and agitates by uttering colorful nonsense to consciously manipulate and maneuver. The body underscores this verbal elasticity by playing with varying notions of time and space. Alterations in direction and pace along with pitch and volume allow us to take others by surprise. They are caught up in our emotional whirlwind before they realize what's happening to them.

Consciousness: Influence

Influence is needed to unearth a secret; to seduce another into doing our bidding; to fulfill a mission or goal. The ability to insinuate one's own feelings into the fabric of another being is essential to bring this about. By using invented language we can sway another to our point of view by bypassing rational discourse and addressing the heart and mind directly. This makes gibberish highly effective in generating spells, invoking magic, fueling enchantment and inciting rage.

This prattle, along with glossolalia, is also known as gromalot, a technique used by *commedia dell'arte* to avoid the censorship of Church and State while slyly undermining their institutional authority in the content of plays. Such a subversive act in itself can be attractive, inviting one to share in the potency of a collective secret. In fact, whenever "the air is charged" we tend to react without reflection. We may unwittingly join in the frenzy of a mob, or be compelled to pursue an illusion or embark on a dangerous path. For better or worse, conscious or unconscious influences raise questions about one's sense of identity, purpose or place in life. A fairy queen falls in love with a donkey. A ghost haunts a dinner party. A troll extracts a deadly promise.

Essence: Psychic

Folklore employs witches and golems and leprechauns from the supernatural world to intervene and influence human destiny. We enter into a dialogue with these spirits by giving voice to the phantoms of our imagination. They often speak the "unspoken" truth without restraint or regard for the conventional rules of social engagement. Our interaction with these ghosts and goblins compels us to dialogue with our desires and fears. We attempt to come to terms with them or eradicate them; to magnify or minimize their hold over our lives. They in turn, are mischievous, wily and utterly determined to confound or clarify our relationship to inner or outer reality. In the psychic state a son sees his mother's ghost whenever he raises a drink to his lips. A child summons an imaginary friend to ward off loneliness. A clairvoyant predicts a celebrity's rise and fall from public adoration.

The three Witches in William Shakespeare's *Macbeth* are manifestations of Macbeth's own inner desires. They speak the unspeakable by addressing the ambition that he dare not name consciously. Their incantations are like a broken record of unresolved want. Their hideous forms are as repulsive as his suppressed desire.

Macbeth: Present fears
          Are less than horrible imaginings.
          My thought, whose murder yet is but fantastical,
          Shakes so my single state of man that function
          Is smothered in surmise, and nothing is
          But what is not.[10]

Mythic

The sixth behavioral state incorporates the animal natures of the first three states with the embodied spirit of the fifth state. It bypasses the limitations of human experience to directly confront fantastical creatures that are aberrant and unsettling.

Elemental Landscape: Light
Shedding light on specters of the mythic world forces one to recognize the power and potency of instinct wedded to intelligence, and intuition to imagination. Our perception of reality is altered by the exchange of these intertwined and often irreconcilable drives. We see things in a new and often disturbing light as these "monsters" upend the status quo, whatever it may be. They elicit responses that can be liberating or terrifying in scope and sensibility. One behaves in a way that is not how one normally sees oneself. One may act as aberrantly as the abstraction one confronts—trying to bite off the head of a grotesquery in a nightmare, subdue an apparition that appears in a daydream or strangle an aberrant creature that suddenly appears in a vision. Such a vision may be the product of extrasensory perception (or "second sight") in which one has a portal into the phantasmal realm. This gift may be as burdensome as it is enlightening since it offers an unvarnished glimpse into a future event over which one may be helpless to intervene.

In "light" explorations our perception of reality is disoriented or even overthrown. Aberrant and extreme sentient beings take shape before our very eyes. Embodying these hybrid creatures requires movement that is highly contrasting and polarized: muscular and delicate, sensual and striking, fluid and forceful. Sound vacillates between unformed utterance and gibberish, creating a mass of competing messages that reflect the turmoil of disparate instincts and inclinations. One may shape-shift with the flick of a tail, a flapping of wings, a screeching song. Exploring the full range of a creature may lead to a complex psycho-physical incarnation. A centaur stamps his hoof with lust. A mermaid stirs up desire with her scaly fin. A sphinx purrs as she poses an impossible riddle.

Consciousness: Alteration

The mythic state contains heightened awareness and heated impulses. This volatile combination brings about alteration of consciousness either by choice or by necessity. Embodying a mythic creature allows one to step outside the "norm." As we engage in behavior that oscillates between instinct and imagination we modify our sense of reality. Erratic and unpredictable behavior throws others "off their beam" by stripping away their "comfort zone." This necessitates a radical change in expectations and patterns of response that may lead to enlightenment or entropy.

Fantastical creatures are symbolic manifestations of the inner life that appear without mediation. They mirror the contents of the core self without offering compromise. It is not surprising that one may encounter the fusion of impulses and awareness in creatures that don't have any recognizable human attributes. These bizarre "crossbreeds" are magnifications of inner conflicts and longings that summon the supernatural world directly. They have great stores of undiluted power and potency. The griffin guards the divine. The chimera feeds on daydreams. The unicorn responds to the heart's promptings.

Essence: Mythic

The fictitious world of mythic creatures is nevertheless a formidable one. It interweaves rational and irrational behavior to provoke disquiet and disorientation. These apparitions—mutations and reconfigurations of human and animal bits and pieces—reorient our vision of the universe and our role within it. They undermine our preconceived ideas about the hierarchy of human and animal needs. The fusion of spirit and animal energies forces us to wrestle with the polar extremes of inspiration and irrationality, reason and desire. For all their naked animality, Pegasus, Cerebus and Ganesh are also imbued with great powers of conscious persuasion. One succumbs to or confronts them with their total being. Their appearance can lead to a kind of death and/or resurrection. In the mythic state a spurned lover becomes Medusa whose anger tumbles out of her head like venomous snakes. A rock star morphs into a centaur that sleeps with a fan then throws her out of the hotel room. A long-forgotten poet rises up like a phoenix when her work is suddenly rediscovered.

The character of Harry Haller in Hermann Hesse's *Steppenwolf* expresses the complexity of this fierce yet fraught state of being. He is a wolf-man, whose two sides of the self are at war with each other. "...the man and the wolf did not go the same way together, but were in continual and deadly enmity. One existed simply and solely to harm the other, and when these are two in one blood and in one soul who are at deadly enmity, then life fares ill."[11]

Cosmic

The seventh behavioral state combines all the attributes of the former six states, and in doing so, transcends them. This is the realm of deities who are infinite and omniscient. See Fig. 5.3.

Elemental Landscape: Ether

Ether was once thought to be the element that suffused the upper reaches of space or the heavens. It also refers to a clear liquid that was once used as an anesthetic to induce sleep before an operation. This is the realm of the "unseen air": somewhere vast and elusive that inspires and intoxicates without making its presence known. We can imagine this place as being the home of the gods who touch our lives without being visible to us. We sense their presence in moments of serenity and suffering as they toy with our lives, creating heaven and hell for us here on earth.

In "ether" explorations we imagine that we are physical embodiments of these omnipresent beings that dwell in the metaphysical realm. We envision ourselves as microcosms of the macrocosmic world. Every utterance and gesture resonates with symbolic weight. Sounds and movements vibrate with the entire universe. We may invoke a healing mantra, a ritual dance or the music of the spheres. Body and breath expands and contracts as we create or destroy with every fiber of our being. A howl grows into a thunderstorm. A stomp stirs up a tsunami. A smile brings out the sun.

Consciousness: Actualization

Actualization is not synonymous with realization. Our final destination may be to arrive at a place of fulfillment or to land in one of fragmentation. We go on a journey in life in which the outcome may or may not lead to awareness and attainment. Whether we realize our potential or not we all certainly arrive at an actual end point.

In the cosmic state we combine inherent nature, experience and imagination to investigate overall paths in life. Rather than entertain a preordained idea of fate we explore actualization in non-dualities. We might also refer to this non-polarization as the two principles of yin and yang, in which seeming opposites actually constitute a whole. Contrasting light and dark energies can be seen in life and death or love and hate. As we embody the ubiquitous presence of the all-knowing and omniscient, we become a force for good or ill, for healing or pain. Yet we include the opposite within the very nature of our "is-ness." Athena is born out of her father's head. Shiva is both a celibate and a lover. The devil is a fallen angel.

Essence: Cosmic

The cosmic state conjures up the embodiment of supra-conscious beings. It is the realm of Kali, goddess of creation and destruction; of Hades, king of the underworld; of Jezebel, a she-devil. It is the realm of all angels and demons; of all gods and goddesses, including those of secular mythology. It resides in all manifestations of heaven and hell: Nirvana, Valhalla, the Great Beyond.

When we human beings get caught up in a "god-complex" we feel as though we are "above" mundane existence. Conversely, when we are touched by the divine, we feel as though we are "at one" with the extraordinary. In the cosmic state a cult leader demands his followers to commit mass suicide. A Wall Street trader drops out of society and gives all his money to charity. A twelfth-century nun translates her visions into a morality play.

In Jose Rivera's *Marisol* an angel descends to earth to directly intervene in the devastation of the human condition. As a guardian from above she exhibited a tender and fierce regard for her charge, Marisol. Now she needs to "spread her wings" and challenge the very hierarchy of heaven, which assigned her an identity as "helpmate" that was ineffective and un-empowering.

Angel: Listen well. Marisol: angels are going to kill the King of Heaven and restore the vitality of the universe with his Blood. And I am going to lead them.[12]

NOTES

1. Michael Agnes, Editor in Chief, *Webster's New World Dictionary*, New York: Hungry Minds, Inc., 2002.
2. Franz Kafka, *Metamorphosis*, trans. and edited by Stanley Corngold, New York: Norton Critical Editions, 1996, p.3
3. Anton Chekhov, *The Seagull*, Act 4, in *The Plays of Anton Chekhov*, trans. Paul Schmidt, New York: Harper Perennial, 1999, p. 159.
4. Frans de Waal, *Our Inner Ape*, New York: Riverhead Books, 2006.
5. Edward Albee, *The Goat, or Who is Sylvia?* in *The Collected Plays of Edward Albee, volume 3, 1978–2003*, New York: Overlook Duckworth, Peter Mayer Publishers, Inc., 2008, sc. 2, p. 598.
6. Cicely Berry, *Voice and the Actor*, London: Harrap & Co. Ltd, 1973, p. 19.
7. Ann and Barry Ulanov, *The Witch and the Clown*, Wilmette, Illinois: Chiron Publications, 1987, p. 192.
8. Rodney Brooks, *Flesh and Machines*, quoted in Robin Marantz Henig, "The Real Transformers," *New York Times Magazine*, July 29, 2007.
9. Bernard Shaw, *Pygmalion*, New York: Penguin, 2003, Act 4, p. 80.
10. William Shakespeare, *Macbeth*, New York: Signet Classics, 1963, Act 1, sc. 3, lines 137–42, p. 46.
11. Hermann Hesse, *Steppenwolf*, trans. Basil Creighton, New York: Picador, 1963, pp. 41–42.
12. Jose Rivera, *Marisol*, New York: Dramatists Play Service Inc., Revised 1999, Act 1, sc. 4, p. 18.

CHAPTER 3

Physiological States

FOUNDATION

The word "physiology" comes from the root word "nature" and is primarily focused on the vital processes of living organisms.[1] We experience our bodily aliveness directly through feeling and sensation. The foundation of the physiological states is based on explorations of body parts, senses and the feelings they generate, which often speak to us in *metaphor*. This indirection allows us to access the intelligence of the body in terms that we might not otherwise be able to express, allowing us to also gain insight into possible underlying issues that affect alignment and dis-ease. There is an elegance in describing a physical state as feeling like "butterflies," or "a lump in the throat" or "a knot in the gut." The use of metaphor helps us to articulate and digest our feelings in the process of identifying and owning them.

Orientation, collective and actor-generated explorations encompass all three aspects of the physiological states: movement landscapes, energy centers and the senses. Orientation explorations are conducted primarily in partnerships, but all participants engage in similar activity as a way to establish a common foundation. Collective explorations are based on suggestions to the group as a whole, but are undertaken individually as the actors experiment with various bodily conditions and sensory stimulation. As an option, or in addition, the senses may be engaged independently through guided sensory explorations with the collective. A sample for each sense is included in this section. Actor-generated explorations use journal

© The Author(s) 2016

E. Hess, *Acting and Being*, DOI 10.1057/978-1-349-95106-2_3

material generated during the orientation and collective explorations to create character studies. Finally, for each exploration I have included an example from a play to illustrate the incorporation of the exploration into specific character work.

Instructions for the implementation of the explorations can be found in Part 2, "Explorations in Embodied Performance."

Movement Landscapes, Energy Centers and Senses

The entry point into the physiological explorations is *movement landscapes*, which are named metaphorically: tree, sculpture, membrane, rubber band, wind instrument, mirror opposites and broken patterns. These metaphors allow the actors to step into an allegorical setting that transcends any self-consciousness that may arise because of the often physically intimate nature of the explorations. They also help us culturally to move beyond a frame of mind where body parts are often compartmentalized or objectified. Even though we are breaking the body down into identifiable states we are doing so to create greater awareness and integration of the whole self.

The process of identifying specific aspects of the body is further explored through *energy centers*: root, sacral, navel, heart, throat, third eye and crown. These "wheels of energy" are also known as chakras. We investigate released and blocked energy using metaphors for body language along with physical conditions and sensory stimulation.

Feelings and sensations color each other and influence our overall response. This symbiosis does not diminish, but rather enhances the connection to our core being through empathetic understanding. The body houses all our individual experience, and the more we relate to its intuitive wisdom, the more it reveals our truth with unembroidered and astonishing transparency.

The *senses*, smell, taste, sight, touch, hearing, intuition, and memory and association, are activated to emphasize the potency of sensory experience as a physical sensation that bypasses intellectual consideration. It is surprising how often we identify something as feeling sensual without recognizing its origin in the senses themselves. As with Stanislavski's teachings on sensory recall, the stimulation of the senses can trigger memories and associations that may be subtle or salient. Once we extract the narrative from these memories and associations we are left with their core emotional contents. This residue can be transferred directly into imaginary circumstances. Our actions are informed by, but independent of, the source material.

I will often say to an actor when they are stuck in a moment, "Throw it into your body!" This is a way of encouraging them to work "on their feet." The more one plays in one's body, the more it will exhibit its grace and power. Our body has the capacity to reveal our "naked" self, since it does not lie. The more we can embrace its innate intelligence, the less we will be tempted to hide from its unflinching gaze. The more grounded we are in the body, the more we are able to soar in the imagination. The mind no longer leads (even though it often feels it is its duty to do so!). It listens to the received knowledge of the body's wisdom and responds to what I like to call the "totality of being."

Many characters, however, never advance beyond the needs of the three lower energy centers, which are focused on the basics of survival, sex and power. Yet not all these characters live solely in the three lower physiological states, root, sacral or navel. Often there is a constricted energy that drives the character, so that even though they may focus on the basics in life, their dominant energy center may be located elsewhere in the body. They may be desperate for love, or hunger for truth, or long for recognition. It is interesting then to investigate how blocked as well as released energy affects the character's state of being. But the actor needs to play actions rather than obstacles, so it's important to discover the character's need to compensate for or overcome those blocks. Also, more than one energy center may be triggered in the body simultaneously, but one center will command more attention at any given moment, if not overall. That center will in turn affect complementary or competing impulses.

INFLUENCES FROM RELATED DISCIPLINES

Kundalini Yoga, Butoh, Contact Improvisation and Viewpoints are all movement-based practices that elucidate the body's intelligence and have been incorporated into these explorations in ways both subtle and substantial.

Kundalini Yoga

Kundalini Yoga, with its emphasis on chakras—energy centers in the body—creates a map whereby it is possible to locate specific feelings and sensations. These locations are often easiest to pinpoint when we are faced with an identifiable bodily condition or symptom. Kundalini seeks to open energy that is blocked and, in so doing, release one into a more mindful state. Sometimes during a yoga session I am aware that my energy is stuck somewhere in my body, but just as often it is not until it vibrates again that I recognize the source of tension. In this way, the approach encourages feelings to flood forth, if and when one is ready to receive them. The eyes are mostly closed during these sessions. This reinforces the very private nature of this practice while still preserving a sense of community as one breathes and moves as a collective.

Butoh

Butoh, with its allegorical investigation of emotions through slow and considered movement, can be a powerful tool for unlocking the innate intelligence of the body. In a workshop called "Sounding the Unsound Body" I participated in an exercise in which I moved within a flexible "membrane" that was created by the collective. Once I totally relaxed within the membrane I was asked to walk forward while the membrane resisted my movement. This demanded a great deal of exertion on my part and fiery feelings began to surface: first frustration, then anger and finally the release of hot tears. The membrane then slowly disengaged and I was asked to stay inside its memory and move within its phantom presence. I continued to struggle, not only physically but also emotionally, as my organs remained actively engaged throughout. This exercise helped me understand the value of bodily activation as a means of engaging viscera itself.

Contact Improvisation and Viewpoints

A series of combined workshops in Contact Improvisation and Viewpoints was conducted for faculty members at New York University's Tisch School of the Arts to familiarize us with these techniques. The sessions focused on kinesthetic awareness by introducing exercises that sparked specific vibrations within the body. We discovered how variables in time and space, and in tempo and duration, affected the emotional connection to ourselves and others in often intangible but very palpable ways.

Not only do actors need to develop their own unique physical expressiveness, but through energetic exchange with others we also learn to interact with empathy and awareness. In an exercise involving weight exchange, I learned to be both flexible and fluid in relation to another's movement. We developed a dialogue with our bodies that felt three-dimensional—communicating not only with our eyes, but also with our backs, hands and breath. Through this "deep listening" we moved with increasing instinctual ease, allowing the movement to initiate within and resonate without while it simultaneously informed our feeling response. I have added vocalization—including tone, pitch and volume— into explorations in the physiological states of being, so that the actors create a call and response whereby the voice is indivisible from the body.

STATES OF BEING

Root

How we stand affects how we make our way in the world. We may be planted or restless, intractable or flexible. The root state of being addresses one's *ground of being* See Fig. 6.3.

Movement Landscape: The Tree

The more we are able to shift our weight around the more influence we can command, whereas rigidity weakens us in the face of opposition. There are times in life when we need to put our foot down and times when we need to accede: to take a stand or give sway.

The "tree" exploration tests our rootedness through weight-exchange, allowing another to lean against our trunk, so to speak, and nudge it gently. Through this exercise we discover sturdiness and stillness, not by being static, but by listening and adjusting in subtle yet supportive ways. Our partner is like tree sap, slowly exploring the curves and contours of our trunk as we root down and respond from our center of gravity. When the partners change roles there is a need to rediscover the dialogue between them. They shift expectations as well as weight in order to find stability, since no one's ground of being is the same. Finally the partners together become the trunk and tree sap, allowing their bodies to intertwine like branches. They lend their weight and support each other as they twist and turn in tandem. In this way they find their ground of being through reciprocity while in continual motion.

Energy Center: Root

Our foundation informs the way we move through life. If our ground of being is shaky so is our presence. But if we are rooted we are more likely to be comfortable in our body and in the world. Life "throws us curves" or "pulls the rug out from under us," which can be unsettling and disruptive. Yet we welcome the feeling of being "swept off our feet." How we respond to change and handle novelty has much to do with both our sense of flexibility and our sense of security.

Laura in Tennessee Williams's *The Glass Menagerie* walks with a limp. Laura herself is hobbled by life. Her hold on reality is tentative and unsure. Yet when Jim, the gentleman caller, teaches her how to dance—to move beyond the limits of her physical handicap—she also experiences a moment of grace. She pays for this experience with a profound realization that she cannot sustain this moment but is frozen in place. She is like the fragile yet rigid creatures of her menagerie. The moment nevertheless does shift her ground of being. Jim's acceptance of her "different nature" allows her be more accepting of her own humanity. She says after the unicorn loses its horn—its fantastical otherness—

Laura: "I'll just imagine he had an operation. The horn was removed to make him feel less freakish!"[2]

Sense: Smell
To inhale is to breathe in inspiration. To exhale is to release into expression. Odors and scents and aromas infuse our experience and color our responses without our conscious consent.

Guided Sensory Exploration
The following sample uses incense to activate sense memory and association through smell.

Incense curls and swirls around in ribbons of smoke. You follow its trail in your mind. In your body. You trace its musky scent. Its pungent aroma. You breathe it in. Looking for clues as to the source of the smell. The origin of its earthiness. Its rich, loamy intensity. You become one with it. One with the smoke. The ashes. Like the incense as it burns. Slowly turning into gray dust. Gray matter. Matter that is now buried someplace inside your rich, loamy interior. You deepen your search. You retrieve bits and piece. Fragments. Feelings. Images. Impressions. Where were you? When was it? Who was there? You follow the tendrils of feeling. There is no distinction between memory and this moment. You are there. You are here. You relive it as you breathe into it. Breathe through it. You bring your discovery, your recovery, with you as you return, like an archeologist with an artifact—an impression, a shard, a full vessel.

Sacral

The sacral state of being, also referred to as the sexual state of being, is the seat of one's *life force*. It houses our most fundamental bodily drives and desires See Fig. 6.1.

Movement Landscape: Sculpture

The sacral, or sexual, state triggers powerful feelings of desire or disgust that are often directed towards another person. We may also be the recipient of another's expression of attraction or aversion. Our experience of connection or alienation can affect our sense of desirability, fostering feelings of acceptance or rejection, inclusion or ostracism. When we move towards or pull away from others we are consciously or unconsciously setting limits and boundaries to inter-relatedness.

"Sculpture" explorations tap into issues of intimacy and attachment, aloofness and separation. The actor observes their partner in a neutral position and then interposes their body in relationship to them, initiating a conversation with them in space. The partner then steps away, creating a void until they interpose their body and re-shape the relationship. As the process continues the actors define and redefine their relationship, discovering—through a dialogue with positive or negative space—that an unspoken narrative emerges that is informed as much by the "gaps" in their relationship as in the "glue."

Energy Center: Sacral

This is the energy center of the pelvic floor, which houses the reproductive organs. "Libido" is a term that the psychoanalyst Sigmund Freud coined to refer not only to sexual drive but to psychic energy, which is affected by both the mind and the body. His theories themselves are a reflection of this, of late nineteenth-century and early twentieth-century European mores which were colored by patriarchal values and sexual repression. Although many of his conclusions are questionable and contested today, it is not surprising that he focused a great deal of attention on sexuality. The impulse to create life (whether it's expressed literally or metaphorically) compels us to act on our drives and desires. We are motivated psychologically as well as biologically to act and react, to create and destroy from often unbidden but vital urges in our bodies.

Regardless of our success or failure in controlling our thoughts and actions, our body always reveals the truth of our desires. Even though our outward appearance and actions may suggest otherwise, we may be in truth a "snake in the grass" or a "hot shot", a "dried-up prune" or "hen-pecked." Our sense of self is often affected by our sexual desirability, especially in a culture that values our marketability and ability to make an external impact on others. But the sacral state is ultimately the seat of one's innate vitality: one's spirited self.

In Henrik Ibsen's *Hedda Gabler* it is easy to forget that Hedda is pregnant since she herself barely acknowledges this "invasion" of her body. She "aborts" Ejlert Lovborg's creative output as a writer and undermines his connection to Thea Elvsted, a woman whose essence is to nurture life. Hedda's destructive acts mirror her unlived passion. She is a magnificent coward who feeds on others' life force, as her own unborn self devours her from within. And so as she feeds the manuscript—the outward expression of Eljert's and Thea's inspired "coupling"—into the fire, her words mock her own deadly conjugation with Jorgen Tesman, her husband.

Hedda: "Now I'm burning your child, Thea. You, with the curly hair. Your child and Ejlert Lovborg's. I'm burning it—burning your child."[3]

Sense: Taste
The tongue itself communicates before it articulates. We chew and swallow, or spit out and reject, and thereby announce our unstudied and honest response.

Guided Sensory Exploration
The following sample uses salt to activate sense memory and association through taste.
Salt sits in the palm of your hand. You lick it with your tongue. It begins to dissolve. Does it have an edge? Bitterness? Bite? Zing? You savor it. Let it marinate. Find its fullness. Its flavor. You swallow it. Take it in. Now you feel the aftertaste. The residue. The resonance. What does this taste bring up for you? Does it remind you of comfort food? Fast food? Where are you? At home? Out in the world? Are you surrounded by salt air? Salt water? Taking a salt bath? Applying salt in a wound? What does it stir up inside you? Does it please you? Or disgust you? Do you digest the experience easily? Relish it? Or is it difficult to absorb? To recall? Take your time and come back, bringing the taste of your adventure with you.

Navel

Our hunger signals the need to be nourished, body and soul. The navel state of being focuses on our *appetite for life*, by looking at how we satiate or starve those needs.

Movement Landscape: Membrane

Our "gut reaction" informs the way we take things in, whether it is nourishment or experience. We can reject it or absorb it, vomit it up or swallow it down. It reveals our unconscious relationship to both abundance and boundaries. A person may be "invisible" if they starve themselves—like a model on a runway who is a "walking coat-hanger" whose form barely detracts from the clothes on her back. But a person may be equally opaque by over-indulging, creating a kind of camouflage by insulating themselves. The more we can trust our "gut" and nurture our genuine needs, the more we are likely to "show up" as a presence in our own lives and in the world.

The "membrane" exploration places the focus on our guts, quite literally. The actor is nourished by the energy of the collective which supports their body as they move freely within the flexible membrane that envelopes them. But once the membrane offers resistance, the actor's innards become knotted or churned up. This may generate feelings of frustration or fierceness as they attempt to free themselves from the restraint. Finally as the membrane slowly disengages the actor moves within its phantom presence. They discover that the engagement of viscera—of intestines, entrails and guts—is indeed one with visceral experience itself.

Energy Center: Navel

By recognizing and responding to our genuine needs we take space in a way that neither deflates nor inflates our presence. We reflect our truth in an undistorted light that neither diminishes us nor obscures others. To digest the food of life fully is neither to "suck the juice out of it" nor to "cram it full of cravings" but to "fuel" it with aliveness.

Garfinkel in Jerry Sterner's *Other People's Money* lives on junk food and junk bonds. He is forever craving more and more since there is no real nourishment in his diet or his ethics. By not addressing his inner needs he confuses them with outer wants, and his relationship to money and power and to energy and love becomes distorted and damaging. But Garfinkel has no desire to change his voracious habits. He says, unrepentantly:

Garfinkel: I love money more than the things it can buy. You know why? Money is unconditional acceptance. It don't care whether I'm good or not, whether I snore or don't, which God I pray to – it still gets me as much interest in the bank as yours does. There's only three things that give that kind of unconditional acceptance – dogs, donuts and money. Only money is better. It doesn't make you fat and it don't shit all over the living room.[4]

Sense: Sight
Eyes are the windows to the soul. The outer world reflects our inner terrain.

Guided Sensory Exploration
The following sample uses a blindfold to activate sense memory and association through sight or, in this case, the deprivation of sight.

You are searching. Searching for something unknown. Something that is alive. Something powerful that needs to be retrieved. Is it an imaginary friend? An animal? A spirit? What does it look like? What form does it take? It dodges you. It darts away. You pursue it. Trying to give it shape. To bring it into focus. Eventually you name it. Identify it clearly. Suddenly it turns towards you. And looks right at you. Its eyes are like human eyes. They are the same color as your own. It beckons for you to follow. You do. It takes you on a journey that feels utterly new and perhaps it is. Or perhaps you've been here before. But you have never seen this place so clearly. Been here so fully. And freely. You look around. You take in your surroundings. You take in your companion, who is really just an aspect of yourself. You see yourself mirrored in them. You are one and the same. You bring them back with you as you return from your journey with new insight and awareness.

Heart

Nothing is higher than the heart. While exploring the seven physiological states of being this is a good time to be reminded of their non-hierarchical relationship (including the behavioral and psychological states of being). The "heart of the matter" is precisely that: it is the *core self*. All other states of being influence and affect each other, but in addition they are also a reflection of the heart's activity See Fig. 6.2.

Movement Landscape: Rubber Band
To love, to hate, to embrace, to spurn: all these actions are influenced by one's degree of self-acceptance and wholeness. Loving kindness is an

expression of integration and empathy, just as hateful cruelty is a reflection of fragmentation and indifference.

The "rubber band" exploration plays with the elasticity and vibrancy of heart-centered exchange. Partners expand and contract the space between them while neither leading nor following, but finding a vibration between them that ignites and enlivens their relationship. They never lose sight of each other, focusing more with the heart than with the eyes, as they feel the presence of an invisible thread that binds them. No matter who or what comes between them spatially their inner connection remains unbroken. They are like lovers who feel each other's presence from across the room. It is only when they doubt themselves or their partner that they falter and the bond is broken.

Energy Center: Heart
Courage (from the French root *coeur*, meaning "heart") is needed to address fear, which often plays an enormous role in robbing an energy center of its vitality. Hate is often an expression of fear, but sometimes the power of love (often gained through self-knowledge as an outcome of suffering) can lead to a life-altering experience.

Love can be transformative but we gain it more often through experience than by epiphany. "Pouring your heart out" to someone who is unsympathetic can turn your heart into "ice." On the other hand, as painful as it is, "heartbreak" can lead to greater self-understanding and empathy for others.

The ecstasy experienced by the lovers in William Shakespeare's *Romeo and Juliet* is initially triggered by passion (the sacral state of being). However, they face terrific obstacles to their relationship that are all rooted in a longstanding tradition of hate between their clans. By refusing to surrender to such toxicity they (especially Juliet) acquire an increasingly heartfelt understanding of the inter-relatedness of pleasure and pain, of "day in night." Even before consummating their marriage Juliet, alone on her balcony, says that her love is like a microcosm of the night sky, the universe itself:

Juliet: Give me my Romeo; and when I shall die
          Take him and cut him out in little stars,
          And he will make the face of heaven so fine
          That all the world will be in love with night,
          And pay no worship to the garish sun.[5]

Sense: Touch
Touch is necessary not only to thrive but also to survive. We need contact in order to feel alive within ourselves and out in the world.

Guided Sensory Exploration
The following sample uses an overcoat to activate sense memory and association through touch.

You are completely encased in your overcoat. Zippered up. Snapped in. Buttoned up. It is dark. Warm. Quiet. You are like a caterpillar in a cocoon, a little pupa. You are small and secure and surrounded. You listen to your heartbeat. You begin to tap the rhythm with your hands. Your feet. You begin to expand. The casing now feels restrictive. You try to break free of its confines. You feel your wings begin to beat against the lining. You push against the gauzy, gray walls. They begin to disintegrate. You step out. Tentatively. Slowly. A new being. Testing your wings. Your antennae. Your toes. Your fingers. You touch the outside world. Discovering who you are as you go. Feeling your way. Hot. Cold. Flat. Round. Hard. Soft. Self. Other.

Throat

To articulate our thoughts and feelings is to bring them into existence. Once they are real we can no longer take them back. The throat state of being is the realm of *self-expression*. Whether we own our words or not, we give voice to our inner nature whenever we speak the truth or tell a lie.

Movement Landscape: Wind Instrument
We may consciously reveal or hide ourselves behind our words but there are sounds we make that are involuntary responses to stimuli: fear, pleasure, surprise, pain, awe. Unsculpted utterances reveal our feelings before we have time to own them. Thus it is hard to laugh at a bad joke or fake an orgasm or yell at an adorable child. Our pitch and tone, volume and rhythm belie our underlying emotions. We may even communicate the opposite of what we intend, or at best send a mixed message.

In the "wind instrument" explorations the actor is like a musician who plays an improvisational "aria" of sounds upon their partner's body as if they were a human flute or clarinet or saxophone. They send a whisper into a knee. A blurt to a shoulder. A trill to a nose. The partner, who acts as the instrument, responds to these "notes" and "phrases" by imagining the vibrations rippling out from their body, creating a dance of jagged and curving and tight and trembling movements. This call and response is like

a jam session in which the musician and their instrument invent composi-
tions as they listen and respond to each other.

Energy Center: Throat

To be "on voice" means that we let our words speak for themselves. They
carry weight since they are grounded in our bodies. But when someone talks "out of the side of their mouth" they slant their truth. When
our voice is unsupported, the views we express are often equally muted.
Women are sometimes encouraged to use only their upper register and
may sometimes "swallow their words" so as not to appear threatening.
Children learn early in life to use their "indoor voices."

Voices can also be consciously altered to gain a desired effect. Lullabies
are sung in hushed tones to soothe and induce sleep. Interrogations are
often delivered in a monotone so as to appear impartial. Yelling may be an
attempt to intimidate or create chaos and confusion.

In Martin McDonagh's *The Pillowman* the two interrogators, Topolski
and Ariel, try to wrestle the truth from their suspect, Katurian, a writer
whose short stories are laced with violence and menace. A gun to his head
would silence him for ever. But what he fears even more than a gun-shot
is that his "voice" will leak out or not live on.

Katurian: I've confessed to everything truthfully, just like I promised I
            would. And I believe that you'll keep all my stories with the
            case file and not release them until fifty years after my death,
            just like you promised you would.[6]

Sense: Hearing

To hear is to be here. Receptive. Attentive. Responsive.

Guided Sensory Exploration

*The following sample uses music to activate sense memory and association
through hearing.*

You hear music in the distance. It is coming to you from your past.
You open the door to your childhood home. You go inside. You are there.
Your body is there. Your thoughts are there. The music is there. You step
into your shoes. Your favorite shoes. How old are you? What room are
you in? You begin to move to the music. You interact with it. Hum with
it. Sing with it. Dance with it. Are you alone? Does someone join you? Is
it a special day? A celebration? Are you light on your feet? Heavy-footed?

Light-hearted? Heavy-hearted? Why? When is this exactly? What does it bring up for you now? The more you interact with it the more it reveals. This music. This time. This place. These people. Maybe things are clear to you that you didn't hear or see the first time. Things that move you now. Or seem silly. Or sweet. Or sad. Or surprising. Things that tell you who you once were. Who you are now. Who you want to become. You bring them together. Bring yourself together. Past. Present. Future. All one.

Third Eye

The third eye is located in the pituitary gland, the seat of intuition. This inner vision lets us understand things through direct perception that is independent of reasoning. The third eye state of being also includes the ears, eyes and nose—a concentration of the senses. Our *presence* is affected by our perception of reality in this intricate and layered exchange between sense and sensibility, awareness and experience, fact and fiction.

Movement Landscape: Mirror Opposites
The third eye state holds a great deal of sensory information: sight, hearing, smell and intuition (the sixth sense), as well as cognitive activity. Our thinking and understanding of the outer world are influenced by our sensory experience. One *feels* connected or alienated. One *feels* clear or confused. How we perceive others is equally subjective, based as much on feeling as on fact.

Explorations in "mirror opposites" can feel odd or even jarring as partners observe each other inhabiting diametrically opposed energies. These are metaphorical embodiments of highly contrasting objects and abstractions that send competing messages. A feather floats towards a stone. A fire blazes as it faces a block of ice. A Pollock painting zigzags towards a Mondrian painting. As partners slowly begin to transition into each other's embodiment something shifts in their perception of themselves from an experiential place. Once the transformation is complete they see each other with different eyes and minds and hearts. They may be more empathetic now that they know what it is to live inside the other's skin, so to speak. Or perhaps they feel a kind of *Schadenfreude*, relieved that their partner is now stuck in their former unpleasant condition while they dance with abandon.

Energy Center: Third Eye
An individual's perception of reality also informs their world view and vice versa. One may question or challenge the unfolding of destiny, like the hero in a fable who overcomes a series of obstacles. Or one may be caught

in, or comply with, the dictates of fate, as in a Greek tragedy where one's path in life is pre-ordained. Perception itself is colored by our experience—by the impediments and opportunities that affect our expectations. If we are called an "air-head" or "space cadet" we may not trust our intuition even when it is "crystal clear." This can lead to a kind of blind-sightedness (in which we stare vacantly before us) or to eventual insight, depending on whether we can "see" the revelations that life presents to us.

It is not surprising that psychoanalysts, and subsequently psychotherapists, place a great deal of importance on the "talking cure." They seek to analyze and uncover a *feeling* response in order to process painful emotions. But there is now a growing reliance in the medical community on prescribing psycho-pharmacological drugs. They address a *feeling* by altering brain chemistry that adjusts thinking and sensation chemically. The *feeling* itself becomes sublimated.

Eugene O'Neill explores the tension between presence and absence, feeling and numbness, in *Long Day's Journey into Night*. Mary Tyrone is a drug addict who lives in a fantasy world filled with dreams that were never realized earlier in her life. Her infatuation with her husband, who was a matinee idol, was based in part on her own need for recognition. Part of her wanted to be in the limelight as a concert pianist, and yet part of her also wanted to disappear into a convent as a nun. Her sense of reality was once dictated by her father and is now prescribed by her surrogate fathers, her husband and her doctor. The fog that rolls in off the ocean is an outer manifestation of the inner haze into which Mary has retreated. Her presence diminishes along with the drugs that numb her senses.

Mary: I've become such a liar. I never lied about anything once upon a time. Now I have to lie, especially to myself. But how can you understand, when I don't myself. I've never understood anything about it, except that one day long ago I found I could no longer call my soul my own.[7]

Sense: Intuition
Intuition is centered in the mind's eye; it is the seat of insight and awareness.

Guided Sensory Exploration
The following sample uses a keepsake to activate sense memory and association through intuition.

You place a keepsake in your hands. It is the projection of your third eye. A manifestation of your intuitive self. You begin to circle the space. As if spiraling outwards from your inner vision. The keepsake circles with you. It is like a ball of energy. A ball of energy in your hands. It carries something that is alive for you. Alive on the inside. You set it down gently. Set it somewhere for safekeeping. Perhaps some secret place. Some hidden space. You close your eyes. There is an image of the keepsake inside your mind's eye. It slowly subsides. You are left alone with the feelings that your keepsake has been holding for you. Something that you wish your keepsake would protect you from. Or grant you. But now you become one with the very thing you fear or desire. You breathe differently. You see differently. You move differently. Finally you come face to face with your deepest secret fear or wish. It whispers something to you. Something you have always known but have never spoken about. And now that thought is released. You are free to reconnect with your keepsake. You search for it by trying to sense its presence. It started you on this inner journey. This inner search. You find it. You open your eyes. You see it with new eyes. New insight. Is it more alive now? Or has it served its purpose?

Crown

The crown encompasses one's *aura*, which reflects the relationship between one's anatomy and autonomy.

Movement Landscape: Breaking Patterns

The life of the mind and the spirit are reflected in the body: it may be bent over with depression, uplifted with self-acceptance or rigid with rules. Our awareness and engagement, or denial and dismissal, of the interplay of the mind, spirit and body can lead to adaptability or ossification.

In the "breaking patterns" explorations, the actors change their physical and vocal expression in quick succession, circumventing any premeditation or planning. The shifts are dramatic and extreme: slow to fast; soft to loud; labored to frenzied; contracted to expansive. An action may be extended or interrupted, magnified or minimized, thereby upending expectations and ideas in mid-formation. By not allowing ourselves the time to make conscious choices, we may be surprised by the wide range of responses that are available to us as we get out of our own way. We may also witness our default positions: the actions we repeat or return to with slight variations, patterns that expose the places in which we are "stuck," but also patterns that reveal our signature persona.

Energy Center: Crown

It is all too easy to make assumptions and judgments about another's physicality that may be limiting or inflating, distorted or embellished. Nevertheless it can be difficult to challenge or change attitudes, especially in a world that prizes beauty and denigrates disability. But being called a "bombshell" is just as destructive as being called a "spastic." We internalize those values, and our body image affects our sense of self-worth. If we can question the heartless way in which objectification contributes to self-loathing we may also be able to shed feelings of victimization and become a "light in the world."

In the play *Richard III*, William Shakespeare's title character was rejected by his mother the moment he was born because of his monstrous appearance. He repays her, and the world, for this fundamental lack of love by turning his physical liability into a weapon. Rather than be the victim, he plays the villain, the only option that seems open to him, since he bears a stigma that would be as difficult to lose as it would be to transcend. He revels in the fear that his repulsiveness arouses in others and uses it as a bid for power. His conscience is as distorted as his spine, leading him to "crooked acts" that expose the soft, unsuspecting underbelly of his opponents. No one is more vulnerable than Lady Anne, who is undone by his sexual advances in which, ironically, all his flattery is focused on physical attractiveness. In the course of wooing her he says,

Richard: Your beauty was the cause of that effect –
          Your beauty, that did haunt me in my sleep
          To undertake the death of all the world,
          So I might live one hour in your sweet bosom.[8]

Sense: Memory and Association

All sensation is stored in the body, ripe for re-collection, re-discovery and reclamation.

Guided Sensory Exploration

The following sample uses a stone to activate sense memory and association.

You are holding a stone. You feel its coolness. Its hardness. Its smoothness. Its roughness. It is part of the natural world. You are part of the natural world. You have a history together. It is like the stone or stick or shell or feather you collected as a child. And kept for a while. And then forgot about. Or did you? Now you rediscover it. It is a reminder of something permanent in the midst of impermanence. You picked it up on your path.

Your path in life. You retrace your steps. Going back. And back. To that moment. That place in time. In space. Now you find your way forward. As if finding your way out of a labyrinth. Returning from some inner sojourn with your stone. With your own story.

NOTES

1. Michael Agnes, Editor in Chief, *Webster's New World Dictionary*, New York: Hungry Minds, Inc., 2002.
2. Tennessee Williams, *The Glass Menagerie*, New York: Dramatists Play Service, Inc., 1945, Act 2, sc. 8, p. 63.
3. Henrik Ibsen, *Hedda Gabler*, Act 3, in *Hedda Gabler and Other Plays*, trans. Una Ellis-Fermor, Harmondsworth, England: Penguin, 1961, p. 345.
4. Jerry Sterner, *Other People's Money*, New York: Samuel French, Inc., 1989, Act 2, p. 78.
5. William Shakespeare, *Romeo and Juliet*, London: Arden Shakespeare, reprinted 2002, Act 3, sc. 2, lines 21–25, p. 170.
6. Martin McDonagh, *The Pillowman*, New York: Dramatists Play Service, Inc., 2003, Act 3, p. 51.
7. Eugene O'Neill, *Long Day's Journey Into Night*, New Haven, Connecticut: Yale University Press, 1968, Act 2, sc. 2, p. 93.
8. William Shakespeare, *Richard III*, New York: Washington Square Press, 1960, Act 1, sc. 2, lines 138–41, p. 12.

CHAPTER 4

Psychological States

FOUNDATION

The word "psychology" comes from the root word *psyche*, meaning "spirit," "soul" and "breath."[1] This term embraces mental and emotional processes that cover the vast range of experiences that comprise the human condition. These processes begin with the expression of basic needs and wants, but are impacted by complexes and constellations that reflect both the individual and the collective unconscious. The foundation of the psychological states of being is based on *myth*, in which personal thoughts and emotions resonate with universal phenomena.

Orientation, collective and actor-generated explorations encompass all three aspects of the psychological states: psychic landscapes, universal themes and archetypes. Orientation explorations are conducted as a group, in which all participants engage in creating a narrative that uncovers archetypal energy. This is monitored by minimal side-coaching, allowing the actors to generate an autonomous world of play. Collective explorations are primarily initiated by the individual actor, who then interacts with the collective, allowing a narrative to further reveal patterns and prototypes. Actor-generated explorations build on the orientation and collective explorations by incorporating original and existing texts with images and objects. This generates character work that is both personally revealing and archetypal in nature. Finally, for each exploration I have included an example from a play to illustrate the incorporation of the exploration into specific character work.

© The Author(s) 2016
E. Hess, *Acting and Being*, DOI 10.1057/978-1-349-95106-2_4

Instructions for implementing the explorations can be found in Part 2, "Explorations in Embodied Performance."

Psychic Landscapes, Universal Themes and Archetypes

The charged nature of explorations into psychological states is tempered by the creation of myths that provide a safe container. The actors enter *psychic landscapes* —exterior environments that are manifestations of interior spaces—which spark heightened awareness and electrifying interaction. These settings include combative, nomadic, transactional, sheltering, communal, collective and liminal.

A setting can be like a character in itself, seeming to be moody or calm or threatening, and plays a significant role in the world of a play. The psyche of a character is reflected in the ways they navigate the space around them as much as the space within them. Their interaction with the environment also informs their relationship to others—whether they chose to hide or invade or accommodate. This interplay between inner and outer reality becomes magnified in a charged environment. It offers one an opportunity to explore an enlarged sense of self through amplified storytelling. This amplification allows the actor to uncover modes of behavior that go beyond individual experience to become archetypal in nature.

In each psychic landscape the actors engage in the *universal theme* of the state. These themes include survival, connection, power, love, communication, awareness and destiny. Carl Jung investigated the relationship between ego and archetype, in which psycho-physical patterns are expressed in universal themes. One or more of these themes is activated during the course of a play. It underscores the super-objective, or overall journey, while simultaneously revealing the arc of the individual characters. One can no more play a super-objective than be an archetype; however, awareness of the universal will inform the particular. This encourages the actor to embrace an expanded sense of self at the same time as they deepen their internal search. Singular work comes from specificity that is as uncommon as it is illuminating.

In the course of the explorations the actors develop relationships in which patterns of conduct begin to suggest a narrative. These patterns gradually lead to the predominance of a specific *archetype*, such as warrior, lover, beggar, nurturer, rebel, visionary and hero/heroine. There is no way to know beforehand which archetype will appear during an exploration, but a prototype eventually reveals itself through ongoing interactions. The archetype one uncovers reveals the actor's core self, as well as that of the character, since it initially arose from their unique instincts, experience and imagination in play with others.

Through embodied experience the actor comes to recognize the vast difference between portraying an archetype and a stereotype. The former is a numinous and resonant representation, while the latter is a clichéd and superficial indication. They begin to understand the difference between work that is illuminating or imitative, provocative or presentational, generous or self-referential.

Curiously enough, many students enter the field of acting looking for an escape from the self, only to discover that this very discipline leads them directly to their core! It is this core being that then goes through an aesthetic fire, so that one's raw material is transformed into an autonomous, living truth. The less one identifies with one's artistic gift, the freer one is to express the inimitable voice and vision moving through them. Archetypes allow the actor to see the universal nature of the human condition at work within them in a recognizable yet transcendent way. Their artistic instrument is then free to vibrate with genuine grace and humility.

INFLUENCES FROM RELATED DISCIPLINES

Mask Work and Puppetry, along with other inanimate objects, are valuable to the explorations into the psychological states. They are tangibles in the outside world that can trigger the inner one. We can see the self reflected on a larger canvas of "otherness"—something different and distinct—that allows for greater perspective on and understanding of our unlived, inferior or shadow contents.

Mask Work

Masks are remarkable in their ability both to reveal and conceal simultaneously. In a mask workshop I attended, the instructor asked that our eyes remain closed while he placed a mask over each of our faces. I was surprised by how alienated I felt when then peering out from behind this unknown façade. I slowly began to investigate who this character might be by gesturing to others to gage their reactions. On the basis of their responses, I altered and adjusted my actions until I found a pattern of behavior that was "other" than that of my known persona. Likewise the other actors looked to me for similar information about themselves in creating their characters. We all became unique yet interdependent beings whose interactions generated a dramatic and enthralling narrative.

Through this mask work we tapped into archetypal behavior that began with the interplay of each person's personality, with projections from others. From here we developed patterns of behavior that took us "outside" our known selves. We found an authentic "otherness" that eclipsed a stereotypical exchange based on unexamined ideas, assumptions and imitations. We might have been tempted to portray these superficial qualities had we seen our masks before putting them on.

I wanted to include archetypal explorations as we delved into the psychological states to encourage actors to elucidate thoughts and emotions that are personally resonant yet equally unselfconscious. Using masks is an effective way of accessing this spacious place, so that without losing sight of their essence an actor can become a "hero" or "murderer" or "seducer" through an expanded sense of self. The actor serves the world of the play not by disappearing into character but by pursuing their character's actions without being self-referential.

Julie Taymor elaborates on this relationship between masks and storytelling: "they [masks] would appear as living statues, emblems of the characters and states of being they represent. They ... transcend the trappings of personality in order to distill the essence of the story."[2]

Puppetry

I have worked with puppets and marionettes since I was a young girl. In many ways they were my introduction to the world of the theater: miniature beings waiting for the breath of life to animate their untold stories. Of course, they were also a projection of all my unspoken wants and needs, and provided a necessary conduit for the release of their stored contents.

I have found that actors are often apt to create an empathetic relationship with a character by first relating to it as something outside themselves. A puppet can hold the dark side of a character—which the actor may have buried or disowned or dismissed—until the actor is able to embrace those prickly or painful contents with greater awareness and ease.

STATES OF BEING

Survival

Survival addresses the most primary issues regarding *life* and *death*. When our existence is called into question, so is our sense of security and safety. We instinctively engage in "fight or flight" activity See Fig. 7.1.

Psychic Landscape: Combative

We are at our most vulnerable when we face the possibility of death. We seek food, shelter, safety and healing. Nothing commands our attention more than securing sustenance, refuge, protection and restoration. Our survival instinct kicks in. We are non-reflective and impulsive, guarded and wary, alert and hyper-aware.

The "combative" exploration begins with actors donning tribal masks while their eyes are closed. They do not know what "face" they are presenting to the world, to which tribe they belong; to whom they are an ally or an enemy, a boon or a threat. They begin to create alliances and test loyalties; to develop strategies to help their cause and hinder others'; to attract followers and outsmart competitors. They find strength in numbers. A leader emerges. A warrior enters combat. A radical challenges authority. An anarchist creates a riot. A refugee seeks asylum. A traitor requests amnesty. A victim surrenders. A martyr is celebrated. All fight for their lives—individually or tribally—to the bitter end.

Universal Theme: Survival

We are capable of de-humanizing the "other" because our own inhumanity may surface when we are in crisis. We do not recognize our behavior and find ways to justify it. Desperation knows no limits. We engage in hoarding and secrecy in an attempt to avert further deprivation and defeat. We find ourselves breaking rules of common decency and compassion in order to outstrip the competition over limited resources.

This struggle becomes more complex the more it moves beyond objective or involuntary conditions such as extreme climate, natural catastrophe and infectious diseases, to encompass subjective or imposed conditions brought on by competing ideologies, religious zealotry and political extremism.

Archetype: Warrior

In the "heat of battle" there is no room for negotiation, no interest in moderation, no investment in co-operation with the enemy. The hierarchy of needs is rigid and inflexible. There are winners and losers. There are allies and opponents. There are friends and foes.

The subtleties of individual expression are absorbed by a collective identity that obscures any deviation from the norm. Individuals become one with their cause, one with their army, one with their tribe—inseparable and inconspicuous. There is safety in unanimity and freedom to act under a specific banner, mission or war.

In Racine's *Britannicus*, Nero is warned by Burrus, his tutor, of embarking on a path that polarizes his people. The choice to take another's life will undermine the security of Nero's own life. By killing another he invites "death" upon himself.

Burrus:

> ...You light
> an endless fire. Feared by the universe,
> you must fear everyone: you must never fail
> to punish, to be uneasy about your plans,
> reckoning all your subjects as enemies.[3]

Connection

The need for connection is fundamental to our sense of belonging. In our search for inclusion our encounters with *intimacy* and *estrangement* deeply affect our feelings of self-worth. These encounters can lead to an increased sense of isolation or communality. They can foster feelings of being an insider or an outsider. Our role in society affects our social skills and standing, and we learn to negotiate with other individuals who are equally influenced by the collective, consciously or not.

Psychic Landscape: Nomadic

Sexual and cultural mores that dictate the nature of sanctioned behavior often inform whether we are socially accepted or outcast. An unmistakable "dance" takes place in which we send out messages that signal our interest or our distaste, our affirmation or our rejection. Body language and gestures invite or repel. Sounds and silence summon or dismiss. Individuals and communities welcome or exclude partners and participants.

In the "nomadic" exploration, the actors are shrouded in sheets or shawls. They are veiled and insulated from the outside world. This may be comforting or claustrophobic, and the idea of connecting with others may feel intrusive or essential. One actor may invite others to hide under their shroud. Or actors may make a tent together. Or they may venture out beyond their "second skin." An extrovert creates extended family. An introvert curls up in a corner. A seducer seeks serial partners. A celibate sits alone. A lover seeks intimacy. A flirt plays the field. A loner tests boundaries. A virgin guards her territory. Finally, the actors unfurl their sheets as they move through the space, using them like extensions of themselves to dance and weave and wrap around each other as they create community in which connection is fluid or binding.

Universal Theme: Connection

The volatile nature of passion often leads to the uncensored expression of desire or disgust. This is due to the restless and unreflective nature of arousal and aversion. It is this very sense of urgency that leads to the procreation of the species, or to its depletion.

This is also the realm of creativity and destruction, literally and metaphorically. We "birth" ideas and works of art as well as generate offspring. Our "creations" may be vital, life-affirming and nurturing or ill-conceived, still-born and poisonous.

All of this creates an atmosphere in which libido—psychic energy—infuses our connections with tremendous pressure or "weight." We flourish or flounder on the basis of our experience of being received or rejected, embraced or repelled, welcomed or dismissed. The sense of our own potential and possibility is greatly influenced by the bonds that endure or break or elude us.

We may project our need to belong onto another, along with our fantasy of fulfillment and the release of our pheromones. This is the allure of the muse, the lover, the mate. We may also envy another's aliveness and attempt to undermine it. This may take the form of trying to "steal their fire," or thwart their creativity, or destroy their autonomy. This too is an expression of passion—passion that invites dangerous, as well as destructive, response. This is the realm of the stalker, the pedophile, the rapist.

Archetype: Lover

Passion lies at the heart of most plays, since competing wants and conflicting desires are central to animated storytelling. In order for a story to "heat up," the characters need to be engaged intensely and intimately. Even though sexuality itself may not be the thematic driving force of a particular play, it is libido—psychic energy—that compels characters to act and react.

Arthur Schnitzler's *La Ronde* is a good example of the combustibility of sexual energy as it races through the play like wild fire. Some of the characters try to label it otherwise, whereas there are those, like the Count, who are remarkably clear-eyed, if not cold-blooded, about their compulsion.

Count: No, dear lady, happiness doesn't exist. In fact, all the things people talk about most don't exist either ... love, for example ... Pleasure ... intoxication ... fine, I've nothing against them ... they're something definite.[4]

Power

The struggle for power fuels the fiery exchange between *strength* and *weakness*. On a purely Darwinian level we all strive to be among the fittest, as our survival depends on it. In the urban jungle this is as true of our mental dexterity as it is of our physical stamina.

Psychic Landscape: Transactional

Displays of strength are meant to relay a message of invulnerability, whereas weakness is often read as a liability. Impenetrability may be confused with strength, flexibility with weakness. Issues of control are often reduced to shows of dominance or submission, whereas in fact they can range from being controlling to being in control, being out of control or letting go of control.

In the "transactional" exploration actors begin with the loose change they have in their pockets and wallets and then barter goods and services in order to improve their financial standing. As their resources increase or diminish they discover that the shift in their status also modifies their behavior. A dictator sets rules. A slave submits. A salesman fawns. A customer demands perks. A thief rips off a bystander. A miser withholds. A boss calls the shots. A beggar pleads.

Universal Theme: Power

If the test of wills moves beyond physical prowess to the engagement of mental acumen, the playing field alters significantly. Open-mindedness may lead to greater avenues of power than rigid thinking ever would. Jonathan Haidt discovered in researching *The Righteous Mind* that in our competition for status the ability to influence others is crucial.[5] To achieve this end one needs to appeal to underlying moral intuitions rather than reason itself. Haidt and his colleagues found several principles that tend to underscore our moral sensibility: care, fairness, liberty, loyalty, authority and sanctity. These principles in turn are married to notions of moral weight, divinity, community, hierarchy, tradition, sin and degradation.

Considerate and caring behavior may serve one better than direct confrontation. However, intimidation, indifference or shaming unfortunately often proves to be just as effective. One may gain ground by force as much as by influence if one is not concerned with moral issues or long-term results, such as loyalty. Regardless of one's chosen tactics, the perception of power is crucial to its maintenance.

Archetype: Master
The ability to effectively assert authority allows an individual or a collective to gain or maintain power. Once a hierarchy is set in place the individual is assigned implicit or explicit status in regards to the collective dictates and rules. This status may be challenged, depending on the individual's role in its creation and its relationship to their sense of well-being. For example, free agency may be willingly sacrificed for heightened security and surveillance. In exchange for the appearance of greater stability, one agrees to limit one's freedom of movement and/or thought.

To express one's personal power it is necessary to have the ability to make an impact—whatever that means in the given circumstances. To be thwarted, or restrained, or undermined, is to no longer be the author of one's destiny. The very word "author," along with "authentic" and "authority," evokes the many variables that exist between autonomy and power.

In Jean Genet's *The Maids* the housemaids and sisters, Solange and Claire, are not free to reveal their authentic feelings: theirs is a love/hate relationship with their mistress. They covet her power over them and yet they are equally contemptuous of the arrangement. They are subversive and secretive and symbiotic. Solange wails with impotent rage to her sister, Claire, against the indifference of their "superior":

Solange: Oh, I hate her! I loathe her. And you, you just stand there! Didn't you see how she sparkled? How disgustingly happy she was? Her joy feeds on our shame.[6]

Love

Our capacity to love is revealed in our displays of *compassion* and *cruelty*. If we have an expansive, open heart we are free to be generous, inclusive and accepting. If, however, our heart is tight and withholding, we are more prone to be limited, exclusive and competitive See Fig. 7.3.

Psychic Landscape: Sheltering
The expansion or contraction of the heart affects all other aspects of our thoughts and feelings. It informs our actions and reveals our "true colors." As mysterious as love is, its expression is the most revealing aspect of our nature. Perhaps this is why we are often cautious and careful about sharing the contents of our heart, since we are at our most naked and vulnerable when it is open.

In the "sheltering" exploration the actors work with a puppet or "homunculus"—a little doll or hand-made figure—that represents a persona that's very different from themselves: a side that may also seem strange, scary or superficial. They create a monologue with their doll or puppet, finding their voice and gestures. They then interact with others' homunculi, exchanging thoughts and observations. Finally, the actors inhabit their homunculus's persona themselves. They consciously look for a home for this character in their heart: for self-acceptance and recognition. They also seek shelter and safety among others. Through this progression the actors are often surprised at the depth of their compassion for their homunculus, even though they originally conceived of a limited sphere for this odd or unfamiliar person. A surrogate mother embraces a child. A stranger is adopted. A nurse tends to a wounded soul. An outsider aids a foreigner. A sister is re-united with an estranged brother. A neighbor takes in an orphan. A roommate makes a friend. A caretaker attends to a refugee.

Universal Theme: Love

It is not surprising that courage is required to live from the heart, and that cowardice is so common. To be fearless is not to live without fear, but to name it and move through it. Yet to "play it safe" is an all too common human trait that we employ in an attempt to avoid undigested feelings. If we are capable of arriving at a place of self-acceptance we also grow in understanding and recognition of our shared humanity with others. But if we are filled with self-loathing for our own failings, we refuse to acknowledge the frailty of others and hold them at arm's length. Or if we refuse to own our issues and we criticize others for their fumbling we may use them as a "punching bag" and rail against them in shows of harsh judgment and recrimination.

Love then is as much the opposite of fear as it is of hate. For we hate what we refuse to accept or don't know or can't explain. Love, however, does not require answers and thrives on investment, engagement and curiosity about the questions life presents. Hate begs to be met with hate, and thereby be reinforced, whereas love does not demand reciprocity—as wonderful as it is when it is acknowledged and returned!

Archetype: Nurturer

We need an experience of love to love in turn. If we are lucky this comes early in life when we are mirrored back to ourselves with the unconditional love of a parent or parents. If we do not receive this birthright, we may spend our lives searching for it from our mothers and fathers—even though they may be incapable of giving it to us. Or we may look elsewhere and find surrogates that fulfill this necessary and central function in our lives. When love is unattainable, so is autonomy, since the center cannot hold without heart.

In Neil LaBute's *the shape of things* Evelyn delivers a long, heady speech about her graduate art thesis project—the evolution of Adam, her lover and "base material"—into a work of art. She is cold, clinical and unfeeling, revealing the lack of love for the contents in her own heart at the same time she catalogues the romantic affects of her "subject." As Evelyn betrays her boyfriend, she also unwittingly exposes the wounded inner masculine energy within herself. Jung referred to this inner masculine energy as the animus of a female, and to inner feminine energy as the anima of a male.

Evelyn: I have no regrets or feelings of remorse for my actions, the man-
          ufactured emotions ... none of it.[7]

Communication

Our need to communicate begins with that primal scream at the moment of our birth. It is only through the civilizing forces of society that we then learn the role that *free-will* and *censorship* plays in our self-expression.

Psychic Landscape: Communal

Words are no more, and no less, than a sophisticated vehicle for relating our wants and needs. But as we begin to shape our thoughts and emotions into verbal responses, we also begin to mold our persona. Language makes it possible for us to voice our truth or to mask it. In contrast to the inarticulate sounds that erupt from us involuntarily, when we speak, we also exercise conscious choice.

In the "communal" exploration, the actors carry protest signs that are often inflammatory and reductive. The more polarizing one's position, the more one tends to use sloganeering and speechifying as a means of persuasion. Dialogue gives way to debate, which gives way to argument, which gives way to chants and rants, which gives way to shouting, or silence, or violence, or chaos. Rarely is there a peaceful resolution or unanimous agreement. Few characters, if any, change positions. If anything, they become more entrenched, although they may align themselves with those of similar beliefs if they think it will strengthen their cause. A teacher tries to enlighten. An agitator stirs up dissent. A politician smears the opposition. A judge passes a sentence. An artist creates a performance piece. A student starts a march. An evangelist preaches. A leader hands out flyers.

Universal Theme: Communication
A picture is worth a thousand words but one word can color the whole world. The words we choose reverberate in the body at the same time as they register in the mind. We can also manipulate the message we wish to convey through modulation of pitch and tone and rhythm and volume. We can select words and expressions and "sound bites" that best represent our intentions, or keep them hidden. We can withhold information, generate buzz, remain silent, expose lies, create rumors, distort facts or report fictions. All these choices allow us to communicate our convictions, our prejudices, our opinions, our likes or our dislikes. Freedom of speech allows us to reveal, betray or distort our inmost thoughts and emotions.

Archetype: Leader
When choice is taken away so is self-expression. Suppression teaches us to be mute or muffled in our responses, except when we are coerced into speaking the truth against our will. In such cases, communication is no longer a vehicle in which to exchange ideas and affection but one in which to alter or eradicate them through force. The gentle art of persuasion is then replaced by harsh interrogation, free press is replaced by propaganda, facts are replaced by fiction, and truth is replaced by lies.

We may also choose to create lies for ourselves when the truth is too painful. A collective may likewise create a mythology that magnifies or minimizes a traumatic piece of its history. The truth itself may not always resemble mere facts. Thus the art of communication is complex, layered and mutable.

In Arthur Miller's *The Crucible*, John Proctor pleads with his wife to affirm his failings, knowing that as long as he is unworthy, he need not speak his truth. Words now have the power to deliver him or kill him, either physically or spirit.ually.

Proctor: My honesty is broke, Elizabeth: I am no good man. Nothing's spoiled by given them this lie that were not rotten long before.[8]

Awareness

To "raise" one's awareness is to engage in a conscious relationship to *mindfulness* and *oblivion*. Wisdom comes from received knowledge— understanding that is grounded in embodied experience. We also need an open mind in order to transform the vast array of events and encounters into a living, breathing whole.

Psychic Landscape: Collective

To know facts and be well read are only a few of the possible avenues we can choose in our search for enlightenment. Curiosity, questioning and the ability to live with the unknown are others. But unknowingness is not synonymous with ignorance or evasion or oblivion. It is a state of active engagement—of searching, of processing, of allowing.

In the "collective" exploration, a placebo stands in for a mind-altering drug that the actors take at a gathering—a party or celebration or fes- tivity. They anticipate the effect the liquid, pill or potion will have on them—whether it will enhance or neutralize or impede their mood. As they socialize they discover that the placebo gives them permission to drop inhibitions, to take risks, to "bliss out," to "clown around," to step out- side their comfort zone and to even be anti-social or alienating. They are experimental and inquisitive or retiring and reticent, all on the basis of the "effect" of some stimulant or depressant that is a placebo. But the power of suggestion gives them the license to go beyond circumscribed social roles and rules. A seer has visions. A clown entertains. A devotee is enlightened. A party animal hoots and hollers. A madman cowers in a corner. A trickster creates chaos. A sage shares pearls of wisdom. A shaman has an epiphany.

Universal Theme: Awareness

Awareness requires that we are able to perceive and react to reality. This may seem obvious but there are many reasons why we may choose not to acknowledge certain events or facts in life. A painful experience may be re-scripted so that it becomes bearable. Wishful thinking may transform a fantasy into a semblance of truth. For example, a New York art dealer made a fortune selling forgeries and never questioned the validity of the works she sold. In fact, one painting hung in her home for many years, and she never noticed that the artist's signature was misspelled.

Clarity comes not through trying to eradicate our wants and needs, but through seeking to acknowledge them. This allows us to see our truth in a new light and move towards a deeper understanding of reality. If we employ our intuition, our sixth sense, we may also be able to "sense" a bigger picture at work: the real beyond the "unreal" of everyday existence, the extraordinary beyond the mundane.

Archetype: Guide

The "dance" between mentors and teachers and their devotees and students is a delicate one. If a guide thrusts their notion of reality onto a follower rather than helping them elicit their own inner truth, it may cause their awareness to be replaced by cult-like conformity; epiphanies may be exchanged for empty mantras, or enlightenment traded for ego-centricity. However, when mindfulness is practiced without an agenda, it frees the individual to find their own path in life, to see their own way forward. When we develop a conscious relationship to our journey we may also recover our core self along the way. Such a gift may come after a difficult passage in which an awakening requires us to let go of past illusions, and to see with new eyes. To be with what *is* rather than live with a fantasy may also be to live with greater acceptance of ourselves and others.

In Anton Chekhov's *Uncle Vanya* Yelena would rather remain oblivious to the promptings of her heart than entertain the possibility of real love, which might transform her longing into genuine aliveness. And Sonya doesn't want to let go of an infatuation that falsely sweetens her life. But when these two women acknowledge each other, the recognition of each other's suffering relieves them, even if only temporarily, from the anger and frustration of inhabiting their small, strangled lives.

Yelena: Sophie...
Sonya: What?
Yelena: How long are you going to stay mad at me? We haven't done anything to hurt each other; it doesn't make sense, being angry like this. Let's stop it, shall we?
Sonya: Oh, I've wanted to... I'm tired of being angry all the time.
Yelena: Oh, I'm so glad![9]

Destiny

Our orientation towards our path in life is greatly influenced by our experience of *hope* and *despair*. We may sense the changeability of destiny as it unfolds or we may feel that our fate is fixed and pre-ordained See Fig. 7.2.

Psychic Landscape: Liminal
Our inner life is exhibited in outer manifestations, and our actions are directly related to our belief system. This interplay includes our overall take on religion and politics and public life, as well as our individual take on ethics and morality and personal responsibility. Our destiny is the confluence of our soul, body and mind.

In the "liminal" exploration, actors enter an in-between place where all is unknown, uncertain and transitional. We know where we have been in the past but not where we may end up in the future. Yet as we take stock of our lives we have a sense of what might be coming that is based on our past actions. But how we view these actions is colored by our thinking. Reward and punishment are part of one person's vocabulary, karmic return is meaningful to someone else, and the hereafter doesn't even exist for yet another. We may feel as though we are being transformed into another being or essence while in this indeterminate time and place. A goddess heals. A demon distracts. A hero is at peace. A doomsayer stokes fear. A penitent prays. A fallen angel revels. A redeemer revives hopes. A cherub lifts a broken spirit.

Universal Theme: Destiny
We may inherit a belief system that reinforces our path in life, or be handed one that is greatly at odds with it. In an article for The New York Times titled 'In Defense of Superstition', Matthew Hutson, the author of "The 7 Laws of Magical Thinking: How Irrational Beliefs Keep Us Happy, Healthy, and Sane" writes that "Belief in destiny helps render your life a coherent narrative, which infuses your goals with a greater sense of purpose."[10]

We crave purposefulness in part because we believe that it will help us attain self-realization. This goal reflects our understanding of salvation and transformation, grace and mercy, good and healing, as well as their opposites—damnation and stagnation, torment and ruthlessness, evil and wounding. How we envision heaven and hell will inform how we attempt to invoke or revoke them.

Our beliefs have a direct bearing on our actions and the outcome of our destiny. For example, a suicide bomber may choose to take his life (and others' lives) in the belief that an act of martyrdom will be honored in the hereafter. Conversely, a terminally ill patient may choose not to be euthanatized in a belief that eternal damnation is worse than a living hell.

Archetype: Hero/Heroine
Beliefs reflect the interface between experience and ideology. We might also want to add the importance of inheritance and essence to this equation.

Our orientation towards both experience and ideology is deeply informed by our issues and how we handle them. A struggle may be life-enhancing to one individual, but debilitating to another. A new approach may seem reasonable to some or completely irrational to others. An epiphany may be heart-felt to a child or heady to an adult. We all search for meaning, whether we name it that or not. We look for heroes to save the day or to save us from ourselves. Or we seek to be the hero in our own lives, hoping that if we take responsibility for the unfolding of our destiny it will lead to fulfillment and freedom.

In *Waiting for Godot* Samuel Beckett introduces us to existentialism in a way that is not passive but profoundly urgent. The characters are restless and in need of meaning, whether they find it or not. The search is necessary even though naming the un-nameable is impossible, but to surrender in silence is equally unbearable. Lucky goes into a torrent of words, words that mask the cosmic dread of emptiness that follows the realization that the old, but known, god is dead.

Lucky: Given the existence as uttered forth in the public works of Puncher and Wattmann of a personal God quaquaquaqua with white beard quaquaquaqua outside time without extension who from the heights of divine apathia divine athambia divine aphasia loves us dearly with some exceptions for reasons unknown ...[11]

NOTES

1. Michael Agnes, Editor in Chief, *Webster's New World Dictionary*, New York: Hungry Minds, Inc., 2002.
2. Julie Taymor, "Music: You Have to Pull a Few Strings to Create these New Opera Stars," *New York Times*, November 19, 2006.
3. Jean Racine, *Britannicus*, Act 4, lines 1350–54, in *Three Plays of Racine: Phaedra, Andromache and Britannicus*, trans. George Dillon, Chicago: University of Chicago Press, 1961, p. 107.
4. Arthur Schnitzler, *La Ronde*, adapted by John Barton from a trans. by Sue Davies, New York: Penguin Books, 1982, sc. 9, p. 56.
5. Jonathan Haidt, *The Righteous Mind: Why Good People are Divided by Politics and Religion*, New York: Pantheon Books, 2013.
6. Jean Genet, *The Maids*, trans. Bernard Frechtman, revised ed., New York: Grove Press, Inc., 1962, pp. 80–81.
7. Neil LaBute, *the shape of things*, London: Faber & Faber Ltd, 2001, p. 122.

8. Arthur Miller, *The Crucible*, New York: Bantam Books, 1959, Act 4, p. 130.
9. Anton Chekhov, *Uncle Vanya*, Act 2, in *The Plays Of Anton Chekhov*, trans. Paul Schmidt, New York: Harper Perennial, 1999, p. 229.
10. Matthew Hutson, "In Defense of Superstition," *New York Times*, April 6, 2012.
11. Samuel Beckett, *Waiting for Godot*, New York: Grove Press, Inc., 1954, Act 1, p. 29.

Explorations in Embodied Performance

The overall objectives of the explorations in embodied performance are transformation, empathy and an expanded sense of self through artistic expression. These are achieved through individual experimentation and collective collaboration. Through physical, vocal and emotive explorations the actor becomes versed in the practice of embodied performance. By accessing the interconnected states of being, they learn to inhabit the immediacy of their instincts, embrace the fullness of their experience and activate the colors of their imagination. Inquiry, inventiveness and interaction leads to a growing awareness of authenticity and openness. This also translates into artistic expression that is a synthesis of a singular vision and supple interpersonal skills.

Explorations, like improvisations, are a tool to unlock the artistic impulses and aliveness of the actor. Improvisations encourage the actor to use their own words and gestures as a way of finding an empathetic relationship to a character. This can be enormously helpful as a means of identifying with the character's circumstances, particularly with contemporary material that reflects day-to-day idioms, expressions and body language. Improvisation has the ability to translate a character's state of being into something that is recognizable and accessible.

Explorations, while also encouraging an empathetic relationship to character, seek to transform the actor in relation to the role, so that the character reflects an expanded sense of self. This skill is particularly helpful for symbolic and heightened works that deal with the embodiment of archetypes. For example, in Greek tragedies (and their re-incarnations by such playwrights as William Shakespeare, Eugene O'Neill and Ann Carson) the actor needs to transcend their everyday experience and tap into an enlarged sense of reality.

Dustin Hoffman said of working on Shylock in *The Merchant of Venice*, "You can't improvise this shit ... First comes the form and second comes the feeling."[1] For this reason I like to use the actual text, including key words or fragments, rather than approximations, so that the language itself becomes inseparable from the reflexes, rhythms and reactions embedded in the behavior, physicality and psychology of a character.

NATURE OF EXPLORATIONS

Behavioral explorations elicit an essence—core identity—by using sympathetic magic (to pretend; as if) in which the actor takes on the qualities of a sentient being they wish to emulate. Through this exchange between nature and invocation we are able to "stir up" instincts directly. Rather than engage the intellect head-on, this allows the actor to gain an understanding of the broad range of human behavior through intuition and incarnation. Unsculpted vocalization and unstudied movement are activated through mirroring, transforming and partnering. These explorations are married to text, image and/or object to further unlock impulses. The interplay between self and otherness—the strange and dissimilar—allows the actor to uncover characters that are expressions of genuine transformation.

Physiological explorations focus on specific energy centers in the body by using metaphor (to compare; as like). Similes for somatic conditions are summoned forth through diverse and dynamic relationships of bodies and voices in space. The actor also inhabits various expressions of physical conditions and sensory stimulations in order to trigger a compassionate and caring relationship to character. As the actor learns to house bodily traits that may initially feel exotic or uncomfortable, they acquire an empathetic relationship to a character that is visceral and grounded.

Psychological explorations bring to light myths (to pattern after; as in) by unpacking a universal theme that is set in an allegorical and charged environment. As a spontaneous narrative unfolds, the actor organically discovers an archetype through a pattern of sustained interactions with others. This archetype is further investigated to illuminate the actor's inner life, as well as their expanded sense of self, as they explore a character's resources and responses through fluid one-on-one imaginative play within the collective.

***

A note on conducting explorations: The instructor may choose to engage both or either of the orientation and collective explorations, on the basis of their specific focus and goals. Orientation explorations build trust and community within the collective. Collective explorations investigate individual autonomy within the collective. In either case, a working definition of the overall state of being—behavioral, physiological or psychological—should precede the explorations. The duration of the explorations is usually somewhere between fifteen and twenty minutes.

***

ORIENTATION EXPLORATIONS

These initial explorations begin with a brief working definition of the overall state of being: behavioral, physiological or psychological. This is followed by an introduction to the particular state (within the three broader categories), which is the focus of the session.

Behavioral explorations take place in an elemental landscape that includes a level of consciousness and an essence. These three interconnected components are evoked through mirroring, transforming and partnering, with the collective gathered in a circle. See Fig. 5.1.

Physiological explorations take place in a movement landscape that focuses on an energy center and sense in the body. These three components are evoked through a "playable" metaphor conducted in partnered and collective exchanges. See Fig. 6.1.

Psychological explorations take place in a psychic landscape that investigates a universal theme in which archetypal patterns of behavior emerge. These three components are evoked through sustained interaction within the collective. See Fig. 7.1.

COLLECTIVE EXPLORATIONS

Working as a whole group, actors uncover individual responses and relationships which unfold against the background of the collective unconscious.

Behavioral explorations utilize text fragments, images and objects to advance the actor's relationship to the essence of a particular state. See Fig. 5.2.

Physiological states encourage the actor to navigate shared space as they inhabit physical and vocal conditions and respond to sensory stimulation. See Fig. 6.2.

Psychological states center on an interior environment which elicits a universal theme from which a character emerges with archetypal energy. See Fig. 7.2.

ACTOR-GENERATED EXPLORATIONS

The actors cull research materials that resonate with the orientation and/ or collective explorations led by the instructor. Working in pairs or small ensembles, the actors interpret the specific state of being according to their own insight, understanding and aesthetics. The actors present their collaboration to the collective as a whole. This collaboration is very much a work-in-progress, which means new and unexpected development often occurs in the moment. Orientation and collective explorations allow the actors to engage in the dynamics of group exchange, while working with a partner or small ensemble now allows for more intimate call and response. See Figs. 5.3, 6.3 and 7.3.

INTERPLAY OF EXPLORATIONS

The unfolding of the explorations can be adapted to suit various teaching curriculums and rehearsal scenarios. Even in circumstances where the explorations are condensed, they are still comprehensive, just not as complex. For example, one might engage behavioral explorations for impulse work, physiological explorations for physical and vocal elasticity and psychological explorations for emotional and imaginative range.

Explorations can be tailored for specific work on character, scene study and production. One can use this framework as a blueprint from which to generate combinations that serve specific artistic needs and visions. These adaptations are the focus of Part 3 "The Interplay of Acting and Being."

SIDE-COACHING AND PROMPTS

The instructor will want to underline key aspects of the actor's craft at work. The instructor's acting philosophy and methodology will, and should, color the way in which these explorations are interpreted. The explorations' intrinsic value lies in the transparent nature in which they unfold. The actor's strengths and weaknesses are immediately apparent and accessible.

I have provided samples of side-coaching and prompts throughout the explorations as possible entry-points or guides for the direction of the explorations. These samples should be fleshed out or reformulated to suit the instructor's specific orientation and objectives.

FEEDBACK

Feedback should be as spontaneous as the explorations themselves. This teaches the actor not to edit raw emotions or unexpected reactions that may not fit into their understanding of their personhood. Often the actor themselves will recognize an underlying issue or a surfacing aliveness. The more they embrace the complexity of their artistic instrument, the more it will resonate with their singular voice and vision.

The instructor may want to critique the work following an exploration, to affirm breakthroughs and highlight challenges. This too should be succinct so as not to disrupt the flow or allow the actors to retreat into their heads. A more thorough analysis of the work may be beneficial at the end of a session, after the completion of a series of explorations and after the presentations of actor-generated explorations.

JOURNALING

It is important that the actors articulate their experience so that they can own it. This is not the same as cataloguing the experience. It is more like responding to the vibrations—feelings and sensations, rhythms and relationships, tenor and tone—that went into its composition. Rather than recording exposition on the basis of the overall theme or shape of the exploration, the writing is sparked by free association and active imagination. This form of journaling can also be referred to as a "free-write."

As the actor becomes more versed in the explorations, and the work becomes more layered, they may generate original characters using the orientation and/or collective exploration as a jumping-off point. This "free-write" may include a pivotal moment in which something of the status quo of the character is eroded, inverted or upended. This may be followed by the creation of an archetypal character who participates in a main event, which leads to a deeper understanding of identity, actions and objectives. The actor may uncover a novel response to a compelling situation that also sheds light on their own inner life.

ACTOR JOURNAL ENTRIES

Following the explorations in embodied performance in each state are samplings of actor journal entries in response to the process.

Entries from behavioral explorations focus on the actor's epiphanies and struggles while learning to "play their instrument." In their growing awareness of self through the interplay of acting and being there is an infinite array of responses from revulsion to resonance, aversion to arousal, resistance to revelation.

Entries from physiological explorations focus on the emergence of a character through stream of consciousness. By inhabiting "playable" metaphors, the actor uncovers a feeling response based on body language and sensation that drives or thwarts their actions and objectives.

Entries from psychological explorations focus on the translation of the individual psyche into archetypal energy. This prototypical behavior may reflect one's deepest and most undiminished needs and wants. An archetypal character may also be the manifestation of a person in the real world, a character in an existing text or a player in the actor's dream or nightmare.

***

One of the gifts of these explorations is the discovery that there is no definitive way of enacting them. This in itself allows the actor to honor the truth of their acting instrument without the interference of their internal critic. This freedom, or the longing for it, becomes evident in the actor's dialogue with others during feedback sessions or self-reflection during journaling. This authorship—this inner authority—can lead to greater risk-taking and revelation in the work itself.

NOTE

1. Peter Hall, *Shakespeare's Advice to the Players*, London: Oberon Books, 2004, p. 8.

CHAPTER 5

Behavioral Explorations

FOUNDATION

The word "behavior" comes from the roots "to be" and "to have."[1] Just as Hamlet wrestles with whether "To be or not to be," how he responds to that question is informed by his essential self and unique experience of the human condition.[2]

Actors are often well versed in the physical and psychological layers that inform character, but unaware of the innate essence that underlies their expression and action. This limits the actor's ability to alter their own behavior and to reveal other perceptions and orientations of selfhood. The explorations into behavioral states provide an opening into various levels of consciousness that elucidate the character's understanding of self, and affect their relationship to the world.

For example, if a character's need is driven by physical survival they may fight *to be* like a tiger—their behavior uncensored or desperate. If their need for social acceptance prevails, they may question what it means *to be* a member of a club—their behavior considered or controlled. If their need is propelled by a morally burning issue, they may struggle with a belief system that encourages them *to be* like a god—their behavior toxic or enlightening.

The explorations into behavioral states are intended to access impulses without mediation or reflection. One just "dives" into the work without a great deal of discussion beforehand. There is room for feedback after the

© The Author(s) 2016
E. Hess, *Acting and Being*, DOI 10.1057/978-1-349-95106-2_5

fact, when the actors can digest their discoveries, but from an organic and visceral place of understanding.

Explorations of behavioral states are impressionistic rather than imitative. The emphasis is on immediate and uncensored expression. This facilitates the release of ingrained or blocked physical and vocal habits and patterns. By moving through the seven states the actor engages in an evolution of embodied experimentation. This leads to an ever-expanding repertoire of behavioral incarnations. The emotional palette is enlarged in the process so that the actor can call upon both strong and subtle feelings when beginning to craft character. The explorations are akin to practicing musical scales, so that the actor can hit any "note" they need effortlessly.

APPROACH TO EXPLORATIONS

Introduction to a Behavioral State

The actors sit in a circle on the floor. The session begins with a working definition of behavior. The instructor explains how it relates to the animation of essence in the most immediate and unstudied way. After this initial session, each subsequent session might begin with a quick review of the previous state before naming the one to follow. This encourages cohesion and a sense of cumulative understanding.

I'll use the primal state as the example throughout the following explorations.

Orientation Explorations: Mirroring, Transforming, Partnering

1. Fig. 5.1 Briefly describe the element that provides the landscape (setting) for the exploration. The elemental landscape is purely imaginative, and the actors throw themselves into an environment that is created within the "mind's eye".

For example, in the primal state the element is earth, which encompasses muck, filth, dirt, ooze, dust and so on.

2. Add in the level of consciousness. There is no hierarchical relationship to the evolution through the seven states. It begins with the most unstudied consciousness and moves through to that of supra-consciousness.

Fig. 5.1 Behavioral orientation exploration: Primal

For example, in the primal state the level of consciousness is instinct, which means the embodiment is uncensored, unselfconscious and unreflective.

3. Ask the actors to suggest sentient beings that exist within the given element and level of consciousness. The evocation of such beings is not intended to imitate sentient reality but to emulate the essence of the behavior, unlocking unpremeditated and imaginative response. This list should be assembled quickly so as not to become labored. It's just to get the imaginative juices flowing and allow the following exploration to be grounded in a specific container.

For example, sentient beings in the primal state would be those such as worms, maggots, rats, hippos, warthogs and so on.

Mirroring
Mirroring frees the actors from anticipating actions, by allowing them to inhabit another's physical and vocal emanations. This also gives the actor

an opportunity to experiment with expression that may expand upon their known repertoire and help to "un-cement" ingrained behavior. Mirroring will change subtly to reflect each actor's signature physical and vocal qualities. But the intention is to observe and mirror another without expectation or judgment.

Mirroring is also a subliminal way to generate empathy. In a study on "Embodied Emotion Perception" the researchers discovered that Botox not only freezes faces but that "reducing facial feedback appears to have broad functional effects on emotional processing, encompassing both emotional reactivity and emotional perception."[3]

1. The instructor initiates the exploration by embodying the physical and vocal qualities that spring from the suggestions by the actors. The instructor's willingness to "jump in" helps to demonstrate the degree of openness and courage required to undertake the work. Before commencing, the instructor acknowledges the actor to whom they will send the behavior. This actor is seated on the opposite side of the circle. In this way the actor is aware of their role in mirroring the instructor before they embody the behavior. It also encourages the actor to take both the time and the space to inhabit the behavior before sending it on to the next actor.

2. Once the first actor has taken the behavior from the instructor, the instructor returns to the circle and side-coaches, as each actor now mirrors the behavior of the previous actor.

For example, side-coaching in the primal state might include the following:

Release that sound from deep in your belly. Let those fingers really dig into the ground. Breathe! Undulate. Writhe. Let it out! Yes, be heavy in your body. Let your belly sink down. Fight up out of the muck. Grovel. Wallow. Enjoy. Don't think!

Side-coaching should never interrupt the flow of the exploration but underline and encourage the discoveries being made. However, the instructor can certainly point out key aspects of craft at work. This may include such qualities as listening and responding, interactive and collaborative skills, commitment and passionate investment, generous and sensitive exchange, risk-taking and bold choices, imaginative and emotional leaps, inclusive and enlivening partnering, and truthful and active storytelling. Referencing the actors' work while in process helps to ground their understanding in instantaneous and recognizable terms.

3. After all the actors have participated, the instructor opens up to the collective for feedback. This too should be as unstudied and unpremeditated as the explorations. A few words or a sentence or two from each actor are plenty.

   It may take a moment for the actors to recover from the exploration before voicing their thoughts and feelings. Give them the necessary room to breathe through this, but don't belabor the exchange. It can be helpful to encourage actors to trust their "gut" reactions rather than attempt to sculpt their responses. This allows them to give voice to inner contents that are often censored. These responses may be surprising as much for their exuberance as for their unsettling or odd nature.

   The instructor will certainly want to encourage self-awareness. They may also want to highlight certain responses or raise certain questions that feel particularly helpful or insightful for the collective as a whole.

Transforming
Transformation occurs when an embodiment shifts without premeditation. Behavior mutates without planning. Essence re-forms without conscious re-orientation. A caterpillar disappears inside a cocoon and re-emerges as a butterfly because it is in its nature to do so. As we open ourselves to our body's wisdom it will initiate action that is unstudied, yet intrinsic to our beingness. Without our conscious intervention, physical movement will affect vocal emanations and vice versa.

Transformation teaches the actor to listen and respond to their internal rhythms. The change in their behavior is sparked by a deeply felt truth that unfolds in the moment. It is often during this exploration that the actor recognizes the blocks that tend to limit their freedom to embody a wide range of responses. This awareness helps to create an inner dialogue with the self that encourages the actor to play outside their "comfort zone."

1. The instructor initiates the action, but this time when the actor mirrors the instructor's behavior they transform it before sending it off to the next actor.

2. Once the first actor has taken the behavior from the instructor, the instructor returns to the circle and side-coaches, encouraging each actor who mirrors and then transforms the behavior of the previous actor.

   Side-coaching from the instructor should focus on unorchestrated and intuitive expression.

For example, side-coaching in the primal state might include the following:

Allow those arms to extend on their own. Yes, let your feet push you forward. Don't know where you are going. Breathe and allow the sound and movement to inform each other. Trust that wave in your belly and back, see where it takes you. Breathe! Deepen! Release!

3. Once all the actors have participated the instructor opens up to the class for unstudied response.

Partnering
Partnering encourages "deep listening" in which the actors engage in a call and response that is sensitive and unscripted. By surrendering control, the actor focuses their attention on their partner, which encourages unselfconscious exchange. A sense of liberation often accompanies this act of generosity, as it helps to dispel self-censorship. This availability in turn sparks an equally generous response from one's partner. The more open and available the interaction becomes, the more at ease and integrated the behavior also becomes. This leads to a dialogue between the actors that can be fluid and fearless.

1. The instructor asks an actor to meet them in the middle of the circle, and the actor listens and responds with the totality of their body and voice.

2. A "round robin" begins as another actor makes their way into the center and the instructor peels back to the circle. The new partner complements or contrasts the earlier partnering simply by the nature of the shift in the energetic exchange.

3. The "round robin" continues until all the actors have been partnered.

Side-coaching from the instructor should encourage whatever is alive in the exchange between the partners.

For example, side-coaching in the primal state might include the following:

Trust that she is there. Yes, dive over his back. Dialogue with sound as well as movement. Play off each other. Diverge. Complement. Contrast. Slither with your arms as one. Listen to each other. Allow. Engage. Challenge. Breathe as one. Move in opposition. Feel free to close your eyes. Listen with your back.

4. After all the actors have partnered, the instructor opens up to the collective for unstudied response. The actors may also want to comment on the progression of the orientation explorations.

Collective Explorations: Text Fragments, Images, Objects

Fig. 5.2 The instructor produces a text, image or object that they want the actors to explore in relation to a particular behavioral state. The instructions are followed with sample materials that are attuned to that particular state of being. The samples throughout all the explorations are culled from a growing catalogue of research materials that I have collected over time. I encourage the instructor to work with materials that inspire their own connection to each state, and ones they also feel will spark their actors' creative fire.

Text Fragments

Words, phrases or sentences are taken from texts that illuminate the essence of a specific behavioral state. The text fragments can come from any source: plays, poems, novels, manuals, advertisements, social media, original and collaged composition and so on.

The text is broken down into small units, and the actors utter the words with very little or no regard for their rational meaning. This allows the actor to let go of their reverence for the words themselves and their symbolic content. The words are free to become the vehicle of inner life rather than the reflection of reasoned thought. Ultimately meaning arises as the exploration continues, but it is meaning that emerges from vocal and physical impulses emanating from the body.

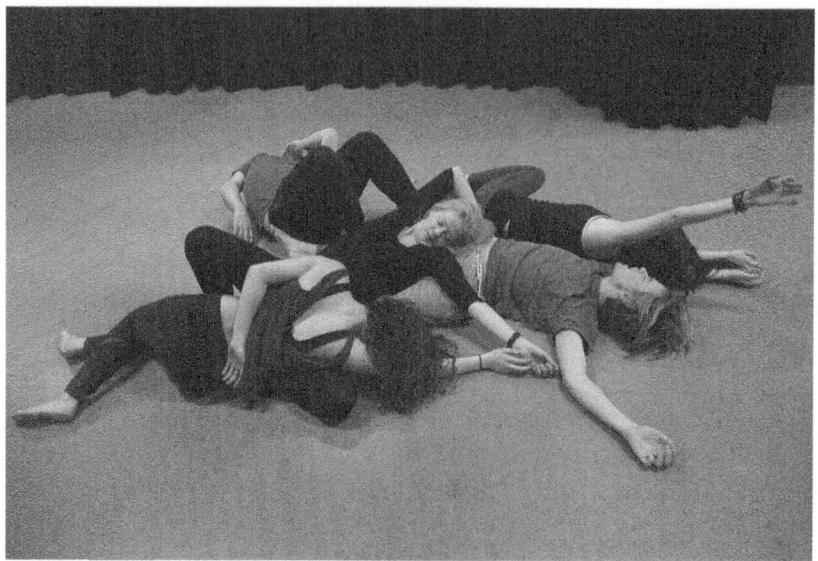

Fig. 5.2   Behavioral collective exploration: Organic

1. The actors form a circle and copies of the text are handed out. A circle facilitates the ease of assigning text, with each actor picking up text where the last one left off. This also encourages the actors not to read ahead but to simply jump in when it is their turn.

2. The instructor embodies the first line, or phrase, and takes the words "off the page," throwing them into their body and voice. They do so with the same freedom that they and the actors discovered during the earlier explorations in mirroring, transforming and partnering.

For example, a possible text for the primal state is an excerpt from *Marat/Sade*, Act 1, scene 15, by Peter Weiss (in this and other text samples, fragments assigned to individual actors are delineated with slashes: /).[4] The instructor would begin with: "A mad animal."

3. The actor sitting next to the instructor takes the following text fragment and interprets it with their own unstudied response to the material.

For example: "Man's a mad animal."

4. The following actor takes the next line, and so on, until all the actors have experimented with the text.

For example: "I'm a thousand years old and in my time," and so on.

5. The actors now know which words belong to them, and during the second or third round, they throw their copies of the text to the side. They have even greater freedom to explore the text now, moving out of the circle into the center of the space when it is their turn.

   Their interpretation should be new each time even though they are working with the same words. This way they won't become attached to a fixed idea and will continue to explore a wide range of possibilities within the given state. The actors simply hang out wherever they land once they have finished their text.

6. The actors are now strewn all over the center of the former circle. From this place they begin to weave their way between each other's bodies as they inhabit their text for the third time. By now they should have a growing sense of ownership of their text, and again, they play with it in new ways as they relate to the other actors directly. After this round, the texts should definitely be set aside.

7. The text is now delivered out of sequence and often overlapping. The instructor may encourage the actors to use just a word or two from their fragment; to feel free to repeat words, to dialogue with others; to take on another's words or exchange them, all depending on the nature of the interaction. The actors move through the space as a whole, interweaving their text, voices and bodies as they listen and respond to each other with an awareness of the particular state they are exploring.

For example, in the primal state, the text from *Marat/Sade* focuses on issues of survival (a theme to be explored from another entry point in the psychological states). The actors writhe and wriggle about each other, looking for ways to marry their words or movements to others in an instinctual way. The text fragments may sound something like this: "mad," "time," "millions of murderers," "spread thick," "human guts," "few survivors," "quaking, quaking, quaking, corpses, sssssssss."

The instructor observes and monitors the arc or journey with minimal side-coaching during the group exploration.

For example, side-coaching in the primal state might include the following:

Fight for your life. Use your words to gain momentum. Explore the space. Where are you? How did you get there? Who is on your side? Who "speaks" your language? Who opposes you, physically, verbally? How can you rise above the heap?

This chaotic struggle may lead to exhaustion or angst as actors surrender or separate from the collective.

8. The instructor winds down the exploration, encouraging the actors to slowly come back to the space. Once all the actors return, the instructor asks for feedback.

For example, prompts in the primal state might include the following:

Where did you go? What did you find there? What happened to your relationship to the text, your body, your fellow actors?

It may take a moment for the actors to digest their experience. Give them space to adjust. The more the instructor encourages the actors to initiate response, they more they spark and encourage each other, discovering in the process that there are no "right" or "wrong" answers. Rather than ask a lot of leading questions, the more the instructor takes their cue from the actors, the more they too will discover surprising and singular responses to the exploration.

Images

Images are selected that directly address the exploration of a specific behavioral state.

The word "imagination" comes from the same root as "image."[5] Thus the use of images can be a very effective way to stimulate visualization and abstract thought. These images can be culled from image banks, computers, newspapers, art books, photographs, advertisements, original drawings and so on.

The image may trigger associations that reveal a theme. I often find there is an inherent duality in the image. I encourage the actors to recognize competing or polar energies as not being mutually exclusive, but compelling in their ability to generate creative tension.

The instructor may wish to provide more than one image to show the breadth of expression for a particular state. They may ask the actors to select two contrasting images from the selection, for further investigation in the collective exploration.

1. The actors gather around the instructor, who sets out the image or multiple images they wish the collective to explore. The instructor asks the actors to free-associate around the image(s) they select by throwing out one word at a time. The instructor repeats the words as they are spoken, so that everyone has a moment to let them sink in.

For example, in the primal state it might be an image like Picasso's *Guernica*. The actors might call out: "chaos," "menace," "desperation," "searching," "light," "jagged," "splintered," "horse," "frenzy," "hand," "frantic" and so on.

2. The instructor looks for contrasting qualities to create a journey that involves a reversal.

For example, using *Guernica*, the journey might be from chaos to light. The instructor shares this arc with the actors and they choose the beginning and end point together. For example, the collective starts in a place of chaos and moves towards one of light.

3. The actors spread out in the space, throwing their impressions into their bodies and voices. They layer in their work from the earlier explorations in mirroring, transformation and partnering.

The actors incorporate moment-to-moment revelations into work that is often non-narrative and proceeds in a non-linear way. Vocal and physical emanations may reveal emotional engagement that is unpredictable, yet purposeful and driven.

4. The instructor observes and monitors the journey with minimal side-coaching that builds on the free associations the actors generated while viewing the image earlier. The actors are encouraged to inhabit its essence as it lives in their imagination and is informed by their interaction with others.

For example, side-coaching using *Guernica* might include the following:

What is pulling you down? Feel your way through the chaos. Who do you trust? What do you most want, hate, love, need right now? Are you alone? Together? Will you make it into the light? What does that mean? Will you live? Die? What do you have to live for? Who will you die for?

5. The instructor winds down the exploration, encouraging the actors to slowly come back to the space. Once all the actors return, the instructor asks for feedback, as in the work on text fragments.

Objects

Objects are collected that express a tangible and/or iconic relationship to the exploration of a specific behavioral state. These objects can be gathered from personal belongings and/or impartial surroundings. They can be imbued with mundane or symbolic import.

As the actors play together with an object they inadvertently create "games" and "meaning" and "ritual." They endow the object with psychosocial import and it becomes emblematic of their collective behavior. In the process of letting go of assumptions about how to view and employ an object, the actors often find hidden, animistic and transformative powers residing within a seemingly lifeless object.

1. There is very little preparation before work with an object. The instructor reiterates the behavioral parameters of the particular state that will be explored.

For example, in the primal state one would emphasize that the actors will want to stay close to the earth or feel a gravitational pull as they work. They may need to be reminded that their understanding of the object itself is purely instinctual. They have no conscious relationship to its purpose or use. They discover how the object's presence affects them and their relationship to each other in unintentional and instinctive ways.

2. The object is put into play. The actors begin to explore it and each other's reaction to it. The instructor encourages them to invest the object with specific meaning and share this awareness with

others, even though the means of communication may be extremely challenging.

For example, the primal state is full of grunts and groans. In this state the actors explore an instinctual, unedited way of relating. There are no obvious powers of reason at work but a great deal of native animal intelligence. If the object is something like play-dough the actors may be drawn to it initially as a lump of clay that is tactile and textured, but then discover that it is also malleable and divisible.

3. The instructor observes and monitors the journey of the exploration with minimal side-coaching. The object may go through a transformation as the collective animates and investigates its numinous qualities. Side-coaching encourages what is already in play.

For example, side-coaching using play-dough might include the following:

What does it feel like? What can it do? Does it smell? Taste? Attract? Repel? Change? Multiply? Divide? Does it bring you together or pull you apart as a group? How? Why?

4. The instructor winds down the exploration, encouraging the actors to slowly come back to the space. Once all the actors return, the instructor asks for feedback, as in the work on text fragments and images.

Combinations of Text Fragment, Image and/or Object
The explorations may be opened up to include any combination of language, visualization and prop. The approach to the exploration is the same, but can certainly be modified on the basis of the instructor's vision. The collective exploration simply takes a moment or two longer to set into motion when introducing more than one material.

In considering whether to work with one or more materials, I find it best to start simply, with one research material per state of being. I might choose to first work with text fragments so that the actors see right away how these explorations can be translated into the actual language of plays and performance pieces.

I build from one material at a time so as not to overwhelm the actors or dilute the specificity of the discoveries. As the process becomes increasingly familiar I add in layers as a way of further addressing the complexity of response to multiple stimuli.

Journaling

Actor journal entries are in response to material(s) that are utilized during explorations into individual states of being

Personal Response

1. The actors retrieve their journals after the explorations are completed. They find a spot in the studio where they can be alone to write about their experience. The instructor may encourage them to focus on the emotions it aroused, the sensations that were triggered and the associations that were made. They have had a chance to bounce undigested responses off each other, so now it is time to dig deeper and allow for greater personal reflection.

2. These reflections often tackle areas that the actor may be reluctant to voice, or resistant to acknowledge publicly. If the instructor wants the actors to share their discoveries, it is important that the actors select the passages they choose to disclose. This respect for privacy encourages the actors to write about the experience in an uncensored and non-judgmental way.

Sentient Being Response

1. The instructor asks the actors to channel their experiences during the explorations through a sentient being and write about them in first person and present tense: "I am ..." For example, in the primal state the essence would be uncensored, raw and instinctive from the point of view of the sentient being.

2. If the instructor wants the actors to share their journal entries it is wonderful to have them do so in the voice and body of the sentient being they have created. Initially this might just be a sound, a word or a phrase. The text may become more sophisticated over the course of the seven states, as the sentient beings evolve in consciousness. As the actors allow this "otherness" to be expressed in their own unorthodox way, they encourage each other to take risks as they exercise their unique and unvarnished creative expression.

Actor-Generated Explorations

Fig. 5.3 These explorations follow the foundational work of the orientation and collective explorations. They are conducted in a separate session since the actors gather research material related to the various combinations of text, image and/or object that were utilized in the initial session(s). They further investigate and personalize their response to the complementary or competing energies within each behavioral state.

I encourage actors to create or collage their own texts, images and objects. This gives them an opportunity to further explore their artistic palette while deepening their investment in the work. It also allows them to contribute a unique point of view to the collaborative creation.

The actors work with a partner or in a small ensemble, which they or the instructor select. I tend to let the actors choose their own collaborators, but ask that they work with different actors and combinations in subsequent sessions, so that they learn to be flexible and adaptable to all kinds of interaction. This hones the actors' interpersonal skills as they practice openness and inclusivity.

Fig. 5.3   Behavioral actor-generated exploration: Cosmic

As in the orientation and collective explorations, the pairs, or small ensembles, create an arc to their exploration, looking for complementary or competing energies. In addition, they include a pivotal moment that leads to a reversal.

Actors may not always agree on the "statement" of the overall journey, but rather than find a happy medium, I encourage them to say "yes" to each other's impulses and ideas. This leads to a dynamic exchange that is not reductive or safe, but challenging, layered and often electric. The "statement" may be open-ended but also more mysterious and compelling.

Preparation
1. The actors pair up and begin to discuss the research materials they have brought to class. This discussion should cover the primary inspiration for their selections or creations and should not be belabored or "academic." Once both actors have shared their thoughts and feelings, they will want to respond to each other's research materials, adding in their own impressions and insights.

2. The actors discuss an arc for their exploration. This requires that they establish a setting or "status quo" for their relationship and then determine the pivotal moment that leads to a reversal—to a conflict or a coming together.

Rehearsal
1. With the barest framework possible the actors explore the relationship "on its feet." The more time they spend exploring in their bodies and voices the richer their exchange will be. This gives them an opportunity to inhabit, rather than indicate, their ideas.

2. The actors explore their relationship and develop a give and take whereby the action is driven and revelatory. They may want to briefly discuss their discoveries and then deepen their exchange or make adjustments to their arc.

Presentation
1. All the actors come together and present their work for the collective. This work-in-progress should be fairly brief—no more than five minutes. It is focused on establishing a relationship that goes through a pivotal moment leading to a reversal. It is not a "skit" and certainly doesn't require a beginning, middle and end. The more

open-ended it is the better, as this helps to keep the work from being result-oriented.

2. The instructor may want to go back and look at a moment in the exploration after the presentation, if there is something buried in the exchange that needs to be illuminated or activated. Often it is the moment after the actors have "tied up the scene" that something genuinely revealing occurs. The instructor may want to extend this moment, since it is outside any expectation that may have been built consciously or unconsciously into the work-in-progress.

3. The instructor asks the partners to share their research materials and talk briefly about their process. The images are sent around the circle so others can inspect them closely. Clearly the text and object(s) have already been shared in the work-in-progress.

4. The instructor, along with the other actors, offer feedback that is based on observation rather than assessment. I encourage actors to raise their hands, to keep their responses short, and to refrain from overlapping. This helps to create an atmosphere of collaboration and community.

   I also generally ask that comments be formed as questions so as to create an atmosphere of curiosity and openness, collaboration and community. This is not to say that comments shouldn't address a feeling response as well as content and form. In fact, it is wonderful when responses reveal the observer's personal point of view, but from a place of ownership rather than instruction or correction.

5. The presentations continue until all the pairings have been presented.

6. The instructor may choose to make closing comments that reinforce the overall work on this particular state, underlining how it also relates to the acquisition of technique and tools of craft. Voice/ speech and movement work is an integral part of the explorations and can be addressed in their own right. The development of an individual artistic process and collaboration skills can be highlighted. Examples of the translation of the explorations into original, devised and/or established worlds of play can be acknowledged and/or discussed.

A Working Definition of Behavior

To Be; To Have

"Behavior" is made up of the words "to be"—one's fundamental nature and essence—and "to have"—to possess or contain. One's fundamental nature is housed in the soul—the essence and spirit of being.[6]

This may be all the definition one needs, but here is further elaboration. "Spirit" is derived from the Latin word *spirare*, "to breathe." "Breath"—the animating principle of life— shares the Latin root *anima* with "soul" and "animal."[7] An animal is defined as any living organism that is typically able to move about, to perform an action. And animism is the belief that all life is produced by a spiritual force, or that all natural phenomena have souls. The essence of life is animation.[8] Animation or action is one of the most fundamental elements of acting and is also a definition of behavior. Thus through action we circle back to behavior. The exploration of behavior allows us to uncover the soul in action, our essence in our fundamental nature.

The Seven Behavioral States

Elemental Landscapes, Levels of Consciousness and Essences

Primal
Elemental landscape: earth
Consciousness: instinct
Essence: primal
Alligator, beetle, cobra, crocodile, cockroach, dinosaur, groundhog, hippopotamus, housefly, leech, mole, mouse, python, rat, slug, snail, toad, turtle, vulture, warthog, worm

Organic
Elemental landscape: water
Consciousness: impulse
Essence: organic
Beaver, clam, crab, crane, crayfish, dolphin, duck, eel, frog, goldfish, goose, heron, lobster, octopus, otter, oyster, salmon, sandpiper, seagull, sea horse, seal, shark, stingray, swan, tadpole, walrus, whale

Willful
Elemental landscape: fire
Consciousness: intent

Essence: willful

Ape, bear, bull, camel, cat, chicken, cow, dog, donkey, elephant, goat, gorilla, horse, lion, monkey, parrot, peacock, rabbit, rooster, sheep, tiger

Humanoid

Elemental landscape: air

Consciousness: affect

Essence: humanoid (pre-conscious baby or human-like replicas or mechanisms)

Action figure, Anime figure, artificial intelligence, Barbie doll, figurine, GI Joe, hand puppet, inflatable doll, mannequin, marionette, mascot, puppet, robot, rag doll, statue, talking doll, tin soldier, wind-up doll

Psychic

Elemental landscape: sound

Consciousness: influence

Essence: psychic

Elf, fairy, genie, ghost, ghoul, goblin, golem, gnome, gremlin, leprechaun, muse, nymph, ogre, pixie, shaman, sibyl, sorcerer, sprite, troll, vampire, witch, wizard, zombie

Mythic

Elemental landscape: light

Consciousness: alteration

Essence: mythic

Basilisk, Bes, bird of paradise, centaur, Cerberus, chimera, dragon, fury, Gorgon, griffin, Karashishi, Minotaur, Pegasus, phoenix, satyr, serpent, siren, unicorn

Elaboration of mythic essences[9]

Basilisk: *lust*—rooster's head and wings, serpent's body
Bes: *sexual potency*—dwarf with erection and animal ears
Bird of paradise: *godliness*—a footless bird
Centaur: *discord*—male upper body, horse's lower body
Cerberus: *guardian of the afterlife*—three-headed dog
Chimera: *danger*—part lion, goat and serpent
Dragon: *chaos*—winged crocodile or snake
Fury: *restores order*—human with snake hair
Gorgon: *the unknown*—female with snake hair and fangs

Griffin: *strength*—lion's body, eagle's head and wings
Karashishi: *vitality, endurance*—lion-like dog
Minotaur: *appetite*—bull's head, male body
Pegasus: *inspiration*—winged horse
Phoenix: *transformative*—footless bird that rises out of the ashes
Satyr: *lust*—upper male body, lower goat body
Serpent: *knowledge*—giant viper or snake
Siren: *seduction*—half woman, half bird
Unicorn: *healing*—a white deer with a spiral horn in forehead

Cosmic
Elemental landscape: ether
Consciousness: actualization
Essence: cosmic
Angel, archangel, Asmodeus, demon, devil, genie, Kali, Kwan Yin, Lilith, Lucifer, Mephistopheles, Vishnu
Greek and Roman gods and goddesses (i.e., the Twelve Olympians): Aphrodite/Venus, Apollo/Phoebus, Ares/Mars, Artemis/Diana, Athena/Minerva, Hades/Pluto, Hephaestus/Vulcan, Hermes/Mercury, Hestia/Vesta, Poseidon/Neptune, Zeus/Jupiter

Elaboration of cosmic essences (including their powers):

Angel: messenger of god
Archangel: celestial being of great power
Asmodeus: king of demons
Demon: evil spirit
Devil: prince of darkness
Genie: guardian spirit
Kali: goddess of creation/destruction
Kwan Yin: goddess of mercy
Lilith: female demon
Lucifer: rebellious archangel
Mephistopheles: medieval devil
Vishnu: supreme god

Greek and Roman gods and goddesses (i.e., the Twelve Olympians):

Aphrodite/Venus: goddess of love and beauty
Apollo/Phoebus: the healer, god of light and truth

Ares/Mars: god of war
Artemis/Diana; lady of wild things, the hunter
Athena /Minerva: sprang from Zeus' head, battle-goddess
Hades/Pluto: king of the dead
Hephaestus/Vulcan: god of fire, both ugly and lame
Hera/Juno: protector of marriage
Hermes/Mercury: Zeus' messenger, shrewd and cunning
Hestia/Vesta: goddess of the hearth
Poseidon/Neptune: ruler of the sea
Zeus/Jupiter: lord of the sky[10]

PRIMAL

Elemental landscape: earth
For example: dirt, dung, dust, filth, garbage, muck, mud, ooze, sand, slime
Consciousness: instinct
Essence: primal
Alligator, beetle, cobra, crocodile, cockroach, dinosaur, groundhog, hip-
    popotamus, housefly, leech, mole, mouse, python, rat, slug, snail, toad,
    turtle, vulture, warthog, worm

Orientation Explorations

Focus: rawness and uncensorship (see Fig. 5.1)

Elemental Landscape: Earth
1. The actors are spread out on the ground.
2. In turn, the actors move on their bellies and backs, staying close to
   the earth. They feel the earth's pull, like molasses or muck, pinning
   them down, sucking them up.
3. The actors struggle against the ground: they submit to it, feel its
   heaviness, resist its gravitational weight. They test their oneness with
   the earth.

Collective Explorations

Focus: desperation and determination

Text Fragment
Sample text: *Marat/Sade* by Peter Weiss, Act 1, scene 15

Patient: A mad animal /
Man's a mad animal /
I'm a thousand years old and in my time /
I've helped commit a million murders /
The earth is spread /
The earth is spread thick /
with squashed human guts / [etc.][11]

Image
Sample image: *Guernica* by Pablo Picasso
The suffering of humans and animals is intertwined and agonizing in this blue, black and white near-monochromatic depiction of the devastation of war. Fragments of body parts and objects are inseparable from the screams of desperation that accompany the horror and pain of senseless violence and impending death.

Object
Sample object: play-dough
Play-dough has the consistency of clay before it hardens. It is tactile and malleable and can be reconfigured and divided, cemented or unstuck. It can be shared or shaped into meaning that becomes a conduit for creative connection and/or destructive alienation.

Actor Journal Entries

Like a snake, we slither and contort ourselves into a super being made up of different consciousnesses and beings and parts that come together to move and dance as one thing which grows and flows and crawls ... We are one. (James Wyrwicz)

Everyone's body is full of hooks and rough edges, tearing into me, pulling at me. They show no mercy and I am left alone. (Gabriel Kadian)

The words I'm hearing are a fright— they're fucking awful and vile—but I'm worming ... I struggle in this massive gross heap of whatever the fuck and I am comfortable. Happy maybe. (Maddie Pollack)

ORGANIC

Elemental landscape: water
For example: blizzard, brook, ice storm, lake, pond, mist, ocean, rain, river, steam, stream, tornado, whirlpool

Consciousness: impulse
Essence: organic
Beaver, clam, crab, crane, crayfish, dolphin, duck, goldfish, eel, frog,
   goose, heron, lobster, octopus, otter, oyster, salmon, sandpiper, seagull,
   seal, sea horse, shark, stingray, swan, tadpole, walrus, whale

Orientation Exploration

Focus: fluidity and changeability

Elemental Landscape: Water
   1. The actors are close to the ground, yet may rise up to their knees or
      to their feet. They allow their bodies to be swept by currents and
      waves.
   2. In turn, the actors feel their bodies float and undulate, crest and fall,
      ebb and flow.
   3. The actors feel the pull of currents, the undertow of a watery tomb,
      the rush of crashing waves. They may ride on waves or return to
      amniotic fluid.

Collective Explorations

Focus: receptivity and rejection (see Fig. 5.2)

Text Fragment
Sample text: *Metamorphoses* by Mary Zimmerman: Alcyone and Ceyx

Narrator: ... as the sun was sinking in the West, / the water
             Everywhere blue / until now, / began to be flecked /
             With the whitecapped waves / sailors dislike. /
             The weather was worse with every moment /
             For the winds were on the loose. /
Ceyx: Reef the sails! / Bail the water! / Secure the spars! /
Narrator: But Poseidon and his Henchman had arrived. / The rest
             was one enormous green catastrophe. / [etc.][12]

Image
Sample image: *Music, Pink and Blue No. 2* by Georgia O'Keeffe
   Swirls of pink and blue seem to undulate and pulse and float in a musi-
cal soup of rhythms and vibrations and emotional undercurrents.

Object
Sample object: hand sanitizer

This slippery clear liquid evaporates quickly. The actors must act quickly if they want to share it or explore its properties. Even though it is a sanitation product, the substance itself is messy and smelly. It may feel velvety and cool, but equally irritating and sterile.

Actor Journal Entries

> I am floating
> I rise with the tides and fall with the waves
> I crash on shores and slither across sand
> I am serene
> I am violent
> I am moved and pressed and pulled
> I ebb and flow (Sarah Lowe)

Swirling, twirling, gnashing, biting waves sweep over me. They throw me against the jagged rocks and rumble their slow lamentations. I tumble against the shore, only to be retched back into the open sea once more. But then, my body dissolves and I lift into the sky, all the particles that were once me flying through the air and rejoining together, clinging for dear life. (Barrett Law)

I am becoming part of a larger body and I am heavy. So heavy. I'm creaking and groaning and feeling colder and colder. I move within the body but can't escape the stiffness. I'm stuck, uncomfortable, stiff. But slowly the warmth comes again. I melt. I melt into my own pool. (Mamie Zwettler)

WILLFUL

Elemental landscape: fire
For example: ashes, embers, flame, flare, flicker, heat, light, smoke, spark
Consciousness: intent
Essence: willful
Ape, bear, bull, camel, cat, chicken, cow, dog, donkey, elephant, goat, gorilla, horse, lion, monkey, parrot, peacock, rabbit, rooster, sheep, tiger

Orientation Exploration

Focus: drive and deliberation

Elemental Landscape: Fire
1. The actors are on their feet. They breathe deep into the fire in their bellies.
2. In turn, the actors take the space, allowing themselves to feel their power, their presence, the immediate response to their internal aliveness.
3. The actors play with the alternating sense of intimidating and submissive behavior. They roar and whimper, expand and contract, attack and retreat.

Collective Explorations

Focus: expansion and contraction

Text Fragment
Sample text: *Baal* by Bertolt Brecht, scene 17

Baal: In the forest eternal / a man lies dead,
        Streams in flood below, / winds screaming overhead. /
        He died like a beast. / He clung to the roots of a tree /
        And he stared at the lofty top of tree on tree. /
        The storm raged on. /
        And those who round about him sat /
        Stood up and said: / "Be calm. This is the end. /
        So let us take you homewards, friend." /
        But he fought back with his knees / and spat /
        And asked those men: / "Home, where is that? /
        Nor child nor land had he. / [etc.]¹³

Image
Sample image: *The Dream* by Henri Rousseau
  Human and animal fantasies and desires reside side by side in this lush, verdant jungle. A snake slithers in the undergrowth, a naked female observes her animal companions, and a lion observes us. Flowers bob their

big heads, and a full moon sheds light on this dense, dark yet strangely serene and sensuous world.

Object
Sample object: a half-empty plastic water bottle

The water bottle is introduced to the collective. The actors begin by exploring individual territorial imperatives, testing their physical strength, agility and vocal power. Eventually they begin to negotiate with others, attracting allies and undermining enemies in their search for possession of the object. The exploration becomes increasingly sophisticated as deceptions come into play along with new alliances. Surprise and suspense are engaged as ways of gaining time and territory. The actors may ultimately engage in a form of "participation mystique" in which a mystical connection develops, making no differentiation between the self and the object. The bottle itself may now become animated and imbued with meaning—a symbol of life or death. The water too may become a healing balm or toxic substance.

Actor Journal Entries

I sweat. Energy pours out of me. Dripping. Seeping out of the pores in me … The pain leaks, the desire remains … I see the washed up remains of people. I see the unvarnished souls in everyone. Heat radiates out of me. I let my breath release. I scream, and all is awakened/unleashed. (Emily Mitzen)

I want to play. I want to understand. I want to collectivize. I want to create. I want to create. I want to imagine. I want to prosper. I want to blossom. I want to care. I want to enliven. I want to evolve. (Kyle Rogers)

The sun is closer than it has ever been before and the light is burning us all to a crisp. I yell, yell, yell to make my voice heard and to force others to back down. There is a heat rumbling in my bones. My brain turns to steam and I howl. (Eli Carpenter)

HUMANOID

Elemental landscape: air
For example: asphyxiation, breath, breeze, contraction, current, exhalation, expansion, inhalation, restriction, space, stillness, suffocation, vastness, wind

Consciousness: affect

Essence: humanoid (pre-conscious baby or human-like replicas or mechanisms)

Action figure, Anime figure, artificial intelligence, Barbie doll, figurine, GI Joe, hand puppet, inflatable doll, mannequin, marionette, mascot, puppet, rag doll, robot, statue, talking doll, tin soldier, wind-up doll

Orientation Exploration

Focus: curiosity and innocence

Elemental Landscape: Air

1. The actors stand, but their stance is unstable, unsure. They carve meaning out of the air, playing with notions of positive and negative space, breath and utterance.
2. In turn, the actors experiment with isolated movements and pre-verbal language. They observe themselves as an arm swings, a leg lurches forward, the torso bends and turns, the spine swivels, the belly collapses. They make percussive sounds and invent words by throwing consonants onto vowels as they try to articulate their discoveries.
3. The actors experiment with pace while moving in space. They are wound up, their batteries die down and their strings jump and snap. They are controlled by some being beyond their own volition.

Collective Explorations

Focus: inviting and alienating

Text Fragment
Sample text: *Blood Wedding* by Federico Garcia Lorca, Act 3, scene 1

Leonardo:	Let's find a dark place /
	Where I can love you forever. /
	People don't matter. /
	The poisons they can pour over us
	Don't matter. /
Bride:	I will sleep at your feet, /
	I will guard your dreams, /

Naked, / looking out at the fields, /
Like a hound bitch. /
That's what I am! /
I look at you /
And your beauty burns me. / [etc.][14]

Image
Sample image: *The Broken Column* by Frida Kahlo
Frida is split down the center of her body. A column of broken concrete replaces her spine. She is wrapped in bandage-like belts that attempt to hold her together. Her face and body are pierced with nails. A white sheet covers her organs. She stares ahead.

Object
Sample object: string
String can be seen metaphorically as an extension of the heart—circulation, nerve endings, messy feelings. Our "heart strings" are easily tangled and intertwined with others as we "jerk them around" or bond with them, manipulating others like puppets as we play with their feelings.

Actor Journal Entries

There is no need to dream. Life is okay. I dance and pull. There is giddiness … A hand from above grasps mine. Like electricity. Soothing. Sleep. Rest. Holding together. Melting into others. Such beauty. Everything is soft. This is waking sleep and dreams. This is love. (Rachel Lepore)

I do love, but I love from afar. I give love to everyone, but I have forgotten to love myself. That's alright, though. I love to love, I live to love, I live to give my love. I lose? (Remi Moses)

i let go and fly. free of all like wisps of wind. skin grazes against mine. the air light. the earth is gleaming. i can reach the sky and feel all my happiness. i am no longer trapped. (Kris Opperman)

Psychic

Elemental landscape: sound
For example: hum, intone, murmur, music, noise, pulse, resonance, reverberation, roar, scream, screech, silence, sing, tone, vibration, whisper
Consciousness: influence
Essence: psychic
Elf, fairy, genie, ghost, ghoul, goblin, golem, gnome, gremlin, leprechaun, muse, nymph, ogre, pixie, shaman, sibyl, sorcerer, sprite, troll, vampire, witch, wizard, zombie

Orientation Exploration

Focus: seduction and ingenuity

Elemental Landscape: Sound
1. The actors are on their feet. They are physically and vocally agile and animated as they fly about the space like voluble sprites, or dance with striking feet like temperamental ogres.
2. In turn, the actors speak gibberish in an attempt to seduce others into doing their bidding, believing their gossip, submitting to their spells, being cowed by their outrage.
3. The actors revel in their ability to directly address their impulses through gibberish. They are impish and excitable, secretive and excessive, given to temper-tantrums and bursts of ecstasy.

Collective Explorations

Focus: volubility and restraint

Text Fragment
Sample text: *A Midsummer Night's Dream* **by William Shakespeare, Act 2, scene 1**

Puck: How now, Spirit; whither wander you? /
Fairy: Over Hill, over Dale, /
        Thorough Bush, thorough Brier, /
        Over Park, Over Pale, /
        Thorough Flood, thorough Fire, /

I do wander everywhere; /
Swifter than the Moon's Sphere; /
And I do serve the Fairy Queen, /
To dew her orbs upon the Green. /
The Cowslips tall her pensioners be: /
In their Gold Coats, spots you see; /
Those be Rubies, Fairy Favours; /
In those Freckles lives their Savours: / [etc.] [15]

Image
Sample image: *Hylas and the Nymphs* by John Waterhouse

Nymphs take human shape to kidnap man for a day and a year. They are spirits of nature seen only by the most sensitive of men. The nymphs seem to possess a quiet strength and mystery that invites intimacy and acquiescence.

Object
Sample object : a pitch pipe

The pitch pipe delivers a single note that the actors hum together, creating aural and emotional unison. They may then choose to harmonize—to generate layers of vibration and musicality. A ritualized dance or invocation may grow out of the aural improvisation.

Actor Journal Entries

I emanate. I am a capsule. I contain. I can spill. I can share. I am magic. I whisper. I open my mouth, I expose myself. You cannot hear me, but it's there. I'm there. If there is no reflection, is there an existence?" (Olivia Daniels)

We are all loving creatures—yet we all do have an edge. Who can ever be truly perfect? Who can only want for someone else? I entered this world of lights, of sparkle and of luminescence. I want a piece of the magic. I want a piece of the light. (Megan Ermilio)

"I am consumed with horrific elation. My passion erupts through my skull and my fingertips. And we dance. We do not dare stop dancing. (Christian Brion)

MYTHIC

Elemental landscape: light
For example: brilliance, chiaroscuro, clarity, color, darkness, illumination,
 incandescence, monochrome, obscurity, shadow, shade, tone
Consciousness: alteration
Essence: mythic
Basilisk, Bes, bird of paradise, centaur, Cerberus, chimera, dragon, fury,
 Gorgon, griffin, Karashishi, Minotaur, Pegasus, phoenix, satyr, serpent,
 siren, unicorn

Orientation Exploration

Focus: aberrance and unsettledness

Elemental Landscape: Light
1. The actors may begin standing but retreat to the ground if their
   animal side takes them there. They alternate between gibberish and
   animalistic utterance.
2. In turn, the actors integrate their animal and spirit natures. They are
   dangerous and free; conscious but uncontrolled, aberrant yet
   alluring.
3. The actors give vent to their desires, their fears, their fantasies. They
   are driven by human and animal wants that are unquenchable and
   urgent.

Collective Explorations

Focus: clarity and obscurity

Text Fragment
Sample text: *Whirligig* by Mac Wellman, Act 1

Girl: I dreamed I had a wicked sister... /
    She was a girl Hun. / She rode her pony, up there
    in the sky. / She rode across the vast empty spaces
    the sky is filled with. /
    Across millions of miles
    of empty sky, / sky so empty and clean you could

never hope to fathom it. / A whole horde of girl
Huns rode with her, / harrying meek ones
of the outer worlds. / They wore only rags; / bows and
arrows were their weapons. / They obeyed no laws /
and had no rules. / For nourishment, they dug up
disgusting roots / and ate them raw. / They laid strips
of raw meat on their ponies' back, / under the saddle
as they rode. / Slap, slap. Slap. / [etc.][16]

Image

Sample image: *The Fireside Angel* by Max Ernst

This colorful but rag-tag grotesquery dances with wild and willful abandon. It is a personification of chaos and madness that is unchecked and imbalanced. It seems to eat up everything in its path with greedy and unabated voraciousness.

Object

Sample object: a mirror

The mirror reflects the viewer back to himself or herself. It can also be trained on others. It can act as an instrument of revelation, of narcissism, of revulsion, of interrogation, of intimidation.

Actor Journal Entries

Are we fire, or are we light? We are darkness. I can see the black ooze congested inside of you free itself from your beauty. We are darkness coming into light, watching the dawn from the hoods of broken-down cars parked before the sand. The ocean stretches in front of us. Can you see it? The first few kisses of dawn blossoming on the horizon. (Linnea Gregg)

I battle with the darkness. It will leave. It must. Slowly it seeps out of me, something I never thought possible. I begin to fly, to float, liberated from myself at last. (Emma Dolhai)

Free ourselves from ourselves. Release our greatest weights. I am not less, and as a result, more. I am opened up and free for light to pass for all eternity. I carry myself home. (Charlie Harrington)

COSMIC

Elemental landscape: ether

For example: agent of enlightenment or obscurity, anesthesia, healing balm, heavens, intoxicant, invisible air, poison, upper air, volatile substance

Consciousness: actualization

Essence: cosmic

Angel, archangel, Asmodeus, demon, devil, genie, Kali, Kwan Yin, Lilith, Lucifer, Mephistopheles, Vishnu

Greek and Roman gods and goddesses (i.e.; the Twelve Olympians): Aphrodite/Venus, Apollo/Phoebus, Ares/Mars, Artemis/Diana, Athena/Minerva, Hades/Pluto, Hephaestus/ Vulcan, Hera/Juno, Hermes/Mercury, Hestia/Vesta, Poseidon/Neptune, Zeus/Jupiter

Orientation Exploration

Focus: infinity and omniscience

Elemental Landscape: Ether

1. The actors stand and breathe deeply through their whole beings, feeling their hearts, their feet, their fingers fill with energy.
2. In turn, the actors move through space with the awareness that every gesture, no matter how large or small, resonates with the whole universe. A finger may send a lightning bolt down to earth, a swish of the hips may stir a gentle breeze, a growl may induce terror. They may intone or sing or create mantras through the use of invented language.
3. The actors feel the subtlety and/or the huge responsibility of every gesture and utterance. They are invincible, experiencing the effects of hubris and humility, divine and demonic power. They wield the ability to invoke good or evil, wholeness or annihilation, integration or polarization.

Collective Explorations

Focus: alignment and crookedness

Text Fragment

Sample text: *A Perfect Ganesha* by Terrence McNally, Act 1

Ganesha: I am in your mind / and in the thoughts you think, / in your heart, whether full or broken, / in your face / and in the very air you breathe. / Inhale, *c'est moi*, Ganesha. / Exhale, *yo soy*, Ganesha. / *Ich bin; io sono. Toujours*, Ganesha! / I am in what you eat / and what you evacuate. / I am sunlight, moonlight, / dawn and dusk. / I am stool. / I am in your kiss. / I am in your cancer. / I am in the smallest insect / that crawls across your picnic blanket towards the potato salad. / I am in your hand / that squashes it. / I am every- where. / I am happy. / [etc.][17]

Image

Sample images: *Paradise* and *Death of the Reprobate* by Hieronymus Bosch

The two images depict the duality of good and evil, of sin and salvation. In *Paradise*, angels and humans intermingle with ease and openness. They are naked yet shameless, serene yet sensuous. In *Death of a Reprobate* aberrant creatures seem to spread infection and disease. The "sinner" is at war with his animality. The word "reprobate" comes from the Latin *reprobatus*, meaning disapproved: "adj. 1 given up to sin, depraved; 2 n depraved person SYN abandoned, condemned, profligate, depraved."[18]

Object

Sample object: a ring

The ring is endowed with supernatural powers. Whoever wears it has the ability to affect the fortunes of others. It can be used as an agent of good or ill. It may become communal property—something that sustains or destroys all that comes within its sphere.

Actor Journal Entries

I know that if we kissed,
Cumulus clouds would crash into cement,
And glass would granulate,
Clovers would shimmy with fever,

Winds would hide,
Angelfish would swim in the stratosphere,
Shadows would clear,
Telephone wires would snap,
An electrical shower would fall,
Because the epitome of sensuality would become a reality,
And there's little use for outside sense when all the sense in the world is centered in the hollow between our hips. (Cherrye Davis)

I have come to the other side of myself. I am flowing, connected, and powerful. I feel good. I am open and whole, I am in my heart. I contain within myself the capacity for both the dark and divine ... I stepped on a new plane of existence. (Lindsay Gitter)

I am alone in a sea of wanderers. It's not evil; it's a breathtaking wind of energy. I find this energy, the energy that is only known to me; the energy that is mine. The others have energy too, but it's different. And together, we become entranced by this mixture of spirits. (Amy King)

NOTES

1. Michael Agnes, Editor in Chief, *Webster's New World Dictionary*, New York: Hungry Minds, Inc., 2002.
2. William Shakespeare, *Hamlet*, New York: Dell Publishing Co., Inc., 1958, Act 3, sc. 1, line 56, p. 111.
3. David Neal and Tanya Chartand, "Embodied Emotion Perception," *Social Psychological and Personality Science*, vol. 2, no. 6, 2011., p.13
4. Peter Weiss, *Marat/Sade*, English version by Geoffrey Skelton, verse adaptation by Adrian Mitchell, Woodstock, Illinois: Dramatic Publishing, 1993, Act 1, sc. 15, p. 37.
5. Agnes, *Webster's New World Dictionary*.
6. Ibid.
7. Ibid.
8. Ibid.
9. Hans Biedermann, *Dictionary of Symbolism*, trans. James Hulbert, New York: Meridian, The Penguin Group, 1994.
10. Edith Hamilton, *Mythology*, New York: Warner Books, 1999.
11. Weiss, *Marat/Sade*, Act 1, sc. 15, p. 37.

12. Mary Zimmerman, *Metamorphoses*, Evanston, Illinois: Northwestern University Press, 2002, p. 23.
13. Bertolt Brecht, *Baal*, ed. Eric Bentley, New York: Grove Press, 1962, pp. 81–82.
14. Federico Garcia Lorca, *Blood Wedding*, version by Ted Hughes, New York: Faber & Faber, Inc., 1996, p. 60.
15. William Shakespeare, *A Midsummer Night's Dream*, London: J. M. Dent, 1993, Act 2, sc. 1, lines 1–13, p. 31.
16. Mac Wellman, *Whirligig*, Baltimore, Maryland: Johns Hopkins University Press, 1994, p. 143.
17. Terrence McNally, *A Perfect Ganesha*, New York: Dramatists Play Service, Inc., 1994, p. 7.
18. Agnes, *Webster's New World Dictionary*.

CHAPTER 6

Physiological Explorations

FOUNDATION

The primary focus of physiology is the vital processes of living organisms and their parts and organs. When we speak of something as being vital we understand that it is both necessary and essential. The word "vital" itself means "life." Vital signs are found in our pulses, our respiration, our body temperatures. Vital statistics mark major life events such as birth, marriage and death. All these measurements are accompanied by our unique relationships to vitality, to our experiences of ease and dis-ease, released and blocked energy, well-being and ill-health.

Actors are often seduced into showing feelings (which are often heightened by obstacles and accompanied by attitudes) rather than playing actions. This isn't surprising since activating our wants and needs means that feelings are summoned simultaneously and unselfconsciously. In fact, the word "feeling" comes from the root word "impel," which means to push into movement. But rather than press on the emotions, the body already has an innate and active response to experience.

The word "feel" refers to a physical sensation as well as to an emotional one. One can "feel cold" or "feel blue." Physical and sensory experience bypasses the intellect, and we often express our state of being in metaphoric language. We "see stars" or have a "knot in our gut" or are as "high as a kite."

The origin of feelings and sensations in the body colors our emotional response. The following are examples from each of the seven physiological states of being.

© The Author(s) 2016

E. Hess, *Acting and Being*, DOI 10.1057/978-1-349-95106-2_6

Root: If my legs are weak, my ground of being may feel shaky.

Sacral: If I'm pregnant, my life force may feel both enervated and enlivened.

Navel: If I lose weight from a stomach virus, I may temporarily lose my appetite for life.

Heart: If my heart is broken, my core self may be shattered.

Throat: If I have a toothache, I may give self-expression to my pain by "biting someone's head off."

Third Eye: If I'm terribly near-sighted and lose my glasses, my presence may shrink as the world around me becomes unrecognizable and threatening.

Crown: If I am chronically depressed, my aura may be as clouded as my spine is bent.

By identifying energy centers in the body—also referred to as chakras, or wheels of energy—we can develop a greater awareness of the specific vibrations moving through us. These vibrations stir within us and generate reactions, creating a "call and response" through body language and vocalization.

Body language is a tool we can use to explore physical and psychological actions through indirection. Vocalization, which also resides in the body, shapes these actions into meaningful utterances. It is said that Shakespeare's use of iambic pentameter replicates the rhythm of a heartbeat. The heart is the center of life itself, and this rhythm becomes more erratic in his later plays, in which the heart is engaged in increasingly complex human conditions.

Our senses are contained within this physical container and are capable of triggering involuntary response, since we cannot control, or filter, a great deal of what we see, hear, touch, smell and even taste, intuit and recall. And so our relationship to our senses is often unedited and illuminating. The interplay between sense and feeling can be as intimate or unnerving as it is intense and immediate. Our uncensored responses to our experiences shape who we are in an unconscious yet revealing way.

Explorations of physiological states are intended to enhance physical awareness, bodily engagement and sensory association. By focusing on individual bodily parts and senses, movement or gesture and voice or speech become specific and salient. This poignancy allows for the recognition and/or release of blocked energy. Libido may be tapped. Memories may be revisited. Emotions may be stirred. The actor moves through the seven physiological states in the body to increase the range and color of available physical and sensory responses, while also developing an empathetic relationship to a character.

Approach to Explorations

Introduction to a Physiological State

Gather the actors together and begin with a working definition of physiology and how it relates to senses and feelings in an embodied and empathetic way. After this initial session, each subsequent session might begin with a quick review of the previous state before naming the one to follow. This encourages cohesion and a sense of cumulative understanding.

I'll use the root state as the example throughout the following explorations.

Orientation Exploration: Movement Landscapes

1. Fig. 6.1 Briefly describe the gestural exploration—based on Butoh, Contact Improvisations or Viewpoints—that provides the basis for the movement landscape. Explain how this movement landscape relates to the specific energy center to be explored.

For example, in the root state "the tree" involves a series of weight-exchanges that focus on the rigidity or flexibility of one's foundation, or ground of being.

2. The instructor demonstrates the movement landscape with a volunteer actor. It is important that the instructor participate in this initial sampling. First, this provides a safe environment by asking and granting permission to make physical contact. Secondly, a demonstration avoids the pitfall of laying out an overly expository and dry explanation of the exploration.

For example, in the root state the volunteer actor will take a relaxed stance as the instructor makes contact with their shoulder and then begins to traverse the body, like sap on a tree. The actor simply needs to maintain their stability while finding ongoing flexibility and grounding.

A note on physical contact: Many of the movement landscapes require the instructor to ask the actor's permission to make physical contact. This can be made easier by outlining very simply and clearly what the exploration will entail before the exploration commences.

3. The actors pair up and begin the gestural exploration focused on the specific movement landscape. The instructor walks among the actors, suggesting adjustments or offering encouragement, rather than side-

Fig. 6.1   Physiological orientation exploration: Sacral

coaching the collective as a whole. Let the actors feel their way and settle into the exploration before bringing the exchange to a close.

For example, in the root state one actor becomes the "tree," the other the "tree sap."

4. Once the exploration is complete, allow for feedback before moving on to another pairing. Keep the comments brief and focused, so as not to lose the momentum of the exploration. By working with more than one partner, the actors gain a sense of the unique exchange of their energies.

5. The movement landscape expands in some form. This may involve another layer based on the original exploration, or a collective exchange. The options will depend on the nature of the movement landscape, which will be clear from the description of each physiological state.

For example, in the root state the actors become both the "tree" and the "tree sap" simultaneously. They grasp a sense of being both adaptable and secure simultaneously. This is also a great opportunity to practice "call and response" between bodies and beings.

6. Allow time for feedback after the exploration.

Collective Explorations: Energy Center, Body Language, Physical Conditions, Sensory Activation, Original Character Embodiment

Fig. 6.2 The explorations of an energy center, body language, physical conditions, sensory activation and original character embodiment should build on each other, moving seamlessly from one to the next. It is also an option to work with some, but not all, of the above sub-categories.

Energy Center
1. Begin by naming the physiological state and identifying which parts and organs of the body are included in this energy center.

For example, in the root state the energy center would include the feet, ankles, legs and buttocks.

2. The actors focus on a specific energy center in the body by engaging a neutral, or habitual, walk and voice.

For example, in the root state the energy center is the ground of being. Prompts might include the following:

Fig. 6.2 Physiological collective exploration: Heart

What story does one tell with their feet? Or legs? Or tail?

3. The actors move through the space allowing the exploration to inform their relationship to weight, alignment, ability, awareness, size, shape and space.

For example, prompts in the root state might include the following:

Start with your own walk. Be conscious of where you place your weight. Do you walk through your whole foot? Are you bow-legged? Are you pigeon-toed? How fast or slow is your natural rhythm?

Body Language

1. The instructor offers metaphors for body language that the actors incorporate into their physical expression. They consider what body language and/or patterns come from heredity or from experience—whether they are new, old, ingrained or novel.

For example, prompts in the root state might include the following:

Are you a pain in the ass? Are you a tight wad? Do you tiptoe around issues? Do you put your foot down?

2. The instructor asks the actors to play with alterations in space, time and sound.

For example:

Space: leaning, sitting, lying down, crouching (including all surfaces or planes—floor, wall, chair, platform, and so on)
Time: slow and fast, half-speed and double speed, repeated and interrupted
Sound: loud and soft, high and low, rough and smooth

The instructor encourages the actors to build and expand upon their existing repertoire of movement and vocalization.

For example, in the root state the actors focus on their ground of being. As they run and meander and sit and tiptoe and lie down, they note the ways in which this movement feels familiar, forced or freeing. They play with vocal patterns that instigate or underline physical response.

Physical Conditions
1. Multiple Physical Conditions

The actors incorporate various released and blocked physical conditions. By exploring qualities, symptoms and/or side-effects, their relationship to balance and well-being is tested. The actors allow the breath to move into vocalization as they give expression to the feelings that accompany the conditions.

As the condition becomes more acute or augmented, it may lead to gibberish or short phrases that complement or contrast with the physical condition. The actors fight their condition or give in to it, exaggerate or inhibit symptoms, release or block energy. They discover whether this condition is a new development, chronic, acute, inherited, inborn, imposed or repetitive.

For example, in the root state an actor may begin by leaping through space, then suddenly hobble on a "sprained" ankle (figuratively, not literally!). However, it's not necessary that there be a logical progression to the movements. One may drag a foot, then double over from constipation, then be bow-legged, then get a blister, then hop on one foot. And so on.

2. Specific Physical Condition

The actors focus on a specific released or blocked physical condition, deepening their relationship to feelings and sensations within the body. The actor seeks to develop an empathetic relationship to the character that emerges from this embodiment.

For example, prompts in the root state might include the following:

Breathe through your feelings. See where the breath takes you. What happens to your voice in response to a stubbed toe? Do you sing as you dance?

3. Alterations in Space, Time and Sound

The actors explore variations with the specific physical condition.

For example, prompts might include the following:

Change your plane—Stand. Sit. Lie down. Crouch. Lean.

Play with different speeds—Slow down. Speed up. Interrupt. Repeat.

Alter your sound—Louder. Softer. Shout. Whisper. Screech. Coo.

Sensory Activation
>   The instructor introduces a sensory activation into the explora-
tion by moving among the actors while they are exploring their chosen physical condition.

For example, in the root state the sensory activation is smell. The
instructor may move through the space with a stick of incense or a room
spray. The instructor may choose not to engage in side-coaching while this
is going on, so that their presence among the actors is unobtrusive.

Original Character Embodiment
1. Interplay of Feeling and Sensation
>   The actors consciously embody a specific character as an outgrowth
of their preceding explorations. They allow the interplay of feelings
and sensations to trigger emotion, recollection and association.

For example, prompts in the root state might include the following:

>   How long have you had this condition? What or who caused it? Was it
an accident? Is it hereditary? How does it make you feel about yourself?
How do you respond to other people?

2. Interplay of Characters
>   The actors explore their character through interplay with others,
enhancing a growing understanding of their character. They should
feel free to include gibberish, but refrain from language. It will only
encourage them to describe their condition and distance themselves
from the experience rather than deepen the connection to the inner
experience of their character.
>   The actors observe the ways in which their physical condition
affects their interactions, on both a physical and a psychological
level. As the actors encounter or engage others they begin to develop
an empathetic relationship to their physical condition, which is now
married to their own impulses. They note what feelings are aroused
by this physical condition and investigate how anger, jealousy, love,
joy and so on are experienced within this character.

For example, prompts in the root state might include the following:

> Do you welcome others? Shun them? Need their help to stand? Want to reach out and dance? Are you secure and grounded? Shaky around others? Do you throw your weight around? Do others throw you off balance?

3. **Journaing**
   The actors retrieve their journals and write an inner monologue based on their original character. This "free-write" reflects the character's stream of consciousness from their point of view in the first person and the present tense. Rather than write exposition that relates the facts of their interactions with others (explanatory narrative), the actor focuses on the interiority of the character. Rather than illustrate outer events, the actor looks for the triggers to those events and the character's response.

Sensory Explorations

Sensory explorations are valuable in and of themselves, as they address the senses specifically while not necessarily focusing on a particular energy center in the body. However, sensory stimulation (or deprivation) is still introduced as a means of engaging physiological response. Emotional connections will invariably arise of their own accord but need to be translated into playable actions.

Sensory stimulation may come from tangible or intangible ingredients. For example, the sense of sight might be explored with the use of a blindfold—a tangible deprivation. Sound might be explored with the use of recorded music—an intangible stimulation. The actors incorporate verbal and physical actions that arise in response to the sensory stimulation, inviting the recollection of memories and associations to deepen their awareness and responses.

Guided Sensory Exploration
Sample sensory guided explorations can be found in Part 1, "Physiological States of Being." For example, incense is used to activate the sense of smell in the following exploration.

1. The actors scatter throughout the space. They may begin with their eyes closed so as to heighten their concentration. However, it is important that they also allow their bodies to respond to the stimulus. The instructor may need to encourage the actors to move through the space during the course of the exploration, so that their journey is as actively engaged as it is internally alive.

For example, as the actors breathe in the scent they react physically.

2. The instructor either offers prompts to the actors as they explore the given sense or takes them on a guided sensory exploration. The actors may be encouraged to let the stimulus elicit images in the "mind's eye" as well as evoke memories and associations.

3. The instructor guides the actors through the collective sensory exploration. The actors are each very much in their own world, following their own trajectory. It is important that the collective not impose a united response to the stimulus.

For example, one actor may love the smell of incense and it may make another want to gag.

4. The actors move through the space inhabiting the provocations of the sense—reliving a moment in depth, layering a feeling, expanding an idea into an embodiment. The instructor may want to carry the incense while wandering among the actors, to give them a more intense or pungent experience.

For example, prompts for smell using incense might include:

Follow your mind's eye. What do you see? Where are you? Is anyone else there? Is this smell special? Routine? Unique? Soothing? Upsetting? Aromatic? Alarming?

Emotional recollections associated with the senses are often personal and private in nature. The instructor may either choose to allow time for feedback after the exploration, or have the actors immediately engage in journaling.

Endowed Object Sensory Exploration
The actors explore the endowment of objects within the context of sensory association. If the instructor chooses to work with these sensory explorations it is necessary to ask the actors to bring in an object related to a specific sense beforehand.

For example, possible objects related to the senses include the following:

Smell: toiletries, perfume, incense, oils, flowers, cleaning fluids
Taste: food, beverages, spices
Sight: all images, mirror, matches, candle, lamp, flashlight, glasses, blindfold, cell phone
Touch: all objects: hot or cold, sharp or dull, soft or hard, smooth or rough, liquid or solid
Hearing: musical instruments, chimes, bells, cymbals, hand tools, drill, hammer, electronic equipment, radio, iPod, beeper, phone, alarm clock, siren
Intuition: mind or mood altering placebos (digestible and inhalable), Tic Tacs, M&Ms, water, sugar, flour
Memory and association: artifact, icon, talisman, photograph, painting, sculpture, charm, venerated or taboo object

1. The actor begins by exploring the object in relation to the specific sense. The instructor may ask them to focus their exploration on sense memory and association. They may then ask them to relate these findings to a character—either an original creation, or one that they are working on in scene study.

For example, using smell as the sensory focus, the actor may have brought in cleaning fluids as part of an exploration into the role of Solange or Claire from Jean Genet's *The Maids*. The actor might begin with their own associations to the smell and then marry them to the character. If the sensory stimulation is unfamiliar to the actor this requires that they set aside emotional recollection and search for novel yet equally salient responses.

2. The actor "throws" their experience into their body and voice, either using gibberish or text to further their relationship to the sensory stimulation.

For example, using cleaning fluids, the actor might find high-pitched and staccato utterances and sharp and angular movements to accompany the smell of ammonia.

3. The instructor may ask the actors to share their sensory object with others, creating complementary and competing stimuli. The actors register their response to the new stimulus through varied physical and vocal exploration. The actors may want to exchange fragments of text as well as gibberish as they interact.

For example, using smell, the actor working on Solange or Claire may want to cover herself in the perfume of another actor to disguise her pungent odor, or to use it in an attempt to imitate "Madame."

4. Option. Through animation of an object the actor mirrors their own, or their character's metaphoric state of being.

For example, object animations might include the following:

Box as retreat
Feather as fickleness
Apple as appetite
Pillow as insulation
Mirror as narcissism
Sleeping mask as escape
Nail file as edginess

5. The instructor may choose to set aside time for feedback, or ask the actors to immediately engage in journaling.

Journaling

1. The actors engage in a "free-write" in which they create a character in first person and the present tense using the collective explorations as a jumping off point. Writing in the character's voice—speaking their truth—often triggers buried material from the actor's own experience. This personal content deepens the interplay between an internal monologue and external events, the marriage of inner life and imaginary circumstances.

The instructor may also ask for the inclusion of a main event—an incident that challenges the "givens" of the character—and necessitates a re-orientation. This change can lead to further character revelation, as well as unexpected actions and objectives.

If the instructor chooses to engage the independent sensory explorations, this may lead to journal entries that are more self-reflective. These explorations often unearth poignant memories and associations that the actor may want to address directly before transforming their emotional core into character work.

2. Actors extract a sentence or phrase from their journal that they wish to explore "on their feet." It needs to be something revealing, but not exposing, so that they are comfortable sharing their discoveries. The actors speak the line out loud as they develop a physical score—five gestures, for example—that are suggested by the text. The actors explore the text and gestures in alterations of space, time and sound.

3. The actors partner and create a short physical and vocal dialogue.

Actor-Generated Explorations

Fig. 6.3 Collective explorations allow the actors to experience physical and psychological presence or absence within a group setting. Now they

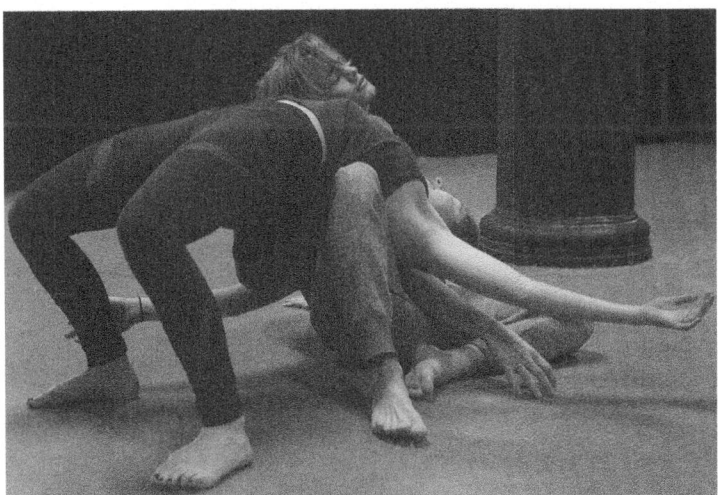

Fig. 6.3 Physiological actor-generated exploration:Root

discover how bodily conditions enhance or alienate interaction on a more intimate scale.

The actor's research begins with their journal entry. They may modify or elaborate their character monologue on the basis of growing empathy. The monologue is supplemented by a sensory object that augments the relationship of character and physiology. This augmentation is further enhanced by an image that "speaks" to the actor about the character, either literally or metaphorically.

Preparation, rehearsal and presentation closely follow the model outlined for the behavioral states, with minor adjustments.

Preparation

1. The actors pair up and begin to discuss the research materials they have brought to class. This includes reading their character monologues out loud to each other, sharing the sensory object and image and briefly stating why they were chosen. This discussion should cover the primary inspiration for their character monologue and object and image selections and should not be belabored or "academic." Once both actors have shared their thoughts and feelings they will want to respond to each other's research materials, adding in their own impressions and insights.

2. The actors look for a primary relationship between their characters, selecting segments from their individual texts and combining them in any way they choose. For example, they can repeat text, share text or meld text—all with the goal of finding an arc for their exploration. This requires that they establish a setting or "status quo" for their relationship and then determine the main event—an incident that challenges the givens of the characters. This event necessitates a re-orientation in the relationship.

Rehearsal

1. With the barest framework possible, the actors explore the relationship "on its feet" using their texts (including fragments or collages) as written, rather than improvised. They may choose to incorporate the sensory object(s) directly or simply use it or them as a reference. The more time they spend exploring in their bodies and voices, the richer their exchange will be, as it gives them an opportunity to inhabit, rather than indicate, their ideas.

2. The actors explore their relationship and develop a give and take whereby the action is driven and revelatory. They briefly discuss their

discoveries and then deepen their exchange or make adjustments to their arc. The work is not set, but does have a shape based on the arc.

Presentation

1. All the actors come together and present their work for the collective. This work-in-progress should be fairly brief—no more than five minutes. It is focused on establishing and developing a relationship that leads to a main event and a new direction to the relationship. It is not a "skit" and certainly doesn't require a beginning, middle and end. The more open-ended it is the better, as this helps to keep the work from being result-oriented.

2. The instructor may ask to go back and look at a moment in the exploration after the presentation, if there is something buried in the exchange that needs to be illuminated or activated, or something particularly alive that begs for further investigation. Often it is in the moment after the actors have "tied up the scene" that something revealing will occur. The instructor may want to extend this moment, since it is outside any expectation that may have been built consciously or unconsciously into the work-in-progress.

3. The instructor asks the partners to share their images and objects (the monologues have already been shared in the presentation itself) and talk briefly about their process. The research materials are sent around the circle so that other actors can inspect them closely.

4. The other actors, along with the instructor, now offer their feedback, which is based on observation rather than assessment. I encourage actors to raise their hands, to keep their responses short, and to refrain from overlapping. This helps to create an atmosphere of collaboration and community.

   I generally ask that comments be formed as questions so as to create a sense of curiosity and openness. This is not to say that comments shouldn't address a feeling response as well as content and form, and it is wonderful when responses reveal the observer's personal perception and point of view, but from a place of complete ownership.

5. This process continues until all the partnerings have been presented.

   At this point the instructor may choose to make closing comments that reinforce the overall work on this particular state, underlining how it relates to the acquisition of technique, tools of craft and character work.

A Working Definition of Physiology

To Feel; To Sense

The primary focus of physiology is the vital processes of living organisms and their parts and organs. To be vital is to live. To live is to feel and sense. The word "feel" comes from the root word "impel," to push into movement. The word "sense" comes from the root word *sentire*, "to feel." Vital processes and parts are dynamic and indivisible.[1]

This may be all the definition one needs, but here is further elaboration.

Movement is perceived through physical sensation and is experienced as an emotion and/or condition. Our awareness of experience may be through intellectual perception or instinctual ability. Consequently, physical sensation can lead us to think or believe, often for unanalyzed reasons, because we are emotionally moved. This conviction allows us to invest in the immediacy of our responses without hesitation since we are impelled. We are moved. We are vital.

The Seven Physiological States

Movement Landscapes, Energy Centers and Senses

Root
Movement landscape: the tree
Energy center: root
Coccyx, feet, immune system, legs, rectum
Sense: smell

Sacral
Movement landscape: sculpture
Energy center: sacral
Appendix, bladder, intestines, pelvis, reproductive organs
Sense: taste

Navel
Movement landscape: membrane
Energy center: navel
Abdomen, diaphragm, gallbladder, kidneys, liver, pancreas, solar plexus, stomach
Sense: sight

Heart
Movement landscape: rubber band
Energy center: heart
Arms, breasts, chest, circulatory system, fingers, heart, lungs, ribs, shoulders
Sense: touch

Throat
Movement landscape: wind instrument
Energy center: throat
Esophagus, gums, jaw, mouth, neck, teeth, throat, thyroid, trachea, vocal
    cords
Sense: hearing

Third Eye
Movement landscape: mirror opposites
Energy center: third eye
Brain, ears, eyes, nervous system, nose, pineal gland, pituitary gland, sinuses
Sense: intuition

Crown
Movement landscape: breaking patterns
Energy center: crown
Aura, hair, joints, muscles, skeleton, skin
Sense: memory and association

ROOT

Movement landscape: the tree
Energy center: root
Coccyx, feet, immune system, legs, rectum
Sense: smell

Orientation Exploration

Focus: balance and imbalance

Movement Landscape: The Tree
   1. The actors are partnered. They engage in a weight exchange whereby
      one actor stands still—the "tree"—while their partner contacts their
      body, the "tree sap," with one pressure point. I like to start with

shoulder to shoulder. The "tree sap" maintains a point of contact while exploring the physical terrain of the rooted bodily shape of the "tree." The exploration is enhanced by closing the eyes, allowing the actors to focus on the exchange of weight rather than on the point of contact.
2. The actors exchange roles and begin again.
3. The instructor allows for a brief feedback session, then actors repeat steps 1 and 2 with new partners.
4. Both actors engage a point of contact while exploring each other's physical terrain simultaneously. They are like intertwined trees or vines.
5. The instructor allows for another brief feedback session before partners are switched again.

Collective Explorations

Focus: ground of being – stability and instability

Energy Center: Root
The actors initially engage neutral and habitual body language as they move through the space.

Body Language
1. The instructor offers a selection of metaphors. The actors embody them one at a time. They may choose to inhabit some, but not all, suggestions.

Prompts:

Are you …
    a push-over, a light weight, a dead weight, the salt of the earth, a rock, a wall flower, a pain in the ass, a stick in the mud, cemented in, wishy-washy, a tight ass, a tight wad, a shit, an ass-kisser?

Do you …
    kick up your heels, throw your weight around, boot others out, shit on another's parade, drag your feet, tiptoe around issues, put your foot down, give everything away, run away from feelings, move as light as a feather, stand your ground, have a bug up your ass, act as though your panties are in a knot, feel as though a rug's been pulled out from under you, feel weak in the knees, have knock-knees, plough through life, put your tail between

your legs, back down, back away, have a pickle up your ass, pull another's leg, fly by the seat of your pants, feel like your world is turned upside down, feel as though you're on top of the world?

2. The instructor asks the actors to include alterations in space, time and sound. The actors add these qualities into their ongoing exploration of multiple physical conditions.

Prompts:

Change your plane—Stand. Sit. Lie down. Crouch. Lean.

Play with different speeds—Slow down. Speed up. Interrupt. Repeat.

Alter your sound—Louder. Softer. Shout. Whisper. Screech. Coo.

Physical Conditions
1. The instructor suggests multiple physical conditions. The actors embody them one at a time. They may choose to inhabit some, but not all, suggestions.

Prompts:

Released energy includes flexibility, regular bowel movements, limberness, strong ankles, aligned knees and good arches.
   Blocked energy includes constipation, diarrhea, corns, club foot, dysentery, worms, hemorrhoids, gas, loose bowels, bed wetting, varicose veins, bunions, hammer toes, pigeon toes, broken toe, sprained ankle and bow-legs.

2. The actors embody a specific physical condition selected from the previous multiple physical conditions.
3. The actors add in alterations in space, time and sound without prompts from the instructor.

Sensory Activation
   The instructor moves among the actors with an object that activates the sense of smell.

Prompts:

Is this smell ...
   pungent, sharp, aromatic, perfumed, fragrant, musky, musty, earthy, salty, fruity, briny, astringent, burning, floral, fresh, clean, pure, stuffy, sweet, sickly sweet, stinky, bitter, acrid, woody, smoky, stale?

Original Character Embodiment
1. The actors explore the interplay of their specific physical condition with the sense of smell.
2. The actors interact with each other, using body language and gibberish to explore the ways in which their character's physiology informs their sense of self in relation to others.

Original Character Journal Entries

ABLE
   What can I say to you? My son, expecting so much from me. I see the way you look at me. I'm your hero, your superman, your god. But how can I teach you to walk when I can't move my legs? One step at a time, son. One foot in front of the other. How can I teach you to stand up for everything you believe in? Be unmovable. Don't let them change you if they try. I can't. You'll have to do as I say and not as I do. I can't. You can. (Anonymous)

THE PRETTY
   Walking down the aisle for graduation no one smiles and claps for me. They all just stare. No one's pretending like they understand. Well good. Cause you don't. None of you do. You can stand proud and tall. You can have boys staring at your legs, but for good reasons only. I want to get good stares. Oh God, I wonder what a good stare feels like. One Halloween I was Cinderella. And I wore this big, gold gown that went all the way to the floor. I was pretty and they smiled. One day ... just pretend I don't exist, ok? (Kerry McEnerney)

SHITHOLE
   I live in a shithole. I'm totally smashed at this point mainly cos my husband is a fucking asshole and I can't deal with him anymore and my kids are shit heads. That's right. Nothing good I can say about them. My husband would have gotten a job today if he wasn't fucking high all the time. I have a job. It's shitty but I have a job—and I'm the woman. I shouldn't be slaving away day after day, morning, noon and fucking night. (Anonymous)

SACRAL

Movement landscape: sculpture
Energy center: sacral
Appendix, bladder, intestines, pelvis, reproductive organs
Sense: taste

Orientation Exploration

Focus: inclusion and exclusion (see Fig. 6.1)

Movement Landscape: Sculpture
1. The actors are partnered. They begin by shaking hands. The first actor steps away while their partner maintains the position of the hand. The first actor begins to sculpt the space that is suggested by the pose, using their own body to reconfigure the interaction.
2. The partner steps away and rearranges their body to create another configuration. The two actors continue to take turns re-shaping their relationship to each other, and to the positive or negative space between them.
3. The instructor holds a brief feedback session, then the actors repeat steps 1 and 2 with new partners.
4. The actors create a "liquid" sculpture in which they move around and through each other's space in continuous movement.
5. Option. The actors create a group sculpture, adding and subtracting numbers until they ultimately create a collective configuration.
6. The instructor holds another brief feedback session.

Collective Explorations

Focus: life force—passion and apathy

Energy Center: Sacral
The actors initially engage neutral and habitual body language as they move through the space.

Body Language
1. The instructor offers a selection of metaphors. The actors embody them one at a time. They may choose to inhabit some, but not all, suggestions.

Prompts:

Are you …
    a go-getter, a slacker, wet behind the ears, deflowered, a shrinking violet, a clinging vine, blossoming, a hipster, a kill-joy, a bitch on wheels, all balled up inside, ballsy, a Juicy Lucy, a cock of the walk, a peacock, a hot mama, a hot shot, a dickhead, a limp dick, a dried-up prune, an infectious asshole, a cuckold, hen-pecked, a ball buster, as tight as a drum, a cold fish, in a pissy mood, pissed off, as stiff as a poker, a snake in the grass, prim and proper, the life of the party, a tart, sour grapes, a mistake?

Do you …
    have ants in your pants, a stick up your ass, a popped cherry, stabbing cramps, blue balls, hot flashes, Red Emma, a hard-on, the hots, a woody, infectious energy, a muffin top, love handles?

2. The instructor asks the actors to include alterations in space, time and sound. The actors add these qualities into their ongoing exploration of multiple physical conditions.

Prompts:

Change your plane—Stand. Sit. Lie down. Crouch. Lean.

Play with different speeds—Slow down. Speed up. Interrupt. Repeat.

Alter your sound—Louder. Softer. Shout. Whisper. Screech. Coo.

Physical Conditions

1. The instructor suggests multiple physical conditions. The actors embody them one at a time. They may choose to inhabit some, but not all, suggestions.

Prompts:

Released energy includes fertility, potency, birth, labor pain, virility, fecundity, pregnancy, erection, peeing, lubrication, wet dreams, orgasm and menstruation.

Blocked energy includes urinary tract infection, sexually transmitted disease (STD), sterility, miscarriage, impotency, castration, barrenness, frigidity, yeast infection and enlarged prostate.

2. The actors embody a specific physical condition selected from the previous multiple physical conditions.
3. The actors add in alterations in space, time and sound without prompts from the instructor.

Sensory Activation

The instructor moves among the actors with an object that activates the sense of taste.

Prompts

Is this taste...

salty, briny, bitter, tart, sweet, spicy, sugary, tangy, tart, zesty, savory, chalky, bland, sharp, syrupy, peppery, off, spoiled, rancid, rotten, rich, creamy, delicious, disgusting, appealing, revolting, nauseating, comforting?

Original Character Embodiment

1. The actors explore the interplay of their specific physical condition with the sense of taste.
2. The actors interact with each other, using body language and gibberish to explore the ways in which their character's physiology informs their sense of self in relation to others.

Original Character Journal Entries

I LOST IT

I lost it. Just now. I was sleeping and dreaming I was drowning in the sea. I mean I tasted the salt. And then I awoke to blood on my sheets, blood in the air. I awoke to nothing. When hours before I had been full and opaque. I was round and lovely and convex. And now I'm lacking. Now I don't exist. I don't know why my body is still here. My soul is lost and my body is useless. I sing the songs I was practicing for my baby. (Sings) "Rock-a-bye baby in the tree tops ..." I hum myself into numbness. (Alison Maddren)

OFF TO WAR

I have the sleekest hair. Swish, swish, swish, swish, through all my hair and all over me. I love being tousled and touched and licked ... Come closer. I'll lick all your war wounds. One by one by one ... Why don't you follow me? It's funny really; I could knock all those girls over. I could knock them all down to the ground and choke them with my soft, soft hair. But that won't get me to you will it? I can lick the dead but I like the warmth of live flesh. (Jordan Baum)

BABY DRAGON

The shell cracks around my middle—why? I suppose I want to move my hips, but the shell is still around me. Except my hips. Is this where I'm supposed to move from? The shell is cracking now. No! No! My home ... my arms. My wings ... I have wings! FREEDOM! I couldn't have known I was not free until I tasted freedom ... Where is my mother? Have I got a mother? Are you my mother? (Ankita Raturi)

NAVEL

Movement landscape: membrane
Energy center: navel
Abdomen, diaphragm, gallbladder, kidneys, liver, pancreas, solar plexus,
    spleen
Sense: sight

Orientation Exploration

Focus: resistance and release

Movement Landscape: Membrane
  1. The actors form a circle around one actor. The central actor closes their eyes. The other actors place their hands on the central actor's body, including their stomach and outstretched palms. The central actor begins to test the "membrane," letting their body move wherever it wants while their feet are planted. The other actors support but do not direct the action. Movement begins slowly and then gathers speed as the "membrane" becomes more elastic and accustomed to the central actor's movement.
  2. The central actor attempts to walk forward. This walk may or may not go far since it is met with resistance now as well as support from the "membrane."
  3. The "membrane" slowly releases from the central actor. The central actor continues to move on the basis of their memory of the

"membrane." The intensity of visceral response to the previous resistance continues as the central actor engages in their own exploration. Slowly the intensity subsides and the actor comes back to the space.

4. The instructor may choose to engage in feedback after each actor has been in the "membrane," or may wish to wait until all the actors have had a turn, so as not to create anticipation or a generalized response.

Collective Explorations

Focus: appetite for life—ingestion and rejection

Energy Center: Navel
The actors initially engage neutral and habitual body language as they move through the space.

Body Language
1. The instructor offers a selection of metaphors. The actors embody them one at a time. They may choose to inhabit some, but not all, suggestions.

Prompts:

Are you ...
   all shook up, a sucker, a vacuum, a leech, a parasite, a bottom-feeder, hungry as a bear, emptied out, tapped out, puckish, peckish, lily-livered, a dynamo like the Energizer Bunny, flat as a pancake, a worry wart?

Do you ...
   have eyes that are bigger than your stomach, a knot in your guts, a Buddha belly, butterflies, a monster appetite, a stitch in your side or a gut like cement or a bowling ball; do you bite off more than you can chew, freak out (anxiety attack), suck up, suck the life out of others, feel as though you were "kicked in the gut, get the wind knocked out of you, eat like a bird, blow up, chew people out, chew the fat?

2. The instructor asks the actors to include alterations in space, time and sound. The actors add these qualities into their ongoing exploration of multiple physical conditions.

Prompts

Change your plane—Stand. Sit. Lie down. Crouch. Lean.

Play with different speeds—Slow down. Speed up. Interrupt. Repeat.

Alter your sound—Louder. Softer. Shout. Whisper. Screech. Coo.

Physical Conditions

1. The instructor suggests multiple physical conditions. The actors embody them one at a time. They may choose to inhabit some, but not all, suggestions.

Prompts:

Released energy includes digestion, stamina, satiation, energy, adrenaline rush, nourishment and invigoration.

Blocked energy includes nausea, diabetes, anxiety attack, bulimia, heartburn, anorexia, emaciation, abdominal cramps, intestinal disorder, fainting, indigestion, starving, bloating, obesity, stomach cramps, hepatitis, diabetes and stomach flu.

2. The actors embody a specific physical condition selected from the previous multiple physical conditions.
3. The actors add in alterations in space, time and sound without prompts from the instructor.

Sensory Activation

The instructor moves among the actors with an object that activates the sense of sight.

Prompts:

Is the sight ...

Bright, dull, iridescent, luminous, foggy, translucent, opaque, hazy, faint, shaded, colorful, neon, monochromatic, sepia, sharp-edged, limpid, filmy, brilliant, dazzling, unfocused, crystal-clear?

Original Character Embodiment

1. The actors explore the interplay of their specific physical condition with the sense of sight.

2. The actors interact with each other, using body language and gibberish to explore the ways in which their character's physiology informs their sense of self in relation to others.

Original Character Journal Entries

DEFEATED

I'm gonna be skinny enough some day, not today, but someday. Doesn't matter how much dizziness I get or if I can't stand up right away, but I'm on the road there. I'll lose this baby fat—that's all this is—baby fat. Only a few more weeks and I think I'll be there. Just have to eat less. Ya know mom always said I ate like a bird. Food tastes like birdseed to me ... Today I looked in the mirror. I think I gained some weight. A lot. Just need to eat less. A little bit less. Just need to eat less. (Chris Andrea)

A BELLY FULL OF PRIDE

Mmm. Hmmmm. These hips are big hips. And this belly, shit this belly housed five little babies. I am proud of this belly. I don't wear a girdle. I like the way I look. People goin' change. They goin' get older, hell, from my face I look about a hundred. But my belly stays the same. It comforts me. Like a bear goin' into hibernation, it nurtures me. It reminds me of my Momma. Now she was good and fat. And you know what Momma always said—"you can never trust a skinny woman" (Lyndsey Bourne)

QUARANTINED

They won't let me out! I need a doctor, please! There's something going on inside of me and they're watching it eat me from the inside out! Why won't you help me? UGH! AHH! I feel like a piece of bread being devoured by a swarm of ants. My body has no chance ... no power over this virus—this demon! They have quarantined me in here to be eaten away like a fucking rack of ribs. UGH! What the fuck is wrong with you people! AHH! I'm still alive, there's still a chance. Help! HELP! HELP! (Javi Perez)

HEART

Movement landscape: rubber band
Energy center: heart
Arms, breasts, chest, circulatory system, fingers, heart, lungs, ribs, shoulders
Sense: touch

Orientation Explorations

Focus: attraction and repulsion

Movement Landscape: Rubber Band
1. The actors form two lines facing their partners from opposite sides of the room. They move simultaneously in a straight line, with soft eye focus, towards and away from their partner. It is as if they are connected by a rubber band—a "kinesthetic" elasticity that expands and contracts as it radiates from the heart. They vary the pace and space between them as they move to and fro.
2. The actors raise their hands to chest level, palms facing out, so that their palms are available to be met by their partner. They can touch palms, or not, as they move to and fro.
3. The actors move throughout the room, never losing the soft eye focus on their partner. They weave in and out of other partnerships as they move to and fro.

* Alternate Exploration: The Hug
Focus: embrace and release

1. The actors are partnered. One actor stands still as the other circles their body, observing their body language and aura. They exchange roles and begin again.
2. The partners move into a hug. They hold this position and then release each other.
3. The actors move throughout the space observing and hugging all the actors individually.

Collective Explorations

Focus: core self—nurturing and numbing (see Fig. 6.2)

Energy Center: Heart
   The actors initially engage neutral and habitual body language as they move through the space.

Body Language
1. The instructor offers a selection of metaphors. The actors embody them one at a time. They may choose to inhabit some, but not all, suggestions.

Prompts:

Are you ...
  heart-sick, heart-broken, tight-fisted, a tight wad, cool as a cucumber, an Ice Queen, an island of calm, cold-hearted, warm-hearted, a block of ice, a love bug, a Mother Hen, a magnet, hot-bloodied?

Do you ...
  have heart burn, a racing pulse, a fluttering heart, a shattered heart, a heart murmur, itchy fingers (a thief), a heart like a fist, a heart that leaps into your throat, a heart that does flip-flops, a heart which pounds like a drum; do you feel as though your heart is wrung out, suffer from heartache, bare your heart, rib people, make others eat their heart out, cut people out of your heart, hold your cards close to chest, wear your heart on your sleeve, beat your chest, cry your heart out, cough your lungs out, pour your heart out, wrap your arms around the world, get the wind knocked out of you?

  2. The instructor asks the actors to include alterations in space, time and sound. The actors add these qualities into their ongoing exploration of multiple physical conditions.

Prompts:

Change your plane—Stand. Sit. Lie down. Crouch. Lean.

Play with different speeds—Slow down. Speed up. Interrupt. Repeat.

Alter your sound—Louder. Softer. Shout. Whisper. Screech. Coo.

Physical Conditions
  1. The instructor suggests multiple physical conditions. The actors embody them one at a time. They may choose to inhabit some, but not all, suggestions.

Prompts:

Released energy includes low blood pressure, regular heartbeat, good circulation, steady pulse, strong lungs and easy breathing.
  Blocked energy includes palpitations, heart attack, numbness, pins and needles, chest pain, rheumatic fever, hypertension, tennis elbow, clogged arteries, poor circulation, hyperventilation, heart murmur, hang-nail and sprained wrist.

2. The actors embody a specific physical condition selected from the previous multiple physical conditions.
3. The actors add in alterations in space, time and sound without prompts from the instructor.

Sensory Activation

The instructor moves among the actors with an object that activates the sense of touch.

Prompts:

Is this touch ...

hard, soft, cold, hot, warm, fuzzy, rough, brittle, smooth, tepid, frigid, scalding, metallic. rubbery, silky, stringy, spongy, greasy, dimpled, concave, convex, curvy, straight, linear, circular, filmy, burning, blistering, soothing, sweaty, slimy, feathery, ticklish, ropey, chalky, stabbing, sticky, electric, shocking, itchy, scratchy, prickly?

Original Character Embodiment

1. The actors explore the interplay of their specific physical condition with the sense of touch.
2. The actors interact with each other, using body language and gibberish to explore the ways in which their character's physiology informs their sense of self in relation to others.

Original Character Journal Entries

CONFUSION

I haven't breathed in months. My chest, it hurts, and every time I try to take in air it feels like someone hitting me with iron. I do not know if this is entirely medical. My doctor says it is, but people can die from a broken heart. So what is that? Medical? Emotional? Both? It's human. My heart is heavy in its emptiness, and so the short, desperate inhalations that my body attempts on a regular basis are not some side effect of whatever condition this man in his white coat can throw at me. They're the physical embodiment of my inability to fully attain what I need, which is love so foreign in its strength and warmth that I will never be able to learn its language. (Francesca Placidi)

IN AND OUT

You really just suck. You know that? Fucking ridiculous. What is this? I can't even breathe I'm so hot and so cold and so trapped in and fuck, why won't you let me out? How can you possibly physically let go of me, but keep me trapped? Keep me in there. Let go of me. Why are you holding on? Why am I holding on? Are you even holding on? Probably not. It's just me. Please just stop. I want you out of my life. I want you in it. (Jenna Dioguardi)

SLICED OPEN

I feel like someone has just sliced me open. But not in a bad way. I'm not sure yet if it's a good way. Right now it has sort of just happened. But I think I wanted that. I wanted people to know because if people know maybe it's true and something can come of it. There is beauty in being exposed which is something that I think we learn with age. My heart is all jumbly and I can't make it stop and I don't know what to do with myself and I feel a great deal of tension over my body, but it's a loose tension. I'm a walking paradox. I'm a blubbering idiot. But can you blame me? Can you blame a woman in love? I just ... I don't know. I don't even know. I think it's just good to finally see my heart. (Jenna Rossman)

THROAT

Movement landscape: wind instrument
Energy center: throat
Esophagus, gums, jaw, mouth, neck, teeth, throat, thyroid, trachea, vocal cords
Sense: hearing

Orientation Exploration

Focus: resonance and response

Movement Landscape: Wind Instrument
  1. The actors are partnered. One actor is the "instrument"; the other is the "wind" (or musician). The "instrument" closes their eyes and responds to the physical and vocal "note" or suggestion from the "wind" as it passes over them. The "wind" makes a sound and contacts some part of the "instrument" simultaneously. The "instrument" responds like a resonating chamber, taking their time to react to each movement or vibration.
  2. The "wind" moves at a pace that allows the "instrument" to fully inhabit each suggestion.

3. The partners exchange roles and begin again.
4. The actors "sound the body" without touching their partner. It is a kind of "sound painting" whereby the "instrument" enacts a physical composition based on the vocal suggestions of the "wind."
5. Option. Sound is accompanied by a word or phrase.

Collective Explorations

Focus: self-expression—clarity and obscurity

Energy Center: Throat
The actors initially engage neutral and habitual body language as they move through the space.

Body Language
1. The instructor offers a selection of metaphors. The actors embody them one at a time. They may choose to inhabit some, but not all, suggestions.

Prompts:

Are you ...
a mess of words, bursting at the seams, tight-lipped, a blabber-mouth, full of hot air, someone who has no edge or bite, a pain in the neck, stung by harsh words, tongue-tied, a garbage mouth?

Do you ...
have a lump in your throat, a slip of the tongue, lock jaw, bee-stung lips, verbal diarrhea, a word on the tip of the tongue, a throat as rough as sandpaper; do you hold your peace, seal your lips, whisper sweet nothings, foam at the mouth, bite people's heads off, rubber-neck, spit things out, swallow feelings, bite your tongue, caress your words, vomit out a stream of nonsense, rip into people, put your foot in your mouth?

2. The instructor asks the actors to include alterations in space, time and sound. The actors add these qualities into their ongoing exploration of multiple physical conditions.

Prompts:

Change your plane—Stand. Sit. Lie down. Crouch. Lean.

Play with different speeds—Slow down. Speed up. Interrupt. Repeat.

Alter your sound—Louder. Softer. Shout. Whisper. Screech. Coo.

Physical Conditions
1. The instructor suggests multiple physical conditions. The actors embody them one at a time. They may choose to inhabit some, but not all, suggestions.

Prompts:

Released energy includes vocal resonance, laughing, crying, singing, articulation, strong teeth, giggling, gurgling, free expression, supported breath, a good bite and relaxed jaw.
   Blocked energy includes congestion, muteness, nodes, lock jaw, thyroid condition, laryngitis, choking, strep throat, gagging, stuttering, sore throat, bad teeth, Tourette's syndrome, a cold, swollen glands, coughing, phlegm, tooth ache and stiff neck.

2. The actors embody a specific physical condition selected from the previous multiple physical conditions.
3. The actors add in alterations in space, time and sound without prompts from the instructor.

Sensory Activation
   The instructor moves among the actors with an object that activates the sense of sound.

Prompts:

Is this sound ...
   loud, soft, jarring. melodic, syncopated, booming, rhythmic, percussive, high-pitched, low-pitched, screeching, ear-splitting, humming, rumbling, rattling, moaning, bellowing, whispering, whistling, resonating, vibrating, harmonic, discordant, mono-tonal, droning, ringing?

Original Character Embodiment
1. The actors explore the interplay of their specific physical condition with the sense of sound.
2. The actors interact with each other, using body language and gibberish to explore the ways in which their character's physiology informs their sense of self in relation to others.

Original Character Journal Entries

OVERTHROWN

Forgive me my trespasses as we forgive those who trespass against us. When the nuclear bomb was first tested one man recalled a mysterious and foreboding quote: "I am become death, destroyer of the world." Give us this day our daily bread. Things have changed, I cannot feel grief or it would take me. I cannot feel happiness or it would destroy me. I can only regret and fear. Hallowed by thy name, thy kingdom come. When the world ends it is interesting to see who you turn to. When war, famine, poverty finally comes, when everyone dies and the dead start to walk. Zombies? Rally? Everyone I have good news! We survived the end of the world. Now our struggle begins. I need food, shelter. May we help ourselves, because God will not. Now is not the time of hope. Now is not the time of thinking. Now it the time of action. Fear not those who are already dead. I have no fear. I only regret. Regret for not having lived before. Regret for wasting my life as a priest. GOD IS DEAD. The time of man has arrived! (Patrick Daly)

LYING

Nobody can see everything. That's impossible. You're lying. Not Santa Claus. Not God. Not the tooth fairy. Not mom with eyes in the back of her head. No one can see everything that happens. I don't believe you. Daddy says that I'm going to grow up to be a hard woman. I don't know what that means, but I won't. I'm going to be what I want, when I want. That's what grown ups can do. Except grown ups who believe. They're dumb. They're afraid of what God is going to think of them. Well, I'm smart. I'm not a hard woman. I just don't believe. (Emily Dixon)

BLOCKAGE

I ... I ... I ... wa .... waannt to ... tttt ... tt ... talk tt .. truly I .. I do. Bbbut it'ssss luh ... luh .... like ... ssss ... suhh ... some ... thing bbbee ... beyond my kkk .... kkon ... contttt ... troll ... isss hhuhhollddinnng me bbbbaaahhhckk ... I nnn ... know wwa .. wa.what I have to sssay, wwannt to ssay, no nnneeed to sssay aand wwhen I kk ... can't it is ffr ... fruuss ...

frustrating. Too sseee yoourr eeager fface mmet wii .. wiith dddiiisssaapp-pointttment just inn .. inn ... furiates me. II waa ... want ttt to yuh... yell, bbut I.... I kk..can't. Kkcann't ggett thhe wworr ... words oout sssooo I ... I ... tt .. try again ... Sss ... ssommee.times ... I..I ffffeell lllike II ... ddd ... don't eeven speak En..english. (Caila Gale)

Third Eye

Movement landscape: mirror opposites
Energy center: third eye
Brain, ears, eyes, nervous system, nose, pineal gland, pituitary gland, sinuses
Sense: intuition

Orientation Exploration

Focus: observation and transformation

Movement Landscape: Mirror Opposites
1. The actors are partnered. A line is taped out to divide the space in half. One side is given a suggestion to embody something hard, immutable or heavy, for example, a soldier in armor, a block of ice, a stone, a mummy or a mannequin. The other side is given a suggestion to embody something soft, fragile or vulnerable, for example, a milkweed pod, a fluttering leaf, a feather, a moth or a flame. The partners slowly approach each other, maintaining eye contact the whole time. As they reach the center line, they begin to assume the essence of their partner and let go of their current incarnation. Once they reach the far side the transformation is complete.
2. The actors turn away from their partner and pursue others in space. Once they make eye contact they begin the process of transformation, slowly inhabiting the others' essence.
3. Option. The actors are shown contrasting images (i.e., abstract or impressionist paintings), which they embody in the same way as the earlier suggestions. After the exploration each side describes the painting they embodied after transforming into their partner's image.

Collective Explorations

Focus: presence—clarity and obscurity

Energy Center: Third Eye
The actors initially engage neutral and habitual body language as they move through the space.

Body Language
   1. The instructor offers a selection of metaphors. The actors embody them one at a time. They may choose to inhabit some, but not all, suggestions.

Prompts:

Are you …
   light-headed, hot-headed, in your head, high, stoned, baked, buzzed, tipsy, hung-over, whacked, poker-faced, red-faced, an airhead, a space cadet, thick, empty-headed, unable to see something in front of your nose, blind as a bat, nosey, eye-candy, a scatter brain, clear-eyed, doe-eyed, open-minded, a nervous Nelly, cottony, wide-eyed, tweaking out, lost in the clouds, a vegetable, in your own world, a daydreamer?

Do you …
   have your head in the clouds, bags under your eyes, dizzy spells, a black out, a brain fart, a brain wave, a brain freeze, a mind like a steel trap, ringing ears, a steady gaze, phantom vision, eyes that cloud over, a stuffy nose, a runny nose; do you put your nose in the air, see stars, see for miles, sniff out trouble, see your way through a rough patch, know how to eyeball a problem, wear rose-colored glasses, glaze over, follow your stream of consciousness?

   2. The instructor asks the actors to include alterations in space, time and sound. The actors add these qualities into their ongoing exploration of multiple physical conditions.

Prompts:

Change your plane—stand. Sit. Lie down. Crouch. Lean.

Play with different speeds—slow down. Speed up. Interrupt. Repeat.

Alter your sound—louder. Softer. Shout. Whisper. Screech. Coo.

Physical Conditions
1. The instructor suggests multiple physical conditions. The actors embody them one at a time. They may choose to inhabit some, but not all, suggestions.

Prompts:

Released energy includes 20/20 vision, memory, alertness, curiosity, brightness, mental balance, wit, second sight, awareness, mental clarity, consciousness, oriented behavior, recollection, dreams, visions, perception and insight.

Blocked energy includes amnesia, migraine, blindness, muteness, deafness, a coma, delusions, schizophrenia, psychosis, Alzheimer's disease, dizziness, blackout, headache, myopia, sinusitis and disorientation.

2. The actors embody a specific physical condition selected from the previous multiple physical conditions.
3. The actors add in alterations in space, time and sound without prompts from the instructor.

Sensory Activation
The instructor moves among the actors with an object that activates the sixth sense, or intuition.

Prompts:

Does this sixth sense activate ...

dread, anticipation, expectation, alarm, questioning, certainty, uncertainty, hopefulness, doubt, a window into the past, the present, the future, a glimpse into the unknown, terror, release, an awakening, an epiphany, impressions, assumptions, an absence, a gap, a gulf, understanding, misunderstanding, a presence, a specter, a vision?

Original Character Embodiment
1. The actors explore the interplay of their specific physical condition with the sixth sense, or intuition.
2. The actors interact with each other, using body language and gibberish to explore the ways in which their character's physiology informs their sense of self in relation to others.

Original Character Journal Entries
SYMPHONY OF SMELL

I shall compose an entire symphony of smell.

To open: an oboe of oozing ochre seeping arpeggios, as pepper cello dust plucks, before the flitter of Jasmine and Rosemary flutes squiggle and sputter and flutter above it, and overpower. And then the crash of the timpani of burnt toast thundering under the blare of candle wax French horns.

In the revolution they shot me.

Coffee grounds violins strumming.

The bullet entered my brain.

Oleander piano plunks.

I lost my sight and hearing.

Horsehair tremolo.

But I am a composer.

Caramel harp.

BUT THEY WON'T TAKE MY MUSIC AWAY FROM ME!

CRESCENDO—SWEAT. A CADENZA OF WET SKIN. FORTE. SIX-EIGHT TIME IN CHALK. CHANGE TO THREE-FOUR IN PINE. A WALTZ OF DRIPPING PINE SAP.

FERMATA!

A GRAND FINALE. A VARIATION ON THE WALTZ; A BOMBASTIC THRIUMPHANT BURNING PINE FOREST. CLARINETS OF ASH. BASSES OF DIRT. VIOLAS OF BLOOD. BUILD TO CACOPHONY. SUSTAIN! Silence ... and a reprise ... the ochre oboe, but this time with fluttering silk and plucking powdered sugar. Fermata! ... and ... off. (Jasper Hirose)

RUFFLED

Should have left two hours ago. He seemed so nice. They seemed so nice. What the fuck did they put in my drink? Asshhole. Goddamn it. I just have to make it home. I just gotta get out my keys—wherever they are—and simply get inside the door. Fuck, my legs, oh god, I'm pathetic. I'm so pathetic. Am I drooling? Ok just ... just crawl home. Can't tell if this is mud or concrete. I'm gonna die oh my god its dark I can't. Ok try the legs again ... nope ok nope just wait ... just rest a second. (Anonymous)

VIRTUE

I can't see a damn thing ... not a single stitch of light. It's almost as if— wait, what are you? Who is it? I'm not used to this ... I'm normally on top of the world. All the world was meant to see me ... Now I can't see a damn thing. Where is this virtue? I can't see it! (Jake Simard)

CROWN

Movement landscape: breaking patterns
Energy center: crown
Aura, hair, joints, muscles, skeleton, skin
Sense: memory and association

Orientation Exploration

Focus: impulse and intention

Movement Landscape: Breaking Patterns
1. The actors work independently. They begin with any movement they wish. The instructor calls out "Change" and the actors abruptly alter their movement. This includes the focus of the eyes, the leading part of the body and the organs that are engaged.
2. The actors add in vocalization. This too is full of immediate shifts in tone, pitch and volume with each change.
3. The actors abruptly change their movement and vocalization without side-coaching.
4. The instructor asks the actors to explore the possibility of moving "beyond their intention" or to "restrain their intention," the possibility of exaggerating or inhibiting their actions. The instructor calls out in a random sequence: "Exaggerate. Inhibit. Change." The movement and vocalization becomes overstated or internalized. The point is to move beyond habitual patterns.
5. The actors work in small ensembles. They "bounce" off each other, looking for complementary and counterpoint patterns in space and time and sound.

Collective Explorations

Focus: aura—clear or clouded

Energy Center: Crown
The actors initially engage neutral and habitual body language as they move through the space.

Body Language
1. The instructor offers a selection of metaphors. The actors embody them one at a time. They may choose to inhabit some, but not all, suggestions.

Prompts:

Are you ...
thick-skinned, a hunchback, stuck-up, a blonde bombshell, raven-haired, a carrot top, out of joint, out of whack, statuesque, willowy, wooden, a stick, built like a brick shit-house, burning up, a light in the world, a shriveled prune?

Do you ...
have the whole world in your hands, a chip on your shoulder, pins and needles, prickly heat, goose-bumps, your back against the wall, muscles that are in a knot, a widow's peak, another's back, skin like sandpaper or silk, a peaches and cream complexion; do you carry the weight of the world on your shoulders, rub people the wrong way, get you back up, muscle your way through things, stab people in the back, light up the room?

2. The instructor asks the actors to include alterations in space, time and sound. The actors add these qualities into their ongoing exploration of multiple physical conditions.

Prompts:

Change your plane—Stand. Sit. Lie down. Crouch. Lean.

Play with different speeds—Slow down. Speed up. Interrupt. Repeat.

Alter your sound—Louder. Softer. Shout. Whisper. Screech. Coo.

Physical Conditions
1. The instructor suggests multiple physical conditions. The actors embody them one at a time. They may choose to inhabit some, but not all, suggestions.

Prompts:

Released energy includes spinal alignment, well-being, co-ordination, good bone density, clear skin, double-joints, elasticity, well-being, autonomy and co-ordination.

Blocked energy includes arthritis, fractures, measles, epilepsy, crippling, hunchback, osteoporosis, rheumatism, cerebral palsy, muscular dystrophy, multiple sclerosis, burns, rashes, acne, balding and bone fractures.

2. The actor s embody a specific physical condition selected from the previous multiple physical conditions.
3. The actors add in alterations in space, time and sound without prompts from the instructor.

Sensory Activation

The instructor moves among the actors with an object that activates memory/association.

Prompts:

How does this object evoke …

recollection, remembrance, fragmentation, a shred of meaning, a remnant of the past, a sliver of memory, palpable understanding, tangible recognition, resonant truth, return, integration, acceptance, split-off thoughts, rejection, PTSD, hazy impressions, faint memories, resurfacing experience, catharsis, gathering of self, conjuring of spirit or soul, compassion, courage?

Original Character Embodiment

1. The actors explore the interplay of their specific physical condition with an object that activates memory and association.
2. The actors interact with each other, using body language and gibberish to explore the ways in which their character's physiology informs their sense of self in relation to others.

Original Character Journal Entries

FALLEN

I OFFICIALLY HATE HUMAN BEINGS. Mistrusting little shits. Tell them you're immortal and what do they do? Shoot you. Assholes. I wanna come back now! I've learned my lesson, alright? Can we cut the banishment crap now? Look, I know you've got some divine plan or whatever but this whole corporeal form thing really doesn't do it for me. Ugh, it's the—what's the word—fatigue, that really gets to me. I'm never gonna get used to that, actually feeling tired. I don't think I can get up. My muscles are rebelling against me. I'm just gonna wait here for a bit, ok? Does that fit into your divine plan? Ten minutes. I'm gonna wait ten minutes. How long is that? What is the experience then of minutes. Is that a blink of an eye, or a lifetime? Are those the same thing in this place? (Anonymous)

BALDING QUEEN

Oh my god, oh my god. I promised myself I wasn't going to cry. Thank you so much. It is such an honor to be your Miss America. I just feel so blessed, so beautiful. Inside and out. This is the most wonderful day of my life.

Ugh. Stupid, stupid. What's that? Shit. My hair, it's getting worse. Stop falling out! I touch it ever so slightly, change my shirt, take a shower and gobs and gobs of hair appear in my hands. My eyelashes, my eyebrows. No, no stop it. You're beautiful. You're okay. You're not sick. Stop crying. Just close your eyes and envision that crown.

What will I do? No one has ever loved me. I'm going bald. Stupid rare disease. Beauty Queens don't get diseases. Beauty Queens don't lose their hair.

This is all I have. My shelter, my mask, my identity. And it's falling away piece by piece and bringing me down with it. Forget the crown I just want to run my fingers through my hair again. (Angela Sclafani)

WALKING DEAD ON A DAY OF SILENCE

Nothing works. Nothing moves. Nothing gives. No color. No light. No stars. I want them to feel how I feel, dead skin and bones. Decrepit, unmoving, unearthly. They'll know because today is the day the earth stood still. It electrified and exploded and died and they'll all know why we are like this. Falling apart, falling within, together as one. Death isn't so bad, it's the waiting, the decaying; the knowing that you're slowly losing parts of yourself, bit by bit, inch by inch. Pieces they have, but not for long, shoved in boxes in the earth, thought of fondly at times, and not at others ... if only they knew the lack of feeling I have, the glimpse of soul I know was once there but only stays at a distance. No heart, no love, no sex, no joy, no sorrow, no grounding. Just a flat horizontal line perpendicular to everything they know. But here it comes. Here we come. Today is the day of the walking dead. (Allie Leonard)

NOTE

1. Michael Agnes, Editor in Chief, *Webster's New World Dictionary*, New York: Hungry Minds, Inc., 2002.

CHAPTER 7

Psychological Explorations

FOUNDATION

The primary focus of the psychological states is mental and emotional processes.[1] The interplay between these processes often feels messy—more complicated than complex. Perhaps it helps to start by looking at the root word *psyche* itself, which means both "spirit" and "soul."[2] To be spirited is to be lively, curious and inquiring. To be soulful is to be moody, reflective and ruminative. The intertwining of thought and emotion can involve a complex dance of ideas and impulses. The following are examples of this interplay from each psychological state of being:

Survival: One may fear for their life and invent coping mechanisms.
Connection: One may be blinded by desire and "lose one's head."
Power: One may lust for power and rationalize methods of torture.
Love: One may fall in love and see the world in a new light.
Communication: One may speak one's mind and feel ostracized.
Awareness: One may envy another's beauty and then critique it to death.
Destiny: One may find serenity through focused introspection.

It seems, however, that the human condition is such that emotions color thoughts in a way that is not as pronounced in reverse. Joseph Le Doux writes in "The Emotional Brain" that "the wiring of the brain at this point in our evolutionary history is such that connections from the emotional systems to the cognitive systems are stronger than connections from

© The Author(s) 2016
E. Hess, *Acting and Being*, DOI 10.1057/978-1-349-95106-2_7

the cognitive systems to the emotional systems."[3] Le Doux discovered that in the complex interplay of reason and emotion, we feel before we think, since reason is considered, whereas emotion is immediate. We can control our thoughts to some extent, but our emotions are often unconscious.

We can also glimpse the interplay of the individual and collective unconscious during heightened events such as wars, rallies and celebrations in which opposition, coercion and collusion are acted out in high relief. A pattern of behavior emerges during this interplay in which the individual taps into an archetype that is triggered in response to the collective.

Psychic landscapes are based on charged environments that elicit the dualities of a universal theme. Examples from the seven psychological states include the following:

Survival: life and death;
Connection: intimacy and estrangement;
Power: strength and weakness;
Love: compassion and cruelty;
Communication: free will and censorship;
Awareness: mindfulness and oblivion;
Destiny: hope and despair.

A narrative gradually unfolds in which the actor taps into archetypal energy through repeated actions. These are actions they undertake in order to realize their individual wants and needs within the collective. The actor attains an expanded sense of self that also reflects their ability to give and take, and to engage in "imaginative play."

APPROACH TO EXPLORATIONS

Introduction to a Psychological State

Gather the actors together and begin with a working definition of psychology and how it relates to thought and emotion as explored through archetypal energy. After this initial definition, each session begins by naming the state to be explored.

I'll use the survival state as the example throughout the following explorations.

Fig. 7.1 Psychological orientation exploration: Survival

Orientation Explorations

1. Fig. 7.1 Begin by naming the psychological state, the psychic landscape and the duality of the universal theme to be explored. The archetypes themselves will emerge in the exploration.

For example, in the survival state the psychic landscape is combative and the duality is life and death (see Fig. 7.1).

2. The instructor and the actors begin to create the psychic landscape of the exploration.

For example, in the survival state the instructor asks the actors to close their eyes and then places a tribal mask over their faces, one by one. They breathe life into a character from within the mask.

3. The actors briefly explore the "world" on their own, discovering their character's initial response to the psychic landscape.

For example, in the survival state the combative psychic landscape may be a war zone, or some variation of an unstable socio-political or environmental setting.

4. The actors begin to engage each other, slowly testing the waters, never forcing the action or following a prescribed direction. They allow their characters' exchanges to unfold on their own within the collective. The less the actors analyze their characters' wants but engage in their immediacy, the more they discover the mythic potential of each specific psychological state.

For example, in the survival states the actors may all be masked and begin to move through the space, sussing out allies and enemies.

5. The instructor side-coaches as the actors explore their characters in relation to the duality of the universal theme.

For example, side-coaching in the survival state focuses on the duality of life and death:

Who is on your side? Who opposes you? What do you do to the one who betrays you? Are you a deserter? A traitor? A dictator? A queen? Is there a power vacuum? Is there a sacrificial lamb? Will you survive? Die? Who accompanies you?

6. The instructor encourages the actors to create situations involving conflict and contrast, so that their characters more fully engage the duality of the universal theme.

For example, side-coaching in the survival state might include the following:

Where did you start? Where are you now? What triggered the change? What happened to you? Your tribe? Your people? Your enemies? Your alliances? How did you lose your way? Why did you take over?

7. The instructor winds down the exploration and allows for brief feedback, encouraging first impressions, thoughts and feelings. The

instructor will then want to focus on the patterns of behavior that emerged and ask the actors to identify the archetypes they inhabited during the unfolding narrative.

For example, in the survival state the actors may have developed a pattern of actions that identify their characters' behavior as a warrior, refugee, protector, victim, traitor, leader and so on.

Collective Explorations

1. Fig. 7.2 The actors focus on illuminating a character's essence in relation to an archetype suggested by the universal theme. The instructor encourages the actors to observe their character's thoughts and feelings without the direct influence of others.

For example, prompts in the survival state might include the following:

Fig. 7.2 Psychological collective exploration: Destiny

Is this character marked for life? Are they outcast? Fierce? Flamboyant? Festive? Camouflaged? Coy?

2. The actors engage each other, moving from individual to collective experience (the opposite direction of the orientation exploration). A scenario emerges in which the character's interior narrative is shaped by the subtle and surprising shifts of multiple relationships, which in turn inform the collective's actions.

3. The instructor winds down the exploration and takes time for feedback. The actors often begin by recounting the overall 'story' or 'narrative' of their character's journey. The instructor will want to guide their responses away from exposition and towards actions, relationships, events and the thoughts and emotions they aroused. Finally, the instructor will ask the actors to identify the archetype they uncovered.

Journaling

1. The actors create an inner monologue that reflects the character's stream of consciousness as evoked by an archetype. They begin by identifying and naming the archetype that emerged from the collective exploration, for example, an ogre, slut, loner, hero and so on.

   The actor deepens their relationship to archetypal energy through this inner monologue by addressing their character's unspoken wants and needs. These may be long-held secrets that the character has never revealed, not even to themselves.

   By engaging in this enlarged palette, the actor may contact aspects of the human condition that were not previously available to them, but are now recognizable in an unselfconscious way. In the process of digging down into the character the actor may hit upon personal memories and associations. This raw material can be crystallized and shaped to reflect the character's frame of mind.

   The instructor may also want to encourage the actor to connect their inner life to the archetype.

For example, side-coaching might include the following:

Do you identify with this archetypal behavior? How do you feel about this identification? Do you recall experiences that resonate with the character's needs? Wants? Actions? Outlook?

The actor looks for a defining moment or main event in the character's life. This may be sparked by suggestions from the instructor.

For example, prompts might include the following:

Did you have a brush with death? Are you harboring a forbidden want? Have you committed a crime? Did you steal someone's heart? Have you spread rumors? Did you ignore your intuition? Were you full of false hope?

2. The actors may find that their character is akin to an existing character from a play, movie or novel. They may be reminded of a celebrity, politician or public figure. The actor will want to infuse these personas with archetypal energy.

3. The actors share their monologues out loud, inhabiting the character's point of view. They may wish to incorporate tangible elements from the collective exploration into their work.

For example, in the survival state the actor may wish to put on the mask as they deliver their text.

4. The actors move through the space interweaving their text and bodies with other characters, expanding upon and altering their earlier relationships from the collective exploration.

Actor-Generated Explorations

Fig. 7.3 The actors use their archetypal character monologues as text and bring in additional research materials—an image and object—to further explore the relationship between inner and outer identity. The image is emblematic of the drives and desires of the character. The object operates as a costume piece or personal prop .

Preparation, rehearsal and presentation closely follow the model outlined for both the behavioral and the physiological states, with some adjustments.

Preparation
1. The actors pair up and discuss the research materials they have brought to class and why these materials were chosen. This discussion includes reading an excerpt from their character monologues to each other and sharing their images and costume and prop choices.

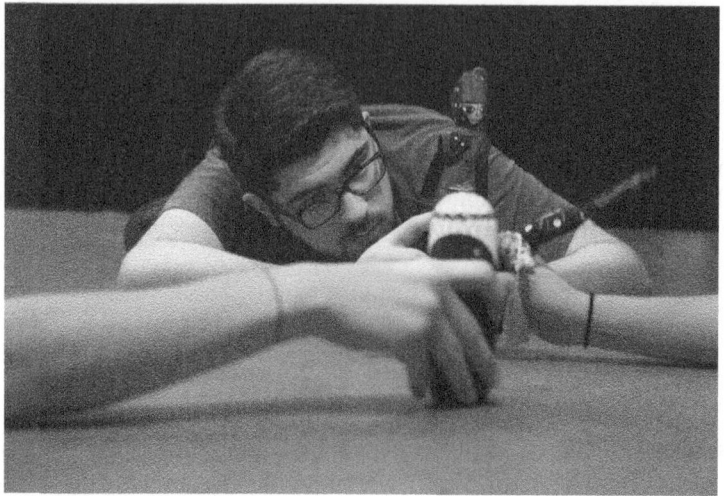

Fig. 7.3 Psychological actor-generated exploration: Love

Option. The instructor may ask the actors to read and prepare each other's monologues as a way of continuing to expand the sense of self, otherness and character range.

2. The actors put on their costume pieces and/or experiment with their props as they investigate the interplay of social expectations and experience of self.

Option. The actors may choose to dress in their partners' costumes and utilize their props.

3. The actors look for a primary relationship between their characters, selecting segments from the individual texts and combining them in any way they choose. They discover a main event based on a duality drawn from the specific psychological state. This often leads to a re-orientation that reveals new rituals, responses and/or rivalries between them.

Status becomes a major focus of these explorations. The actors uncover who drives each moment and how other archetypal energies complement and conflict with their own psychological state.

Rehearsal
1. With the barest framework possible the actors explore the relation-ship "on its feet" using their text as written, rather than improvised. The props and costumes are an integral part of the exploration.

2. After the actors have had an opportunity to explore their relation-ship they may want to briefly discuss the duality that is in play and then deepen their exchange or make adjustments to their arc.

Presentation
1. The actors form a circle and present their partnered work for the collective. This work-in-progress should be fairly brief—no more than five minutes. It is focused on establishing and developing a relationship that leads up to a main event and requires a re-orienta-tion. It is not a "skit" and certainly doesn't require a beginning, middle and end. The more open-ended it is, in some ways the bet-ter, as this helps to keep the work from being result-oriented.

2. The instructor may ask to go back and look at a moment in the exploration after the presentation, if there is something buried in the exchange that needs to be illuminated or activated, or if there is something particularly alive that begs for further investigation.

   If work on the psychological states follow the physiological and behavioral states, these actor-generated explorations might also include a more conscious relationship to beat work: actions, objec-tives and obstacles.

   Often, the moment after the actors have "tied up the scene," some-thing genuinely revealing will occur, and the instructor may want to extend this moment, since it goes beyond any expectation that may have been built consciously or unconsciously into the work-in-progress.

3. The instructor asks the partners to share their images (the mono-logues, costumes and props have already been shared in the presen-tation itself) and talk briefly about their process. The images may be sent around the circle so other actors can inspect them closely.

4. The other actors, along with the instructor, now offer their feed-back, which is based on observation rather than assessment. I encourage actors to raise their hands, to keep their responses short, and to refrain from overlapping. This helps to create an atmosphere of collaboration and community.

I generally ask that comments be formed as questions so as to create a sense of curiosity and openness. This is not to say that comments shouldn't address a feeling response as well as content and form. It is wonderful when responses reveal the observer's personal perception and point of view, but from a place of complete ownership.

5. This process continues until all the pairings have been presented.
   At this point the instructor may choose to make closing comments that reinforce the overall work on the particular state, underlining how it relates to the acquisition of technique, tools of craft, character work and storytelling.

A Working Definition of Psychology

To Think; To Emote

Mental and emotional processes, as expressed in human and animal behavior, are at the heart of psychological explorations. Curiously enough, the root word, *psyche*, means both "spirit" and "soul."[4] Spirit is otherworldly; soul is indwelling. Spirit is intoxicating; soul is ruminative. Spirit is visionary; soul is visceral.

This may be all the definition one needs, but here is further elaboration.

The psyche's dialogue between thought and emotion can be either polarizing or non-dualistic. The mind translates emotions into beliefs and opinions, considerations and judgments, memories and epiphanies. The emotions translate thoughts into joy and fear, rashness and reserve, sentiment and conviction.

Psyche also means "breath." Breath animates behavior and activates physiology, creating action. Also, the word "emotion" comes from the Latin root *emouvoir*—to agitate, stir up, move.[5] Therefore we do not need to press on our emotions, but trust them to reflect the totality of our being. We are moved to act.

Psychology expands on behavior and physiology by examining the complex and layered thoughts and emotions of a person or group. The focus of the psychological states is individuation and/or the collective unconsciousness. This is expressed through ideas, assumptions, expectations, attitudes, prejudices, projections, convictions and so on.

Archetypes illuminate character paradigms by describing a perfect example of a type or person based on an original pattern.[6] These patterns arise out of actions performed by the individual and/or the collective that propel one forward as they embrace, confront or resist change. What ignites and necessitates change is emotion charged by thought, or vice versa. Given circumstances provide the framework in which this change occurs.

THE SEVEN PSYCHOLOGICAL STATES

Psychic Landscapes, Universal Themes and Archetypes

Survival
Psychic landscape: combative
Universal theme: survival
Archetype: Angel of Death, captor, comrade, enemy, grim reaper, guard, hero/heroine, hunter, liberator, prisoner, protector, soldier, victim, warrior

Connection
Psychic landscape: nomadic
Universal theme: connection
Archetype: Casanova, castrator, celibate, damsel in distress, dominatrix, Don Juan, Gigolo, lover, pedophile, pimp, rapist, seducer, virgin, whore

Power
Psychic landscape: transactional
Universal theme: power
Archetype: beggar, boss, celebrity, client, dictator, dowager, employee, follower, groupie, jailer, king, leader, master, miser, patron, prisoner, queen, subject, servant, slave, terrorist, thief, victim

Love
Psychic landscape: sheltering
Universal theme: love
Archetype: brother, caretaker, child, companion, doctor, father, friend, foe, guest, helpmate, host, intimate, helpmate, misanthrope, mother,

neighbor, nurse, parent, philanthropist, roommate, sister, stranger, tormentor, torturer

Communication
Psychic landscape: communal
Universal theme: communication
Archetype: agitator, apprentice, artist, dictator, disciple, elected official, exhibitionist, follower, judge, jury, law enforcer, lawyer, leader, maverick, mentor, provocateur, rebel, revolutionary, student, teacher

Awareness
Psychic landscape: collective
Universal theme: awareness
Archetype: clown, crone, cultist, fortune teller, madman, magician, orator, preacher, prophet, proselytizer, sage, seer, shaman, trickster, visionary

Destiny
Psychic landscape: liminal
Universal theme: destiny
Archetype: angel, damned, deliverer, devil, demon, doomsayer, god, goddess, healer, hero/heroine, saint, saved, savior, sinner

SURVIVAL

Psychic landscape: combative
Universal theme: survival
Archetype: Angel of Death, captor, comrade, enemy, Grim Reaper, guard, hero/heroine, hunter, liberator, prisoner, protector, soldier, victim, warrior

Orientation Exploration

Focus: life and death (see Fig. 7.1)

Psychic Landscape: Combative—War Zone
Further examples: battlefield, detention center, disaster area, earthquake, flood, prison, quarantined area, restricted area.

1. The actors close their eyes as the instructor places a "tribal mask" over each of their faces. Some of these masks are duplicates; some are not, so the actors do not know who is from their "tribe" and who is "alien." The actors sense what energy the mask gives them and breathe into their character from the inside out.
2. Once all the masks are in place the actors create the psychic landscape of the exploration. All the characters are uprooted—in unknown or unsafe territory. They look for those they can approach or should avoid. They find ways to signal their vulnerability or dominance, their resourcefulness and restriction, their resilience and resistance.
3. The actors begin to interact with each other. Each allows their character's relationships to be informed by physical and vocal clues, since there are no pre-established allies, enemies or status.
4. The actors further investigate their characters "tribal" alliances. They protect or threaten; become victim or victimizer; are loyal or traitorous. Battle lines are drawn and redrawn, and a resolution may or may not take place.

Collective Exploration

Focus: security and vulnerability

Survival
1. The actors paint each other's faces, illuminating a character's archetypal energy in their partner that is based on the theme of survival, such as a warrior, victim and so on. The mask may include prosthesis (i.e., noses, ears and lips), hair-pieces, face paints, removable tattoos, face jewelry and/or extreme street make-up.
2. The actors react to each other's masked characters through gibberish and gesture. Their interaction informs and molds their identities in relationship to the collective.
3. The characters' interaction becomes heightened so as to uncover the unspoken allegiances and alienations between them.
4. The actors may wish to see themselves in a mirror at the end of the exploration in order to process the relationship between inner understanding and outer perception.

Archetypal Character Journal Entries

MURDERER
Through eyes of Oedipus
seeping seething silky blood
gushes
from thine eyes
My father, naked skin
and hidden heart
beneath rotting bones.
sweat drips down my
crevices
sinking sores
pores in my face.
Now I am farther away
I can write the explosion of sound
My ocean
my deep blue ocean
eternal
boundless
destructive
dangerous.
the world is round you see
and it will spin
spin
no matter how hard I force flat. (Danielle Sacks)

SAVIOUR
Different doesn't mean bad, why can't they just understand? He probably needs help! I WANT to help him, but everyone is trying to make me
stop. The only way I can get to him is to sneak to him, and he doesn't trust
me because I look like one of them. Why are people so narrow-minded
or empty headed? Why can't they see that just because he looks different
doesn't mean he doesn't feel like us? "I won't let them hurt you" I whisper.
(Sierra Duncan)

VICTIM
There is no point … to anything. Life is ridiculous. We are, each and
every one of us, we are all just a blade of grass. We grow, we flourish, we
wither, we die. New blades take our place. But the sick thing is that all the

other blades besides me think there is something more to it. Something more to life ... that son of a bitch sucked the world away. Sucked the promise of my life away. (Lindsey White)

CONNECTION

Psychic landscape: nomadic
Universal theme: connection
Archetype: Casanova, castrator, celibate, damsel in distress, dominatrix, Don Juan, Gigolo, lover, pedophile, pimp, rapist, seducer, virgin, whore

Orientation Exploration

Focus: intimacy and estrangement

Psychic Landscape: Nomadic—Motel
Further examples: hostel, hotel, motel, whorehouse, flop house, stopover, squatter's quarters, tent.

1. The actors begin by being completely shrouded in a veil. It may be a sheet, blanket, throw, large scarf or curtain—anything that drapes the whole body like a second skin. They investigate their character's feelings of transience, isolation and aloneness.
2. The actors each explore their character's relationship to others through various degrees of exposure and revelation; inclusion and exclusion; invisibility and accessibility; attraction and repulsion, by testing their boundaries within and without the shroud, with and without others.
3. The actors further explore the veil as an extension of their characters' wants and needs by using it to envelop other characters or expose them and so on.
4. The actors each widen their character's "net", engaging each other by using their veils to make and take space.
5. The characters engage in some form of a communal "dance" that welcomes and/or shuns members of the collective.

Collective Exploration

Focus: creativity and destruction

Connection

1. The actors work in costume and/or everyday clothing that conveys something overt about their characters' presentation of self and how it reveals, promotes or distorts their identity. They may reconfigure clothing to further explore the effect of altering image and identity. For example, a shoe is worn as a hat. A jacket becomes pants. A wire cage is a dress. A box is a coat.

2. The actors explore the size and possibility of their character's outer "shell." This may mean that they expand or shrink in presence, include or exclude others. They move beyond their "idea" of self-expression to inhabit the message their costume communicates about their identity and their interface with others.

3. The actors exchange costume pieces, trying to get "under the skin" of another character by insinuating themselves into their world. They alter their earlier understanding of desirability and disgust, personal space and projection.

Archetypal Character Journal Entries

WHORE

There's no hope in living when there's nothing to love for. I just want to belong to something. Belong somewhere. Fuck everyone that hurt me, that took all I had, they have no idea what it's like to be me. I hate them, I hate them all. I hope they all burn in hell. Maybe they will. I'll drag them down with me. I'll make them pay for what they did and I'll enjoy every moment of it. They will finally know what it's like to be somewhere you don't belong … Have fun bitches. (Alexandra Grossi)

OUTSIDER

My mother stands outside my doorway begging me to conform. She says my rebelliousness is like me asking her to stop breathing. BREATHING? Except motherhood was thrown at her and she keeps denying who she is! I am what my parents denied … My dad thinks he understands me completely, that I'm in some phase. Fuck that shit. He extends his hand to me. What am I gonna grab his hand? And run off like some fucking faggot? I don't even know why I care 'cause I don't. (Ryan Szelong)

QUEEN BEE

God, who are these people and why are they talking to me? I have a boy-friend and he can beat you up. Boyfriend? Where is he? Where is everyone?

Why did everyone leave me? Everyone knows I am Bernice so why did they leave? I don't need anyone. I'm Bernice. (Korey-Elizabeth Rushing-Parker)

POWER

Psychic landscape: transactional
Universal theme: power
Archetype: beggar, boss, celebrity, client, dictator, dowager, employee, follower, groupie, jailer, king, leader, master, miser, patron, prisoner, queen, subject, servant, slave, terrorist, thief, victim

Orientation Exploration

Focus: strength and weakness

Psychic Landscape: Transactional—Marketplace
Further examples: antiques mall, auction house, black market, fair, flea market, mall, trading floor, urban jungle, "Wall Street."

1. The actors take out all the loose change in their wallets and pockets. They tally the total amount of money they have on their person. They imagine that their character is facing bankruptcy unless they increase their revenue.
2. The actors attempt to multiply their character's amount of money by bartering in any way possible—offering services, goods, entertainments, thefts, collective bargaining and so on. They observe their characters experiencing of plenty and deprivation.
3. The actors engage in at least six exchanges. Holding onto what they have initially is not an option.
4. The actors count up their profits or losses and return the change while discussing the power plays and exchanges of energy.

Collective Exploration

Focus: vitality and exhaustion

Power
1. The actors bring in objects that allow them to create boundaries, for example rope, tape, box, chalk, clothesline, paper. They imagine a

circumstance in which their character has once been invaded or evicted and now feels vulnerable.

2. The actors begin to define their characters' spaces and choose whom they will include and exclude. They observe their characters' feelings of inflation or deflation, of value or worthlessness.

3. The actors begin to negotiate in any way possible to save or increase their characters' territory, in order to expand their influence and power.

Archetypal Character Journal Entries

ENFORCER

I am here to protect the land we live in. I make sure that everything stays in order. There is no greater pleasure than knowing all is safe. I have to enforce even the strictest laws because that is simply a part of the job I so truly love. It is good to have those who appreciate what I do applaud me for my work. However, some just don't understand that the rules must be followed. It's their ignorance and I'm not looking to make any friends. The law is my one and only true friend. (Martin Mundzik)

OPTIMIST

People think I'm a nobody and maybe I am, but not for long. I'm gonna make something of myself. I'm gonna add something to this world, they'll see. And when I'm rich and successful they'll all be dyin' to get in on it. See, I have something that nobody else does. With my brains and vision I can offer so much; so much that they never thought they could have. All they have to do is give me a chance. (Courtney Barnes)

RICH BITCH

Why are you so obsessed with me? It's like everybody sees what's mine and wants to be a part of it. I mean, I'm hot and rich. So why wouldn't they want a piece of this? But what just irritates the hell out of me is when people defy me. No. You're not "Just as good as me" and you never will be. But it's not that hard to get rid of these people. Just start a rumor or insult them. That usually works and if it doesn't a little seduction can't hurt. Sweet little Dan is like my personal guard dog. He knows his place and knows the best way to live is by listening to me. (Jenna Antoniades)

LOVE

Psychic landscape: sheltering

Universal theme: love

Archetype: brother, caretaker, child, companion, doctor, father, friend, foe, guest, helpmate, host, intimate, helpmate, misanthrope, mother, neighbor, nurse, parent, philanthropist, roommate, sister, stranger, tormentor, torturer

Orientation Exploration

Focus: compassion and cruelty

Psychic Landscape: Sheltering—Home

Further examples: apartment, boarding house, detention center, dormitory, house, immigration center, mansion, room, refugee camp, residence.

1. The actors each bring in a homunculus (a puppet, doll, action figure or effigy) that is an expression of otherness. This character represents some form of "otherness." It may be an inferior side, a light or dark energy, a different sex, a foreigner, a stranger. They observe this homunculus closely, discovering something of their own relationship to their inner opposite—their anima or animus, or their shadow side. They engaged in an inner monologue in the voice of their character, the homunculus.

2. The actors take their homunculi on a journey through the space. They present them to others. The homunculi themselves carry on a dialogue—the actors are the conduit for their thoughts and actions. They share their back story, situation and secrets.

3. The actors incarnate their homunculi, adopting their body language, actions, voice, image and attitude. They interact with others, never letting go of their homunculus. They may conduct interrogations and interviews with each other to determine whether or not to accept a "foreigner" as extended family, to embrace an outsider as an equal.

Collective Exploration

Focus: courage and cowardice

Love

1. The actors become the puppet and puppeteers for each other. The puppet presents the external actions of the puppeteer's internal monologue.

2. The actors engage their character's "inner opposite" directly. This is an opportunity for the actors to explore their character's "inferior" or "inhibited" or "diminished" qualities in a conscious way—to bring their greatest fears and desires about themselves to light—and project them onto the "other."
3. The actors explore the outer edges of gender identity, finding out what it means to be ultra-masculine and *uber*-feminine.
4. The actors explore notions of pan-sexuality by playing with stereotypes and moving beyond them to uncover a more nuanced understanding of gender fluidity.

Archetypal Character Journal Entries

COWARD

Some of my earliest memories are going to the rallies. Proudly waving my American Flag and wearing my big baggy GOD HATES FAGS t-shirt that used to be my brother, Jimmy's, until he grew out of it. There was one slogan especially that I remember loving—DIE FAGS DIE. I loved it because every time I yelled it out my father would pat me proudly on the head and say good job son. It was the only time he really showed affection … I'll never forget the look in Jimmy's eyes when he saw me raise that bat above my head. Betrayal. Pain. Disbelief. But in my head I heard my father's voice telling me that fags were bad and they must die. And I brought the bat down on Jimmy's head. (Luke Perkins)

MUSE

I am you. I am flexible. I am whatever you want me to be. I am You. I move. I occupy whatever pose you ask me to. I am anyone for you. I take any position you place me. I am everyone and I am also no one. I am distinctly nondescript. You are me. I am you. I am your changeable chess piece. Move me where you will. I speak volumes. Ask and you will receive. (Jasper Hirose)

OUTCAST

People don't know what I'm feeling since I have no face. So I have to do a lot of work to get people to come to me. I want them to stay—unless they're mean, in which case I don't mind the hassle of moving. Sometimes when I'm with people who suddenly need to rush somewhere it sucks, because I can't keep up. But I don't want them to think I'm weak, so I walk along anyways. The key is not to let it get in the way, and if people notice, just acknowledge that it's there … the clipped wings of a bird. I feel guilty for yearning for more, but I can't help it. (Thomas Hedlund)

COMMUNICATION

Psychic landscape: communal
Universal theme: communication
Archetype: agitator, apprentice, artist, dictator, disciple, elected official, exhibitionist, follower, judge, jury, law enforcer, lawyer, leader, maverick, mentor, provocateur, rebel, revolutionary, student, teacher

Orientation Exploration

Focus: free will and censorship

Psychic Landscape: Communal—Public Square
Further examples: atrium, church, conference center, court, forum, lobby, meeting room, mosque, park, plaza, police headquarters, speaker's corner, temple.

1. The actors each generate a "message" that is a conscious object of provocation. It is prompted by some affront or injury to their character in which their rights were violated. The message may be composed of one of the following:

   a. Words, such as protest posters, love poem, chant;
   b. Images, such as anti-fur photo, anti-porn image or pro-life or abortion rights slogan;
   c. Objects, such as effigy, puppet, flag.

   The point of view does not need to reflect the actor's own beliefs. In fact, a character's "message" that is in stark contrast to their personal convictions may lead to greater revelation since the actor is no longer obliged to be politically correct.

2. The actors begin to explore their character's "message" with increasing investment. The more heightened the conviction, the stronger the message.

3. The actors collaborate with other characters to create a collage of "messages." The actor observes how their character's original "mes-

sage" morphs to gain the support or validation of the collective. The final "messages" may end up being contradictory or corrective, reductive or layered.

Collective Exploration

Focus: expression and suppression

Communication
1. The actor works with a talisman that is numinous and alive for their character and has a specific history and meaning for them. This talisman may be one of the following:

   a. Religious symbol, such as prayer beads, cross, Star of David;
   b. Fetish article, such as shoe, stocking, soother;
   c. Sex-related object, such as condom, X-rated photo, pregnancy test;
   d. Written statement, such as love letter, hate mail, manifesto;
   e. Political item, such as insignia, flag or military pin.

2. The actor is secretive and protective of their character's talisman. They explore the character's personal history of the talisman—how it came to be secretive and whether it fills them with joy or dread, excitement or shame.
3. The actors "feel each other out," each deciding when and how to reveal their character's talismans. It is essential that their character's secret be shared or it will die with them. In the course of exchanging secrets the characters may choose to collude or diffuse the information they gather by supporting or betraying each other's confessions.

Archetypal Character Journal Entries

CARETAKER
We need to get rid of the commies. My dad went to war to fight them in 'Nam and it fucked my mother up. I had to spend days out of school just to take care of her and make sure she didn't injure herself with the kitchen knives. I learned to cook when I was 11 so mom didn't have to be in the kitchen. Mom just wasn't the same person after dad died. She

would sit in the living room and just mutter to herself. Half the time I didn't even know what she said, but that was the better half of the time. (Anna P. Crouch)

ANARCHIST
Bring down the system!
FUCK the system!
These people think they're revolutionary
But the revolution is in the same fucking system
Inside of the same fucking system that made them
That controls you
That makes you
Then leaves you
I never even got a chance in this world
This system rejected me from the beginning.
Never even gave me a chance
... and ... I never really had a family ... orphan
WELL, I guess I turned into exactly what they wanted me to. (Antonio Barrera-Mejia)

FEMINIST
My father didn't allow my mother to watch the news or read the newspaper. He would wake up first to get the paper and throw it away before she could read it. But after he left for work, my mother would take the paper out of the wastebasket and read for hours about what was going on in the outside world to educate herself. We would discuss what she read about—she wanted me to be stronger and more opinionated than she allowed herself to be. And that is what I stand for. A world where a woman is actually equal to a man; where she is free to vocalize her own opinions without a man's instructions. (Victoria Sumrall)

AWARENESS

Psychic landscape: collective
Universal theme: awareness
Archetype: clown, crone, cultist, fortune teller, madman, magician, orator, preacher, prophet, proselytizer, sage, seer, shaman, trickster, visionary

Orientation Exploration

Focus: mindfulness and oblivion

Psychic Landscape: Collective—Party
Further examples: celebration, concert, ceremony, circus, cult headquarters, flash mob, gathering, opium den, party, psych ward.

1. The actors bring in a placebo that represents altered consciousness. The placebo reveals their character's need to address some social issue or awkwardness that may be temporary or long-term. The placebo may be one of the following;

   a. Tic-Tacs, M&M's or other pill-like simulation of a prescription or recreational drug;
   b. Empty beer, wine or liquor bottle filled with water or other simulation of an alcoholic beverage;
   c. Flour, sugar, or other simulation of a powder drug.

2. The actors prepare to ingest the placebo. They imagine the character's expectations in regard to the advertised, expected or promised qualities of the substance.
3. The actors partake of the substance, noting the sensations in their character's body.
4. The characters explore each other's realities in their altered state of consciousness. The external world becomes a reflection of their inner landscape.

Collective Exploration

Focus: wisdom and stupidity

Awareness
1. The actor works with an "everyday" stimulant or relaxant that speaks to their character's need for distraction or alleviation. This may be a mood-altering substance or activity such as one of the following:

   a. Coffee, tea, cigarette, comfort food;

b. Music, meditation;
c. Video game, TV, movie;
d. Dancing, working-out;
e. Reading, crossword puzzle.

2. The actor explores the stimulant or relaxant on as many sensory levels as possible and note its effect on their character's body rhythms and breathing. They observe whether or not this activity is habit-forming, a ritual, a reward, a punishment, an escape, or a release for their character.
3. The actors take in other characters around them and include or exclude them in their activities. They are consciously aware of the mood they wish to create, of who they choose to witness or avoid, entertain or overlook.

Archetypal Character Journal Entries

MISFIT

Did you know my doctor told me that my brain was too fast for the normal world? True story. He said, what did he say, uh "I'm giving you these pills because you're too good for us mortals." Ha! Take that, mortals. And it's hard. I forget sometimes. Six times a day? It's too much. Funny story. I was at a Christmas party and I might have forgotten my pills, I don't know. Anyway I held my father up to the wall with a knife. I don't know. It was a blur. Now I always take an extra pill each day to be careful. (Ben Langhorst)

DISPOSSESSED

I love the feeling when my eyes glaze over, when everything in my body goes heavy, turns numb. I love melting into the ground, loosening my grasp on this hell of a reality, letting my heart slow down, beat drowsily, work at the edge of exhaustion. There is nothing I want more than to lie down and sleep, unmoving. Oh to be content. I used to think it was possible to be happy during the day, to smile and enjoy the sun and the people and the hum of normal life … All I have now are growing kids and a dwindling settlement staring me in the eyes when it's 9 pm and I haven't gotten out of bed all day. (Anonymous)

EVANGELIST

Her energy beaming through my veins ricocheting off the walls of my heart and out of my navel like a smile. My body smiling out-loud. I want to feel this always. This is life. Completeness. Connection. Melting into one! My eyes can see through my eyelids. I just want to be here with everyone. They need to know! You need to know this connection! Open your eyes! Open your eyes! (Javier Perez)

DESTINY

Psychic landscape: liminal
Universal theme: destiny
Archetype: angel, damned, deliverer, devil, demon, doomsayer, god, goddess, healer, hero/heroine, saint, saved, savior, sinner

Orientation Exploration

Focus: hope and despair

Psychic Landscape: Liminal—Limbo
Further examples: cave, Hades, Heaven, Hell, mountain, Olympus, Purgatory, River Styx, threshold, Valhalla, Valley of Death.

1. The actor brings in a collection of "artifacts." Aspects of all or any of the preceding psychological explorations come into play: masks, face-paints, scarves, costumes, money, ropes, tapes or string, homunculi, messages, talismans and substances. The actors begin by assembling their artifacts into an outer expression of their character's inner life. They look for ways in which their character comes together or falls apart. They seek elements of integration or fragmentation. This is a final reckoning in which a major life event of their character may be replayed.
2. The actor explores the expansive or contracted nature of their character in space. They may want to add or subtract artifacts as they refine their interior and exterior presence.
3. The actors begin to relate to each other. They explore aspects of the dualities of some of the previous psychological states that most affect their character's life.
4. The actors explore the duality of hope and despair as they discover how their character's personal expression reflects their world views,

how their outer realities mirror their inner truths and how others enlighten, aid or undermine them.

Collective Exploration

Focus: faith and doubt (see Fig. 7.2)

Destiny
  1. The actors create a god/goddess-like character that is a symbolic but tangible replication of wholeness or brokenness. This replication depicts an "evolved" or "atrophied" character based on the actor's imagination, but it may be inspired by paintings, carvings or stories based on existing deities.
  2. The actors investigate the ramifications of their character's overall statement. They ask themselves if this god/goddess-like character is meditative or manic, enlightened or confused, serene or agitated.
  3. The actors invite others to enter the world of their character. Their character may be accessible and attractive, or alienating and disturbing. They may be empathetic and embracing, or rigid and removed. The actors discover spirited and soulful ways in which their character interacts with the archetypal energy of others.

Archetypal Character Journal Entries

PRISONER
  I'm not supposed to be here. I'm definitely not supposed to be here. Where is here, exactly? No I need to go back. I have to go back! I need one more day! I have to find love! Love! It went away! I need to see my wife again. She don't wanna see me, but I gotta see her. Jail? How did I end up in jail? Why was I—no no no I can't remember, I don't want to. I can't … I got home. I found her. On the couch. Naked. With another man. The neighbors said they heard screaming. No no no no I don't want to remember. I can't … I can't remember. Love I need to find love! (Patrick Daly)

DELUDED
  Mom always told me the love of the group above all other things. So I gave them everything I had, or could have had, and gladly. Everything was control and moderation. Dad said birthday parties were unnecessary. Why celebrate one when we could celebrate all? Besides, we must put God first

and never falter in the truth even for a day. So I never had a birthday party … I must be honest now when I say that I did not want to die. But when there's a cup in your hand and a cup in everybody else's, there's not much else. (Francesca Placidi)

BETRAYED

People are evil, they're mean … my dad … asked me if I loved him. I said of course I do, you're my daddy. But he said no, you don't love me enough. Can you show me you love me more? Yes. Yes. I gave him a big hug. But that wasn't enough. And he took me and he threw me down, and he hit me and beat me. He did things I will never be able to un-feel or un-see or un-hear. And two days later … gave me this necklace. There, he said, this means I'm sorry. (Anonymous)

NOTES

1. Michael Agnes, Editor in Chief, *Webster's New World Dictionary*, New York: Hungry Minds, Inc., 2002.
2. Ibid.
3. Joseph Le Doux, "The Emotional Brain" in Rita Carter, *Mapping the Mind*, London: University of California Press, 1998, p. 98.
4. Agnes, *Webster's New World Dictionary*.
5. Ibid.
6. Ibid.

PART 3

The Interplay of Acting & Being

The interplay of acting and being—of behavioral, physiological and psychological states of being with explorations in embodied performance—encourages creative expression that is authentic, flexible and multi-dimensional. This is true whether one's focus is on single or multiple disciplines. In Part 1, "States of Being," I included influences from related disciplines to emphasize the importance of adopting an open and inclusive frame of mind. Through experimentation, inventiveness and collaboration we expand our interpersonal skills while enhancing our artistic aliveness. Both our individual and world views are enlarged.

This expansiveness can take many forms, and what follows are some of my observations of theatrical events from a world that continues to grow in complexity, even as the globe continues to shrink. Interdisciplinary pieces blur distinctions between artistic fields to generate work that is enlarged by hybridization. Mixed-media installations straddle various art forms to transcend artificial boundaries. Cross-cultural collaborations interweave artistic traditions to speak to a diverse audience. Original works spring from collectives to share a timely message. Devised works deconstruct a taboo subject to bring it to light. Immersive works break down boundaries between performers and spectators to create intimacy among strangers. Established works re-visit universal themes to imbue them with new urgency.

Elasticity and integrity in form and content, whatever their source or expression, will always enliven a theatrical event. Explorations into states of being are meant to support and encourage this aliveness. This begins with the actor's instrument itself. The more the actor understands how to fully engage the individual "notes of the scale," the more they can access the considerable color and range of their impulses, experience and imagination. Complex and layered acting choices reflect a spontaneous yet informed and resonant truth.

Character work allows the actor to then marry this truth to the circumstances of the world of the play. The states of being are numerous in their variability, yet they are distilled within a character in a specific and coherent combination that includes their essence, energy center and archetype. This doesn't mean that a character can't be unpredictable or conflicted, but their state of being will always support their overall journey throughout the course of a play.

This journey is informed by what I will call "elements" that either are stated, are inferred or need to be unearthed within the world of the play. I have generated seven character elements based on Stanislavski's teachings: origins, drives, issues, relationships, age, ability and arc. They resonate with the states of being, leading to strong and specific character choices that serve the storyline.

The most exhilarating acting involves a dynamic exchange between characters. I recall that when I was a student at LAMDA, Sir Alec Guinness gave a talk in which he remarked that an actor's best moments on stage are shared ones. When actors are available and generous with each other, the ease and excitement of their chemistry is palpable. The trust, willingness and vulnerability that accompany such dynamism lie at the heart of our art. We move others as much as we are willing to be moved ourselves.

Scene study is the arena in which characters engage each other in the often volatile circumstances of a play. For this reason it is important that scene study explorations are based clearly on the play elements so as to create a safe space in which to play dangerously. Again, these elements may be stated or inferred, or may need to be unearthed. They often generate conflict between characters, driving actions forward with urgency and intensity.

I have identified seven play elements that are also based on Stanislavski's teachings: setting, actions, objectives, characters, time, activities and super-objective. These elements are interwoven with the character elements to illuminate the interplay between characters on and off stage. This means that, for example, a character may pick a fight with their best friend on stage because they were fired off stage. Or a character may be madly infatuated with a stranger off stage and mask their feelings with their lover on stage. Also, a character is more than likely in conflict with another character on stage at any given moment, but may also be at war within themselves. All these variables may lead to seemingly contradictory or irrational acting choices that, in fact, reflect a multi-faceted yet cohesive whole.

Production of a theatrical event, including the rehearsal process, weaves together multiple creative strands to arrive at a whole of even greater complexity. However, working on a specific theatrical event in which all the characters have a shared reality (unlike scene study, in which the characters live in disparate worlds) creates a beautiful interconnectedness. Despite all the characters divergent wants and needs there is an overall journey—a super-objective—that unites and drives them all forward. As each actor explores the complexity of their character, the interplay with other characters will inform and influence their individual arc and the collective experience.

During research and table work, the collaborators—creative team (director, playwrights, designers) and ensemble members (performers)—may focus on the mechanics of the theatrical event, including plot structure and narrative arc, especially if there is established text. For this reason I have included story elements as a way of identifying possible key moments for explorations. I have generated seven story elements that are inspired by aspects of Jung's theory on Individuation and are also loosely based on my understanding of the hero/heroine's journey. Although not all theatrical events are based on a linear storyline, certain story elements may serve aspects of its trajectory. The seven story elements are reality, search, rebellion, rupture, involution, evolution and return.

Explorations offer an opportunity to investigate moments that are referenced but not witnessed during the course of the theatrical event. They encourage performers to investigate on-stage and off-stage relationships to better understand how they trigger actions and events. They give directors, playwrights and designers the time and space to test ideas, insights and materials. They inform the rehearsal process in a way that allows multi-layered interactions to resonate with a depth that is palpable and "reads" on stage. Finally, they help to hone inter-personal skills by generating an atmosphere of receptivity within the collective through shared experience.

Explorations can find their way, with refinement, into the production itself. Not only can they be illuminating for the ensemble members, but they may further enhance the creative team's vision. The performers then become an integral part of a very collaborative process in building original work or expanding upon an existing vision.

On that note, explorations are designed to be as inclusive as they are inventive. The unique insight of all the collaborators involved is essential to the activation and unfolding of these explorations, regardless of who initiates them or how they are implemented. The interplay of acting and being is like a symphony of complex harmonies that resonate on many levels simultaneously.

CHAPTER 8

Character Work

FOUNDATION

In the course of researching and rehearsing a role, it is often by accident that I discover a specific essence, energy center and archetype that slowly come together to create a "meta-physical" whole.

Insight most often comes while I'm working "on my feet" in rehearsal. In time I have learned to trust this more visceral and intuitive approach to character development. Table work and dramaturgical research are not diminished, but both processes become more vital if the facts do not feel concretized, but color my work while I move, speak and breathe life into the character.

Explorations allow one to do their "homework" and then let it go, allowing meaning to emerge from embodied experience in an unpremeditated but consciously considered way. Relinquishing predetermined choices allows subtle or even startling discoveries to occur throughout the run of a performance, as well as during the rehearsal process. Consistency does not negate novelty along with complexity of response. If a character is housed in a specific yet flexible psycho-physical container they are capable of ongoing growth that is organic and non-linear.

Certain aspects of a character will surface before others. How the character's state of being interacts with our inner life depends greatly on our openness and emotional availability. We are also influenced by our fellow actors' interpretation of their characters, which in turn reflects their relationship to their inner lives. Thus, the interplay of acting and being

© The Author(s) 2016
E. Hess, *Acting and Being*, DOI 10.1057/978-1-349-95106-2_8

may take place on multiple levels if we radiate and receive from a place of generosity and wonderment. Characters are capable of continually evolving—just as we are ourselves—if we marry our inner lives to their imaginary circumstances. This means that every time one steps into a role it is an opportunity to gain in self-knowledge. What a gift it is then to "fire up the soul" as one also embodies a role!

CHARACTER RESEARCH

I like to begin character work by focusing on character elements based on Stanislavski's teachings. The framework has seven interlocking principles that resonate with the states of being. These elements are also informed by play elements (see Chap. 9, "Scene Study") from the world of the play. As I read through the text I make notes on stated or implied character elements from all sources: what the character says about themselves, what they say about other characters, what other characters say about them, plus exposition and authorial notes. Often the information is unreliable: lies, wishes, fantasies, rumors, half-truths and suppressed memories may all compete to speak the "truth" of the character. How the character hears, promotes, denies or accepts the information is in itself significant. Underneath these conflicting points of view resides the character's indisputable, though multi-dimensional, sense of self.

Character Elements

Origins	Ethnicity, race, nationality, language, dialect
	Social, religious, economic, political roots
Drives	Actions: conscious physical and/or psychological *wants* based on passions, appetites
	External behavior, psychic energy
Issues	Objectives: conscious and unconscious *needs* based on issues and complexes
	Internal motivations, intentions, justifications

   Drives and issues are often met with *obstacles*

Relationships	Essence, persona, identity, gender, traits
	Status, authority, reputation, position, entitlement, sociability
Age	Experience, maturity

Ability	Education, occupation, opportunity, intelligence
	Health, skills, talents, habits
Arc	Super-objective, destiny, fate, actualization
	Impact of ethics, morality, philosophy, beliefs, values

The interplay between character, play and story elements is explored in Chap. 10, "Production"

EXPLORATIONS IN ACTING AND BEING

Character explorations allow us to identify and inhabit the behavioral, physiological and psychological states within the character that combine to create a complex whole. For example, in a fully realized character, essence will color feeling, just as experience will color thought, just as sense will color emotion and so on. This character interacts with others who are also multi-dimensional. All these characters together affect and are affected by the world in which they co-exist.

Often a character's search for autonomy is realized during the course of the play, but just as often it is shattered. One character may rise above obstacles while another succumbs in defeat. Their fate mirrors their overall state of being in relation to the circumstances of the play. What destroys one character inspires another to find fulfillment. The interplay of acting and being within the actor generates characters that are multi-layered, yet contain a singular truth.

I have formulated areas for explorations that investigate character through behavioral, physiological and psychological states, in that order. But all states of being are inter-related and inform each other. Ultimately one breaks a character open during research and rehearsal to uncover their layers, only to stitch them back together again in a seamless, but surprising whole.

Behavioral Explorations

Comb through the text looking for references to the essence of the character. For example, are they referred to as a "bull," a "frigid bitch," an "angel"? If no such description is available, search for clues in the text about their behavior—their inherent animality or spiritedness, their bearing and demeanor. You may need to collect or create images and objects that illuminate the character's essence to further stimulate the imaginative juices. Once you have a sense of the character's dominant behavioral state, work out loud with the text and embody their essence through emulation. Observe the vocal colorings that emerge along with signature gestures and note how this activates behavior that is raw and undigested, or considered and conscious.

Investigate the intertwining of the character's level of consciousness and sentient nature. Consider how aware they are of their behavior—whether they accept responsibility for their drives and issues or avoid them. Review their personal history to see how their level of consciousness mirrors their coping mechanisms. Look at their interactions with other characters to see how their sentient nature is affected and altered, consciously or not. Likewise find ways in which the character influences the behavior of others. Question whether their native intelligence is utilized or underserved, whether their thinking is flexible or rigid. No matter what their level of consciousness, find out what excites the character's curiosity or keeps them from questioning. Discover how their sentient nature and level of consciousness affects their love of self, and how that love, or its lack, is manifested in or compensated for in their relationship with others.

Physiological Explorations

Search for the energy center that triggers the character's actions and ask why they are compelled to move from this place in the body. For example, are they in labor, nursing a hang-over, protecting a bad back? The above physical conditions are urgent and obvious. When the character has less pronounced physical conditions, observe the habits and/or tics embedded in their body language. For example, do they lick their lips, swivel their hips walk on tiptoe? The text may also provide metaphors that illuminate the character's relationship to their physical condition. For example, do they have "butterflies," a "lump in the throat," "pins and needles"? Observe the character's interaction with others to see what it reveals about their physical boundaries. For example, are they "touchy-feely" or withdrawn? Ask yourself what their physical expression reveals about their past and present relationships to others and the world around them.

Further examine the character's relationship to feeling and sensation. For example, do they have a voracious appetite, and if so what flavors appeal to them—sweet, savory, briny? Consider whether they wear a specific perfume or cologne. Be curious about their aesthetics and sense of style—their taste in art and music and dance and design and fashion. Note what activities excite or calm them, are simple or complicated, are sanctioned or taboo, and how they respond to conventions and challenges.

Psychological Explorations

Take a look at the underlying patterns of the character's behavior in order to identify their archetype. This is revealed in the consistent—even if competing and complex—ways in which they pursue their psycho-physical actions and objectives. Consider how their journey is informed by the collective unconscious and whether their inner life is aligned or out of balance with the larger world. For example, do they feel a need to uphold the status quo or to rebel against it? Observe how their actions reflect their belief system. Discover whether their present circumstances are new to them or all too familiar, comforting, jarring or precarious. One may need to create a more detailed back story in order to understand the character's philosophy of life.

Further explore the interaction between the character's thought and emotion by looking at their sense of self-worth. Find out how sensitive and soulful they are, how resilient and resourceful, how loving and open. Look at events and experiences in their life that may enhance or impede their greater self-fulfillment. Consider whether their wants and needs are complementary or in conflict, and whether their most basic needs are being met. If they are not, observe how desperation unmasks raw emotions and strategies for survival. If survival is not a burning issue, determine what drives the character, mentally and emotionally. One may want to review universal themes to see whether the character's needs and wants are predominately related to connection, power, love, communication, awareness or destiny. Finally, one may want to keep an eye on their dreams, to see if anything emerges from journaling that will provide further insights into the character's psychic landscape.

CHARACTER NOTES

How might the interplay of acting and being come together in a specific role? The following examples are from characters I have played in various productions. My own discoveries are just that (not to be replicated) and are meant as illustrations of a way to approach this work. They also represent points of entry that require further character development.

These discoveries emerged in their own way and in their own time. Sometimes they appeared in dreams. Sometimes they morphed in subtle or startling ways. Sometimes I wasn't able to articulate my discoveries until they were fleshed out in rehearsal or performance.

Molly in *Molly Sweeney* by Brian Friel[1]

Molly, who was born with minimal sight, recovers partial vision, but eventually succumbs to "blind-sightedness." She unconsciously refuses to process outer reality and retreats into an inner vision. The naked truth of "everyday reality" is too painful for her to process, much like as was for her mother, who retreated mentally from the world.

Molly's *essence* is akin to that of an owl. In her original blindness she was able to see clearly in the dark. She sensed the aura of others in a sensuous and insightful way. She was wise and still with an inner, expansive "wing-span" that allowed her imagination to soar.

Her *energy center* is the third eye. Her sense of sight is hyper-sensitive and subjected to experimentation. Her husband and her doctor have much to prove to themselves at her expense. As Molly divests herself of her own inner vision and self-understanding, she loses her ability to "feel" her way, even as she gains her footing in the outside world. But it is a false footing that undermines her intuitive self. She can no longer recognize her own interior as she stares at the stranger in the mirror.

Molly's *archetype* is the ultimate help-mate. In her willingness to assist others in their journey towards self-fulfillment, she loses her ground of being, her foundational self. Her tenderness and empathy are both a gift and a liability. Once she is no longer attached to her native instincts, she trades in her acute awareness for detached oblivion.

Arkadina in *The Seagull* by Anton Chekhov[2]

Arkadina is an aging actress who still has an enormous appetite for life. She fosters the attention that has always followed her, partly owing to her extroversion, but also to the exacting demands of a financially precarious profession. Consequently, she is loath to step aside and let the spotlight shine elsewhere. It can only mean a diminishment of her own radiant presence both as a woman and an artist.

Arkadina is tenacious and tender, funny and fierce, sexy and strident. Her *essence* is that of a de-clawed tiger. She's incapable of seriously ripping her lover apart emotionally, but can still lung at him, scratch him and kiss him with her rough tongue. Likewise she has no trouble with sinking her teeth into her son with biting words right after licking his wounds like an attentive mother. She rubs up against everyone, insisting that they pamper her, and meows when she's ignored or upstaged. No one dares to mess with her rather large and potentially menacing presence.

Arkadina's appetite is insatiable. Maybe it's that divine dissatisfaction of being an artist, but it's just as likely a lack of self-reflection. Her *energy center* is the navel. She is a powerful presence yet senses that she's also somehow impotent. But even though she is inwardly unconvinced of her unrivaled state she dares not admit it, so she is restless and bossy and voracious.

Arkadina is a curious mix of what are for her irreconcilable roles: an actress, a lover and a mother. But in all her various incarnations she embodies the *archetype* of the entertainer. Not only must she be the center of attention in all her spheres, but she feels obliged to entertain. Things will fall apart if she doesn't keep them light and buoyant. It is her curse and her gift. She keeps everyone riveted and distracted and yet she also manages to suck the energy out of the room—and out of some lives.

Amanda in *The Glass Menagerie* by Tennessee Williams[3]

Amanda is wily and resourceful, but also desperate and traumatized. She is both flighty and earthy—a duality that is spelled out in her last name, Wingfield. But her wings are too tattered to soar and she is too old to play the 'field"—not that she doesn't try to "fly" back to the past and revive her prowess with gentleman callers.

Her *essence* is akin to a battered griffin: "A fabulous animal, symbolically significant for its domination of both the earth and the sky – because of its Lion's body and Eagle's head and wings."[4] But rather than be mistress of both earth and sky, Amanda has an "eagle" call that is strident, and her "lioness-like" ferocity mauls her cubs more than protects them.

The Glass Menagerie was inspired by Tennessee Williams's relationship with his sister, Rose, who was mentally unstable, and his mother, Edwina, who was physically abused by her husband. In the play, the matriarch has been transformed into a single mother who clings to a romantic fantasy about her absentee husband. But something happened during their actual marriage that was deeply damaging—psychically, if not physically. Amanda's *energy center* is the heart, which has been broken beyond repair. She replays the dynamics of this trauma with her children. She dismisses the sensitivity of her daughter, Laura, and demands that her son, Tom, act as her surrogate lover and partner.

At first I thought it was obvious that Amanda was the ultimate, if complicated mother—a woman whose life revolved around her children. As I dug deeper into her psyche, her narcissism felt clinical to me—meaning that the world revolved around her and that her children were simply extensions of her reality. She embodies the *archetype* of the dreamer, a woman who is wrapped in veils of illusions and spins fantastical tales in order to survive. Her last words to her son are: "Then go to the moon – you selfish dreamer!"[5] Her taunt feels like a painful and angry projection of her own state of being, as much as a reflection of the truth about her husband and son.

NOTES

1. Brian Friel, *Molly Sweeney*, New York: Dramatists Play Service, Inc., 1994.
2. Chekhov, Anton, *The Seagull*, Act 4, in *The Plays of Anton Chekhov*, trans. Paul Schmidt, New York: Harper Perennial, 1999, p. 159.
3. Tennessee Williams, *The Glass Menagerie*, New York: Dramatists Play Service, Inc., 1945.
4. Hans Biedermann, Hans, *Dictionary of Symbolism*, trans. James Hulbert, New York: Meridian, The Penguin Group, 1994, p. 159.
5. Williams, *The Glass Menagerie*, Act 2, sc. 8, p. 67.

CHAPTER 9

Scene Study

Foundation

Chemistry between actors is never a given, but if one is able to radiate and receive, there is a chance that sparks will ignite. Explorations into states of being offer lots of resources for firing up one's acting instrument, but also for fueling the relationship to one's scene partner. They allow the exchange to be inventive, yet accountable to the world of the play. This encourages a sense of hard play, rather than hard work, so that the overall process is informed by joy, resilience and a spirit of generosity.

If another actor is inaccessible, for whatever reason, we still have room to be wily, to make space, to say "yes." We can continue to radiate as we remain in a state of receptivity. To play the truth as it unfolds means "to be" with what *is*, not with what one wishes would be. If scene partners listen and respond honestly, the exchange between them can be playful as well as unpredictable. Such flexibility nurtures ingenuity and adaptability, which also encourage ensemble building.

It is important that scene study begin with a thorough reading of the script. Explorations are meant to complement, not replace, research and text analysis. Such inquiry is not an academic exercise but an active excavation. It enables the actor to marry their inner life to the imaginary circumstances of the world of the play. The actor's interpretation of their role, and their character's relationship to other characters, needs to support the overall journey—the super-objective—of the play. This leads to character choices that are fully informed, as well as in tune with the actor's impulses.

© The Author(s) 2016
E. Hess, *Acting and Being*, DOI 10.1057/978-1-349-95106-2_9

The process is akin to a musician who scores a composition that will influence their interpretation, but not dictate the expression of their soul.

Explorations augment research into the world of the play in a number of ways. They flesh out unscripted back story. They reinforce the given circumstances that happen between characters on and off stage. They unearth subtext in order to ignite its direct influence on a character's needs and wants. They affect behavioral and psycho-physical actions by mirroring the soul, sensibility and psyche of the character.

Explorations also further the insights that are gleaned in text analysis through imaginative play. This allows the process to be layered yet surprising, since the actor's work is informed but not limited to the stated facts and fictions of the text. This can also help the actor to overcome prejudices and pre-conceived ideas about a character, since their understanding is based on empathy as well as dramaturgy.

Research based on works that are non-naturalistic, or set in a different time period, has the added challenge of making the play come to life in the present tense. Actors often struggle with the notion of "style," which can feel synonymous with artificiality. They may sacrifice their character's genuinity in a need to honor a symbolic or historical setting. Explorations can address abstract worlds, or the spirit of another age, by giving actors the space to breathe and move within these foreign environments. Gestures become familiar rather than imposed, activities become necessary rather than novel, actions become urgent rather than archaic. The divide between self and strangeness is bridged through an embodied experience of shared humanity across time and space.

The actors apply their discoveries from the explorations directly to their characters' lives. They may embody the omniscience of a ghost, or engage their lover in a dangerous dance, or torture the unraveling mind of an enemy. As they transition from beat to beat—moving from one action, objective and obstacle to the next—they investigate the character and play elements through active, rather than passive, choices that are informed organically.

The explorations also develop trust with one's partner allowing the exchange to be surprising and supple. When the instructor makes time in class for explorations, actors can then be witnessed in a safe space, which frees them to take greater risks. They can then incorporate their discoveries into private rehearsals outside the class.

An inner monologue begins to emerge over the course of multiple explorations, as the character's arc becomes more layered and their actions and objectives more complex. Ultimately, the actor wants to arrive at a place where every action vibrates with character consistency and mystery, every relationship is essential and unknowable, every action necessary and unpredictable. In the world of Shakespeare's plays and many works of heightened realism, this complex whole lives and breathes not only in the mind and body of the character, but also "on the line."

SCENE RESEARCH

Scene study begins with a shared understanding of the character elements (see Chap. 8, "Character Work") and play elements of the text. This ensures that advanced students who come from various training backgrounds can arrive at a common language in which to work together.

The play elements are also based on seven interlocking principles, which resonate with the states of being. The framework is filled in with specifics of the world of each play.

Play Elements

Setting	Place, atmosphere, location, surroundings, interior or exterior, near, mid or far
	Geographical, social, religious, economic and political environment
Actions	Conscious physical and/or psychological *wants* based on collective drives
	Collective behavior, driving forces
Objectives	Conscious and unconscious *needs* based on collective issues
	Collective motivations, intentions, justifications

Actions and objectives are often met with *obstacles*.

Characters	Collective identity
	Relationship to self, other and circumstances
Time	Minutes, hours, days, weeks, seasons
	Past, present, future—period, era, century
Activities	Collective tasks, routines, habits, rituals, rites
Super-objective	Overall journey, theme, message

The interplay between character, play and story elements is explored in Chap. 10, "Production."

EXPLORATIONS IN ACTING AND BEING

Scene study explorations engage the whole class simultaneously. This means that actors are working against the backdrop of the other actors, who are not a part of the world of their play. Nevertheless these "strangers" affect them in character, much in the way we adjust to strangers with "unknown scripts" in our everyday lives. However, the actors may be asked to work individually or with their scene partner, within the broader context of the whole class.

Any state of being can serve as an entry point into scene study explorations and be tailored to address the needs of a specific play or genre. A detailed description of the approach and application of behavioral, physical and psychological explorations can be found in Part 2, "Explorations in Embodied Performance."

The instructor will want to announce the focus of an exploration beforehand if it draws on particular aspects of the various plays covered in a scene study class. This allows the actors time to collect and incorporate research materials that relate to the specified orientation, activity or environment of the exploration. The actors may also be asked to work on states that differ from those assigned to their fellow actors and/or scene partners. For example, one actor might explore their character's animality; another, their character's physical challenges; a third, their character's afterlife. And so on.

The explorations may run from five to twenty minutes, depending on curricular needs. Additional time may be set aside at the conclusion of an exploration for actors to articulate their discoveries, to generate an inner monologue through journaling and to interweave excerpts with scene partners through embodied exchange.

I also encourage the actors to journal outside the class. These ruminations may include dreams that reveal character traits with numinous and emotionally charged energy. Before final presentations I ask the actors to hand in a stream-of-consciousness "free-write." This inner monologue is told from their character's point of view and is based on the interplay between the explorations and formal work on the scene.

Behavioral Explorations

The actors extract words or phrases from their assigned scenes that illuminate the sentient nature of their character. These text fragments are augmented by an image and/or object that mirrors their character's sense of self in an allegorical way. The actors morph into the metaphorical power of the images, or shape-shift into a symbolic replica of the objects. For example, they might scurry like a rat that is as chaotic as a Pollock painting, or flit about like a sprite that is as weightless as a feather-duster. They revel in their character's animality or spiritedness, their density or lightness, their rigidity or fluidity. In the process they may also unearth taboo or untapped desires and drives.

The character's level of consciousness is revealed as the actors now interact with others. The actors discover, for example, how aware, aggressive or articulate they are in expressing their wants and needs through physical and vocal play. The instructor may encourage the actors to exaggerate or inhibit their character's essence to uncover a greater range of response. Actors may also oscillate between playing off their scene partners and interacting with "strangers," to test the range of their characters' resourcefulness, resilience and responsiveness.

Physiological Explorations

The actors begin by investigating their character's dominant energy center. They experiment with variations of space, time and sound, using aural and body language to express their physical nature. They may whimper as they curl up in a fetal position, grunt as they clench their fists or laugh as they dance wildly. They test the limits of their character's physical expression—including habits, tics and gestures—noting how released or blocked energy informs their sense of self in relation to others.

The instructor may ask the actors to engage in a movement landscape, such as "sculpture," to express their characters' physical boundaries, while also observing the ease or awkwardness with which they give and take space; to transform into the physicality of their scene partner, as in the movement landscape "mirror opposites," to create empathy with their partner's somatic experience; or to exchange weight, as in the "tree," to discover ways in which their relationship may be symbiotic or sustaining, collapsed or supportive, intimate or questioning.

The actors may be asked to collect and incorporate research materials related to sense activation. These materials may include endowed objects and activities that arouse a strong feeling response. For example, the character's attire, personal items and pastimes may ignite specific memories and associations. They may also trigger attraction or aversion as the actors impose or share these properties and propensities with others.

Psychological Explorations

The instructor will want to determine the universal themes that are most poignant in relation to the various plays covered in the scene study class.

They might look for a central event, strong subject matter or issue of urgency addressed by the various playwrights, that best meets the needs of all the actors. For example, if characters are struggling with destructive choices, unmet need and/or lost love, it might be interesting to focus on the theme of "destiny'" using limbo as the psychic landscape. The actors would enter this space and relive moments in their character's journey in life, returning to events and relationships that require some kind of personal reckoning.

An actors may gravitate towards their scene partner during psychological explorations, in a desire to address their character's unresolved conflicts. However, they may find unexpected insights into their character's pattern of behavior by sharing their deepest wants and needs with "strangers." A new alliance or alienation may reinforce or challenge their archetypal energy. This may lead to a rekindling or re-examination of their convictions. As they then engage their scene partner, their attempts to meet their character's goals will be infused with invigorated and/or novel tactics.

Multiple Playwrights and Genres

When working with beginning actors, scene study that encompasses multiple playwrights and/or genres may best be accompanied by explorations that cover all the states of being in some form. This allows the actors to unearth impulses, awaken experience and enliven the imagination, so that their acting choices are active and embodied rather than static and analytical. When working with advanced students who already have considerable access to their acting instrument, the instructor can focus on the states of being that best address the genre of the scene work to follow.

Behavioral explorations, with their emphasis on impulse work, may be well suited to plays based on surrealism, absurdism or magic realism that demand bold and unexpected choices. Examples from these genres include *Ghost Sonata* by August Strindberg, *Rhinoceros* by Eugène Ionesco and *The Skriker* by Caryl Churchill.

Physiological explorations, with their intense and often intimate physical exchange, may be well suited to plays that are comedic, expressionistic or heightened and require intense physicality. Examples from these genres include *The Lieutenant of Inishmore* by Martin McDonagh, *Blasted* by Sarah Kane and *The Swan* by Elizabeth Egloff.

Psychological explorations, with their examination of unconscious and/or shadow contents, may be well suited to plays that are naturalistic, gothic or realist dramas and are driven by internal struggle. Examples of these genres include *Hedda Gabler* by Henrik Ibsen, *Cat on a Hot Tin Roof* by Tennessee Williams and *Betrayal* by Harold Pinter.

If scene study covers a number of different genres within one course, the instructor may want to conduct a condensed version of all the states of being, combining the same level from each of the three broad categories of behavioral, physiological and psychological states. The explorations would focus on an aspect of each state that best serves the class as a whole.

Descriptions of all the states of being can be found in Part 1. Templates for all explorations are covered in Part 2. Tailored investigations can be fleshed out and/or modified from the chart "States of Being" on p. 225.

Single Playwright and Genre

Scene study that concentrates on a single playwright allows explorations to engage in an even more fluid interplay of various states of being. In Chap. 10, "Production," the notes on *The Crucible* offer an example of explorations that are tailored specifically to the world of an Arthur Miller play. These notes can also serve as an in-depth example of explorations for scene study based on one text. More often, however, scene study covers several works of a playwright simultaneously. The focus on a single dramatist is particularly prevalent in the study of Anton Chekhov and William Shakespeare, whose worlds are ripe for customized explorations involving various states of being.

Chekhov

Chekhov's characters constantly struggle for recognition, release and return of self and others. Chekhov states: "My Holy of holies is the human body, health, intelligence, talent, inspiration, love and the most absolute freedom imaginable – freedom from violence and lies no matter what form they take."[1]

Freedom, as we know so well from Chekhov's plays, can be very elusive. Our inner life and outer reality often compete for supremacy, leaving us full of restlessness and longing, rather than ease and acceptance. The psychologist Daniel Kahneman, who conducted research into happiness, discovered:

> What makes the "experiencing self" happy is not the same as what makes the "remembering self" happy. In particular, the remembering self does not care

about duration – how long a pleasant or unpleasant experience lasts. Rather, it retrospectively rates an experience by the peak level of pain or pleasure in the course of the experience, and by the way the experience ends.[2]

The interplay between the "experiencing self" and "remembering self" is ever-present in Chekhov's plays. With this insight in mind, Chekhov explorations might focus on emotional recall, engaging the senses (from the physiological states), through endowed objects and activities, in relation to the duality of a universal theme (from the psychological states). Such interplay of states may help to elucidate the characters' inner struggle as they navigate the tangled web of truth and deception, deliverance and entrapment, health and disease—some of the dualities that are so central to Chekhov's plays.

For example, one might combine the sense of *sight* with the duality of security or vulnerability from the theme of *survival*. The actors would bring in an image that speaks directly to their character's history and experience, like a portrait of a dead mother, or a photo from a military parade, or an icon of a patron saint. These images might help to arouse powerful recollections and lead to complex responses, especially if the characters' worlds are being uprooted simultaneously, as when a soul mate is leaving town, or possessions are being packed up for a move, or a fiancé prepares for a duel. Explorations can be fleshed out, tailored and transposed from the following framework, which combines sample sensory objects and activities with psychological dualities:

Smell: perfume, vodka, tobacco	Connection: intimacy or estrangement
Taste: eating, drinking, smoking	Awareness: mindfulness or oblivion
Sight: portrait, photo, icon	Survival: security or vulnerability
Touch: dancing, care-giving, parlor games	Love: compassion or cruelty
Hearing: folk songs, instrumental music, litanies	Power: vitality or exhaustion
Intuition: rituals, prayers, superstitions	Communication: expression or suppression
Memory and association: gift, talisman, letter	Destiny: hope or despair

Shakespeare

As mentioned earlier, it is important that scene study begin with an examination of the text. This is particularly true of the works of Shakespeare, whose characters reveal their inner and outer thoughts "on the line." Scansion illuminates their emotional state through the rhythms and rhetoric of their speech, but the actors' interpretations are entirely their own invention. As Peter Hall writes in *Shakespeare's Advice to the Players*

> Shakespeare tells the actor when to go fast and when to go slow, when to come in on cue, and when to accent a particular word ... he always tells him *when* to do it ... But he never tells him *why*. The motive, the *why*, remains the creative task of the actor. He has to endorse feelings in himself which support the form that Shakespeare's text has given him.[3]

Shakespeare explorations might engage universal themes (from the psychological states), through archetypes—whose polarity he investigated with tremendous range and depth—with levels of consciousness (from the behavioral states). Working in tandem with words and phrases from the text, the explorations might help to address the enormous breadth of Shakespeare's understanding of the human condition by further illuminating the subtext that already exists "on the line."

For example, one might combine the archetype of the cross-dresser or imposter from the theme of love, with impulse from the levels of consciousness. The actors would bring in costume bits and pieces that reveal or conceal their essence. They might don a mask to hide the contents of their heart, or wear clothes of the opposite sex as an act of empowerment, or dress in the attire of another character or persona in an attempt to deceive. Disguised, they are free to activate their impulses—to unleash their irrational wants, hidden desires, or shadow side—and perhaps also escape with another into a dream, or disappear into the woods, or venture into foreign territory.

Explorations can be fleshed out, tailored and transposed from the following framework which combines universal themes through polarized archetypes, with a level of consciousness:

Survival: kin or bastard	Level of consciousness: actualization
Connection: lover or loner	Level of consciousness: intent
Power: warrior or peacemaker	Level of consciousness: affect
Love: cross-dresser or imposter	Level of consciousness: impulse
Communication: gossip-monger or seer	Level of consciousness: alteration
Awareness: dreamer or destroyer	Level of consciousness: instinct
Destiny: saint or sinner	Level of consciousness: influence

SCENE NOTES

The following notes are a combination of models that I have written for scene study that covers multiple playwrights and genres, followed by actors' "free-writes" for Chekhov and Shakespeare scenes. These examples and excerpts illuminate the possible and actual interplay of explorations and formal work on scenes. Words and phrases in the texts underscore various essences, energy centers and archetypes embedded within the characters. The language itself reflects the cadence and consciousness of the characters' inner voices and vision.

Both the models and the actor journal entries reflect the interplay of acting and being within the particular character. They also embrace the interplay with other characters, uncovering ways in which the relationships are both necessary and nuanced. The entries are not necessarily narrowed down to the scene itself but may reflect other moments in the character's life and thought that impact the scene.

These character revelations need not be shared between scene partners, but they will add texture and resonance to overt and concealed needs and wants between their characters. What remains unspoken or subliminal will be as palpable and persuasive as the conscious psycho-physical actions that drive the scene forward, moment by moment.

Multiple Playwrights and Genres

Southern Gothic
Blanche and Mitch in *A Streetcar Named Desire* by Tennessee Williams, Act 2, scene 2[4]

> Blanche: Mother turned into a wicked witch when she was pregnant with my baby sister. She was so ugly and bloated and rude. Like the day I brought home that dusty little boy – both of us five at the time – and she croaked, "What's that sewer rat doing in my kitchen?" We both started to cry. I bathed him down in the laundry room and he re-emerged as this little pink prince. Later I married that prince and the only thing "gray" about him was his last name.

Dark Comedy
Padriac and Mairead in *The Lieutenant of Inishmore* by Martin McDonagh, scene 6[5]

Padriac: I had to rip out that fecker's finger nails 'cause I know what he does with his hands when he's not dealing dope to little kids. Son-of-a-bitch is wankin' off. And that's just not right. Should get himself a wife. A girl who'd shoot his balls off if he got out of hand. Yeah. And a girl shouldn't waste her talents on blinding cows but should keep her sight on a man instead. Should be like my pussy cat – sweet and savage.

Magic Realism
Lily and Skriker in *The Skriker* by Caryl Churchill, underground[6]

Lily: Whispering wanting weird.
Sister self one burning being split splat.
Incest bad baby dying inside.
Lost lover secret smothered.
Specter salivating secreting bleeding.
Let me out, out, out.
Jumping out of my skin.
Dancing inside my mind.
Skriker and I are one.

Chekhov
Konstantin and Nina in *The Seagull* , Act 1[7]

Konstantin: I am making an attempt to change the state of the theater today. It is a stifled art, stripped bare of its potential and instead clothed with convention and compromise. There is no longer any meaning in it ... and whatever little can be gathered is cliché, commercial and shallow. Yet the public praises their work of monotony ... Even my own mother thrives on the starving populace. Their love for her is the only thing she ever truly cared about. To her, there is nothing else – either in the world or in art ... she resents me for my refusal to sacrifice my morals and theories for public adoration. (Evan Newman)

Anya and Trofimov in *The Cherry Orchard* , Act 2[8]

Anya: ... I always notice this particular smell in the nursery. It's this wonderful freshness that is just so comforting to me ... I fall right back into being a little girl again and I long to run outside through the orchard. I sometimes wish I could return to that young me ... a life completely full of possibility ... maybe I could convince Trofimov that no one is above love ... (Julia Rosenbaum)

Sonya and Yelena in *Uncle Vanya*, Act 3[9]

Sonya: ... I made up with Yelena ... but I can't help feeling like it's all her fault. Everyone is entranced by her. It makes me sick! But I cannot hate her, for she doesn't create such great fusses on purpose. It's her beauty – something over which she has no control – that drives everyone mad. Oh, were I cursed with such beauty! (Leigh Jones)

Shakespeare
Celia and Rosalind in *As You Like It*, Act 3, scene 2[10]

Celia: The other evening I had this really scary dream ... a giant bird appeared and started pecking. I tried to shield myself but the bird was too fast and I was cut up all over and my nightdress was all torn up. Suddenly I realized tiny trees were growing from my cuts and soon I was covered in a forest with tiny woodland creatures and everything! ... I called for help ... and there she [Rosalind] stood, ten feet tall! (Lauren Adleman)

Macbeth and Lady Macbeth in *Macbeth*, Act 1, scene 7[11]

Macbeth: She [Lady Macbeth] is my everything, and without her I would not be who I am, and with her I will become the man I need to be ... It is my destiny, and I have been told that I must. I cannot go against fate. We are doing this for the greater good of the people. (Ryan Lefton)

Desdemona and Emilia in *Othello*, Act 4, scene 3[12]

Desdemona: I have not denied you love, so why do you turn from me, spurn me, call me whore?
Whores do not love.
Whores lust.
Whores and trust don't go together.
I love.
I trust. I can be trusted.
And my love is beautiful.
Like Barbary's love was beautiful. (Abby Broch)

NOTES

1. Anton Chekhov, *Chekhov for the Stage*, trans. Milton Ehre, Evanston, Illinois: Northwestern University Press, 1992, p. 2.

2. Jim Holt, review of *Thinking, Fast and Slow* by Daniel Kahneman, *New York Times*, November 27, 2011.
3. Peter Hall, *Shakespeare's Advice to the Players*, London: Oberon Books, 2004, p. 4.
4. Tennessee Williams, *A Streetcar Named Desire*, New York: Dramatists Play Service, Inc., 1947.
5. Martin McDonagh, *The Lieutenant of Inishmore*, New York: Dramatists Play Service, Inc., 2003.
6. Caryl Churchill, *The Skriker*, London: Nick Hern Books, 1995.
7. Anton Chekhov, *The Plays of Anton Chekhov*, trans. Paul Schmidt, New York: Harper Perennial, 1999.
8. Ibid.
9. Ibid.
10. William Shakespeare, *The Complete Plays and Poems of William Shakespeare*, Cambridge, Massachusetts: Houghton Mifflin Company, 1942.
11. Ibid.
12. Ibid.

CHAPTER 10

Production

FOUNDATION

My experience, as both a teacher and a director, has taught me that the best way to realize one's vision is to relinquish control. This is not the same as dismissing one's convictions; it is embracing them in a spirit of collaboration. The more one is inclusive and inviting, the more one's vision may move beyond a personal artistic lens to reflect a transpersonal perspective. The mirror we hold up to life may magnify it rather than make it myopic.

Our aesthetic as well as personal expression is colored by our life experience. In order to transform the ordinary into the extra-ordinary we need to slowly peel away the layers of self-protection in order to see what pulses at the core. As Jerzy Grotowski writes in *Towards a Poor Theatre*, "Why are we concerned with art? To cross our frontiers, exceed our limitations, fill our emptiness – fulfill ourselves. This is not a condition but a process in which the dark in us slowly becomes transparent."[1]

This dawning awareness requires both patience and passion, so that we can digest our discoveries as we go, rather than fixate on a detail or swallow everything at once. I recall a life-drawing class I took once in which I was determined to sketch a hand with beautiful accuracy. I quickly "roughed in" the whole model and then immediately went to work on her draped hand. I was totally consumed and thrilled with the life that began to emanate from the page. The instructor came over and observed my work in progress. I beamed with pride at the expressive hand I'd drawn

© The Author(s) 2016
E. Hess, *Acting and Being*, DOI 10.1057/978-1-349-95106-2_10

with its exquisitely animated fingers. The instructor nodded in agreement and said that it was indeed alive. But then he asked me to step back and look at the whole sketch. You can imagine my surprise when I realized that the hand was huge and disproportionate! I learned from this experience to circle in, from the big picture to the specific, over and over again, so as to allow details to emerge as part of a slowly evolving, breathing whole.

Often what compels us to originate, devise or reinterpret a play or theatrical event in the first place, is a burning desire to address a truth that we may not have yet fully accessed. This is partly why we embrace a new project with such a sense of necessity and zeal. There is something alive and unknown that wants to be acknowledged. Even if it is an uncomfortable truth, we need it to be understood and enacted. The rehearsal process may then begin with a kind of hubris or self-protection along with all the excitement, but that should, it is hoped, evolve into a sense of humility and wonder.

Artistic peers can also offer much-needed expertise that enhances a project, generating greater dimensionality and depth, as well as resonance and revelation. Steven Dietz, a director and playwright, addresses the artificiality of the "hyphenization" of artists' roles such as "director-playwright" and seeks to integrate disciplines. He writes in "On Directing: A Modest Proposal":

> We must acknowledge the centrality of the *explicit* elements which comprise the theatrical event: text, performance and design. In an effort to embrace these central elements, the director – the *implicit* element in the process – must be trained to be a *unifying* rather that *stratifying* presence in the artistic workplace we call the theatre.[2]

It is in this spirit of shared discovery that one enters the collaborative process. The word "rehearsal" itself can be broken down into syllables: "re-hears-al(l)." The more we uncover shades of meaning buried beneath the surface reality the better. Explorations encourage collaborators—creative teams and ensemble members—to "unpack" a theatrical event from many vantage points. I am loosely referring to the director, playwright and designers as the creative team, and to the performers as the ensemble members. But these are just place-holders for an infinite variety of collaborative scenarios.

Directors may wish to conduct the explorations, but it's also wonderful when they are initiated by fellow collaborators and ensemble members. For example, a playwright may want to investigate a story idea through movement. A choreographer may want to animate a prop. A composer may want to experiment with *Sprechstimme* (speech-song). A designer may want to project images on bodies. An actor may want to initiate a collective ritual, and so on.

The director may utilize explorations to create a collaborative environment as well as to crack open the world of the theatrical event. Thus after an exploration it is good for all involved to take time to talk about the experience together. This is particularly true of established works that need to be re-envisioned. Often this feedback session can be as long as the exploration itself, as certain discoveries and epiphanies are made after digesting the experience. If, on the other hand, explorations are an integral part of creating original or devised work, less feedback may be desirable until late in the process, to keep discoveries fresh, focused and unselfconscious.

I encourage the collaborators and ensemble each to keep a journal to record thoughts, feelings and impressions that they may not necessarily wish to share with the collective. These entries might be musings, sketches or soundscapes that feel "random" and have yet to be fleshed out and integrated into the collective process. They may also contain "secrets"—character impulses and inner narratives that need to remain private in order to retain their personal potency and persuasiveness.

However, the theater is a public, rather than private, art form. Even secrets need to "read"—to be palpable and "in play." A theatrical event needs to be seen and felt to be believable and moving. In "Art as a Catharsis" Theodor Lipps says that as a member of an audience he feels himself and his own human value more intensely when it is reflected in someone else.[3] Paradoxically, an individual feels safe within a collective to access their unique experience through the witnessing, recognition and release that come with communal sharing.

PRODUCTION RESEARCH

The rehearsal process often begins with a table-read of the script. If there is no pre-existing or set text, one may begin by talking about the theme and concept of the theatrical event. The director (or initiator) may ask for immediate feedback following the reading (if there is text), when emotions are still fresh, thoughts are undigested, and questions are as valuable as insights and observations.

It is important for the collaborators to recognize the entry point into the theatrical event. Even if one is creating a hybrid work, such as a dance-theater piece, one will want to ask if this is a movement-based or text-driven work. If a work is collaborative from its inception, the team will want to bring their specific "know-how," as well as their individual voices and visions, to the venture. In other words, it is helpful to honor the original impulse and orientation of the piece. From there, anything is possible. Since my own background is in the theater, storytelling for me springs initially from the spoken word. One may wish to expand one's "toolbox" to include other artistic modes of expression, such as visual and gestural language. However, unless one is a multi-disciplinary artist, one doesn't want to embrace new tools by abandoning the skill-set of one's field of expertise. Even a collage of various art forms requires one or more sound organizing principles. By establishing a strong foundation, one can then entertain and incorporate multiple orientations. This encourages all collaborators to have confidence in their area of expertise as they step outside their comfort zone to explore an enlarged artistic palette.

A presentation of research materials may follow the table-read and discussion. The collaborators may offer music samples, costume sketches or set models, as well as images, videos and props. However, it is preferable not to "set things in stone" before conducting explorations of the theatrical event. If possible, it is good to utilize the research materials directly in the explorations. This gives the ensemble an opportunity to experiment, personalize and possibly expand upon the collaborators' initial vision.

If the theatrical event involves a clear journey or arc, I may want to familiarize the ensemble with story elements. Some, but not all, of the elements may be relevant to the explorations of the theatrical event. If, for example it is a collage of scenes rather than a single plot, there may nevertheless be some overriding theme or internal logic that underlies the piece.

Plot focuses on the *development* of events that shape the theatrical event. Story focuses on the *dynamics* of events that shape plot and character. These dynamics are the focus of the explorations since they allow each member of the ensemble to invest in their character's role in informing, and being informed by, the theatrical event.

I have laid out story elements in terms of the hero/heroine's journey against the backdrop of the collective. Characters tend to oscillate between heroic and unheroic attributes as a story unfolds. This is what makes them complex and compelling and all too human. Of course, the collective can also undergo a heroic or unheroic journey; a chorus or community can support or undermine individual and group goals.

The story elements include seven interlocking steps that resonate with the states of being. Some or all of them may be either critical or marginal to the theatrical event. They are inspired by aspects of Jungian theory on Individuation and loosely based on my understanding of the hero/heroine's journey.

Story Elements

Reality	Heroic: acknowledges given circumstances
	Unheroic: adheres to status quo
Search	Heroic: curious, inquisitive, investigatory
	Unheroic: obedient, complacent,
	acquiescent
Rebellion	Heroic: questioning, dissenting,
	experimental
	Unheroic: bombastic, reactive, explosive
Rupture	Heroic: in revolt, in crisis, disoriented
	Unheroic: inert, reductive, rigid
Involution	Heroic: inward-looking, reflective,
	contemplative
	Unheroic: implosive, numb, insulated
Evolution	Heroic: transformed, reborn, reformed
	Unheroic stagnant, atrophied, stifled
Return	Heroic: whole, realized, individuated
	Unheroic: fragmented, unfulfilled, lost

The Interplay of Character, Play and Story Elements

Extracting relevant character, play and story elements can help to identify areas within a specific theatrical event that are ripe for exploration. Most theatrical events are based on conflict, which is central to dynamic storytelling. The interplay of elements can help to illuminate the tensions that lead to these conflicts. Explorations uncover and/or activate these tensions by utilizing the states of being that best serve the needs of the work.

Character and play elements determine the nature of the conflict between the life of the character and the world of the collective. Story elements determine their expression.

A character's drives may be aligned with, or in opposition to, others' drives and/or the collective's actions. For example, a hero/heroine may be invested in upholding the status quo while the anti-hero/heroine fights to destroy it. Or conversely, the hero/heroine may be committed to overthrowing the status quo while the anti-hero/heroine fights to maintain it.

The play elements may in themselves be cohesive or fragmented. For example, the collective may be content with its lot but opposed by an outside force. Or the collective may want change but not have the means to bring it into effect.

The character elements can also be harmonious or discordant. For example, a character may be driven to break free from a relationship (which may be an unhealthy one with self), but may stay within it to survive, physically or psychologically. Or a character may want to sustain a relationship but need to leave it in order to find autonomy.

At every moment the storyline either reveals character or advances plot, often doing both simultaneously. Collaborators will want to address several overriding questions as they investigate a theatrical event.

Who is heroic? Who is unheroic? If that question feels too reductive then ask: who are these characters and how do they perceive their role and destiny in relation to others, and to events?

What drives the characters passionately?

Who (or what circumstances) opposes one or more characters with equal, though different and conflicting, investment?

What is at stake, urgently and immediately?

What is the pivotal moment, crisis or main event?

How are the characters arrested or transformed?

What is the outcome and overall theme?

Chekhov states that there are no angels or villains in his plays. Yet the consequences of his characters' actions are profound, both to themselves and to others. Chekhov was a doctor and knew the importance of asking essential questions as an integral part of examining a patient. Explorations also need to uncover the complexities, struggles and variations within the human condition that make every story unique.

EXPLORATIONS IN ACTING AND BEING

Explorations enhance a rehearsal process and production by generating ideas for original and devised work, or excavating motifs within existing text. Whether a theatrical event is naturalistic or heightened, realistic or impressionistic, a distillation or a collage, it will contain some form of internal logic or outer pattern, even if it is not a linear narrative.

Explorations geared towards production goals may share some commonality with those pursued in Chap. 9, "Scene Study." States of being that may be suited to specific theatrical styles can be found under the subheading "Multiple Playwrights and Genres."

It may also be valuable to review Part 1, "States of Being," to determine which states of being resonate with the theatrical event under investigation. One can also use the chart "States of Being" for quick reference.

Behavioral Explorations

These explorations require that performers each bring in an image and/ or object that speak to the sentient nature—essence—of their character. Designers may also wish to present materials that resonate with their vision regarding the "world" of the theatrical event.

For example, if the "world" deals with characters that live in some version of a "lower depth," the image may be of an ape; the object, a wash rag. If the "world" is one of numbing routine, the image may be of a robot; the object, a cell phone. If the "world" is suffused with the supernatural, the image may be of a sylph; the object, finger lights.

The performers consider the numinous nature of their individual image and/or object. The initiator of the exploration may wish to offer prompts such as; "What behavior does this image or object elicit in the character? How is it reflected in their drives and issues? What special energy does it carry for them, for others? How do they feel about this image of themselves, or of this world? How is this object alive and animated?"

The performers begin to inhabit the image and/or endow the object, encountering each other as they move through the space. They allow an animal, humanoid or spirit sentience to infuse their work, discovering ways in which their essence provokes response in others. They consider the character's level of consciousness. The initiator may ask: "How aware is the character of their wants and needs? How do they negotiate with others? Are they oblivious or self-conscious, overt or covert in their behavior?"

Physiological Explorations

These explorations begin by asking the performers to "throw the character into their bodies." The designers may also want to activate the space so that it is evocative of the world of the theatrical event.

The performers move through the space. Starting with a neutral or habitual walk, they slowly transform their own body language into that of their character. They observe how much space they take up as they "come into their own." The initiator talks them through all the energy centers, one at a time, as they weave in, out and around each other.

As the performers progress from the root to the crown, the initiator may offer suggestions that come from the world of the theatrical event. For example, if the event concerns starvation, a character may keep their eyes on the ground looking for crumbs. If the event involves heresy, a character on their way to the execution block may find an inner resolve that straightens their spine. If the event deals with displacement, a character who is about to be reunited with a long-lost loved one may try to calm their pounding heart.

The performers may also experiment with aural and body language as they activate different energy centers of the body. For example, their character might mumble as they grovel, sing as they strut or whisper as they cower. This might organically evolve into speech in which the actors include a line of their text as vocalizations become one with physical expression.

Psychological Explorations

These explorations are tailored to illuminate the dualities within the universal theme of the theatrical event. The collaborators' understanding of the play will influence the point of view of the production, and the physical setting for these explorations will deeply affect the psychic landscape, and vice versa. Performers are encouraged to be in rehearsal clothes and to bring personal props—materials that they provide themselves or that have been gathered by the designers—so they can put their character's unique stamp on the environment.

The initiator begins by addressing the main theme of the theatrical event. For example, if the theme is forbidden love, they may separate characters who long to be together. If the theme is censorship, they may dare everyone to sing a national anthem that has been banned. If the theme is privilege, they may allow only one character to eat, while others look on with hunger. The initiator may also suggest that the characters enact their unspoken desires, to see what effect they have on the collective. In every case, the exploration seeks to heighten and expose the underlying tensions of the overall theme.

PRODUCTION NOTES

These following explorations are taken from work with university theater students and international professional actors. They reflect my work conducting explorations in three distinct creative capacities: as an acting consultant for another director on an established American classic, as the creator and director of a devised ensemble performance piece and as director and playwright in collaboration with a composer, choreographer and designer on a collective multi-disciplinary work.

Established Play

The Crucible[4]
    Playwright: Arthur Miller
    Director: Mary Robinson
    The director, Mary Robinson, asked me to generate several explorations with her cast during the rehearsal process. Early in the text of the play, Arthur Miller alludes to the conjuring of dead spirits in an inciting incident that occurs before the opening of the play. Mary asked me to conduct an exploration with the female cast members involved in this off-stage scenario. Using the text as a reference point, we created a dance in the dark around a large bowl filled with "blood" (tomato juice) to the singing of a Yoruba chant (researched by the actor playing Tituba). The cast transformed the blood into a "brew" of forbidden and fearful desires by endowing it with the "magic if"—the phrase Stanislavski uses so beautifully and simply to express our ability to suspend disbelief. Their giggles and screams and whispers and singing were filled with terror and delight as they explored a ritual that was as titillating as it was taboo. This shared secret informed their collective outcries during the court scene later in the play. They had a shared experience of the unspoken understanding that fueled their underlying hysteria, and that truly made them an unstoppable force.

Here, is the response of the director, Mary Robinson, to the incorporation of this and another exploration into the overall fabric of the rehearsal and production process.

In a production of Arthur Miller's *The Crucible*, which I directed at Playwrights Horizons Theater School (an affiliate of NYU) I had in the cast a mix of current students, recently graduated students, and faculty. Elizabeth Hess took our performers through a series of off-text explorations that turned out to be essential and integral not only to the actors' work but to the production overall.

In the early days of rehearsal, she took most of the 20 member cast through a community building exploration, in which they experienced the joys and restraints of being part of a religious community. They sat, segregated by gender, in a church-like setting, meditating, singing together, and observing each other. She then had them explore and act out on their fantasies towards each other, bringing to the surface the hidden tensions that are buried throughout most of the play. This enabled the actors to have a three-dimensional sense of what exactly they are suppressing, both as individuals and as a group, and I heard from the actors over and over how much this helped them as we worked our way through the play and its complicated relationships.

About halfway into the rehearsal process, Elizabeth led an exploration on what happened in the woods before the play begins, with the actresses playing the young girls and Tituba. Her preparation for this exploration was incredibly impressive. She discussed what might want to happen with the actress playing Tituba, and we brought in some props, including tomato juice to stand in for the blood drunk by Abigail, mentioned in the play. Then Elizabeth let the exploration unfold, prepared to step in and do some side-coaching if necessary—but as it turned out, because she had set it up so beautifully, there was little she needed to do because the actresses followed their impulses so well. An organic event was created which surprised, thrilled and scared us all. We then launched into a run-through of Act One, and discovered for the first time the incredibly high stakes, as well as the erotic charge, of the act. This was entirely due to Elizabeth's work with the actors.

These explorations were so integral to the work that I incorporated streamlined versions of both of them into the production's beginning. When the audience entered the actors were sitting, as at a service, and a feeling of community was established through the humming of a psalm just as the play began. This was juxtaposed in the blackout leading to the first act, when we heard sounds of the ritual in the woods, startling and unnerving the audience.

Though I had planned to start with some sort of pre-show moment, I had only a sketchy sense of what this might be before Elizabeth's work. My ideas were entirely fleshed out and inspired by these wonderful explorations Elizabeth planned and led which so enhanced the experience of the actors, myself and finally, the audience.

Devised Performance Piece

Internally Displaced

Direction and conception: Elizabeth Hess
Dramaturge: Doruntina Basha
Collaborators and performers: Dhurata Hoti, Fjolla Hoxha, Vlora Nikci, Vesa Qena, Vjosa Shala, Alketa Sylaj, Lola Sylaj

I met Doruntina (Dori) Basha, a soulful and singular playwright from Kosovo, at a conference of Women Playwrights International (WPI). Both our plays had been selected for presentation—addressing the trauma of the war-torn Balkans in unique ways—and thus we became familiar with each other's voice and vision. Dori remarked that my solo play, *Dust To Dust*—based on the systematic rape of women during the Bosnian war—broke through the silence of an issue that was still very taboo in Kosovo. She invited me to lead sessions based on the same subject matter in an atelier in Prishtina, with local actors and playwrights.

The atelier was part of a five-part art-based action research investigation called "Recollecting the Past in Kosovo: Cultural Memory between Facts and Fiction," implemented by forumZFD (Ziviler Friedensdienst). Dori worked for this non-partisan organization and, along with her co-worker Jane Felber, approached Lina Andeer of Kvinna til Kvinna (Woman to Woman), a non-governmental organization which supported my participation as well as contributed to the research and overall concept of the atelier.

Our atelier was called "Transforming Trauma through Art: War Rapes and the Re-Collection of Self and Community." We began the process with information-gathering, including a discussion with Sevdie Ahmeti, a human rights activist who conducted extensive interviews with rape survivors and witnesses of the Kosovo war of 1998–99. Her insight into the specifics of these crimes, committed during internal displacement and deportations, and at rape camps, was harrowing, yet it helped to particularize the women who had suffered. Sevdie remarked that survivors remain silent not only out of a sense of personal shame, but also out of a sense of duty, expected within Muslim culture, to preserve one's family's honor.

The members of the ensemble then talked about their wish to not only give voice and visibility to these survivors, who cannot speak for themselves or reveal their identities, but to also restore their dignity and re-integrate them into society as women who are so much more than the ostracizing label of "victim." By moving beyond a narrow definition of these women as victims to an expanded understanding, the members of the ensemble were able to uncover the depth and complexity of these women's individual and collective experiences as they then struggled to excavate their dark secrets.

I then led the actors in a series of behavioral explorations—from primal to cosmic—to generate a shared physical and vocal language that was instinctive and visceral. These explorations were followed by actors reading aloud from selected archival rape testimonies. These archives became the basis for our piece. We chose to use only the words of the survivors, working mostly in the original Albanian language, but also sprinkling the text with the English translation, to give the work resonance on a global scale.

Further explorations focused on the psychological states of being that were evoked by the various women's testimonies. The actors worked with fragments of the testimonies, thus underlining the "splitting off" of the self during rape. These fragments were invested physically, as the ensemble inhabited the text in an allegorical way. The actors also brought in mundane, everyday objects to express the benign nature of "normalcy." These objects became transformative, as reality also became warped and unrecognizable.

We discovered, as we began to interweave the text, that no one had chosen to focus on the rapes themselves, but rather on all the details of degradation and humiliation that accompany such violence. In this way the ensemble made it clear, without spelling it out, that rape is less about sex than it is about power.

As the piece began to take shape, a heightened reality emerged that took the form of three short acts.

Act 1: Everyday Life and Interaction. Suspicion and Evacuation. Hiding and Exposure.
Act 2: Impact and Invasion. Reaction and Resistance. Aftermath and Emptiness.
Act 3: Cleansing and Community. Restoration and Recollection. Witness and Oneness.

Initially the ensemble moved though the empty space with shopping bags, back-packs and purses that were filled with water bottles, make-up and articles of clothing. These few objects became transformative in surprising ways. A water bottle was poured over someone's head as she spoke of being thrown in a well. Lipstick was smeared on ankles as another spoke of being stabbed in the legs so that she couldn't run away. Baby clothes that were ripped out from under a T-shirt became an abortion. Hair was tucked into a baseball cap for a disguise as a boy. Eye-shadow became bruises. A bra became a blindfold. Sweatpants became a restraint. A scarf became a ghostly veil.

In the aftermath of the rape all the women covered their faces with their hands in a gesture of collective shame. They then began to reach out to each other: washing one another with water, combing hair, restoring a piece of clothing, rocking each other in their arms, offering water to drink. We actually referred to this section as "ethnic cleansing," reversing the notion of objectification and eradication and instead introducing recognition and restoration. Once all the women were attended to, they picked up all the "fragments" and restored the space to its original neutrality. Only now it was filled with their voices as they sang a traditional Albanian folksong. Finally they all come together and faced the audience to be witnessed as women in the world.

On the final day of the atelier we presented our performance piece to a small invited audience. After the performance Dori led a dialogue with those present; the response was evocative and emotional, as the material released buried contents that have festered in the culture for many years. Rather than offering an intellectual response, the audience expressed insights and observations that resonated personally and profoundly.

The piece was then performed at POLIP, a literary festival in Priština. The sensitive yet transparent approach to the material astounded one journalist, who asked Dori if she was aware that there were Serbs in the audience; Dori replied that we wanted to reach out in a spirit of reconciliation.

Original Multi-Disciplinary Work

Perfect Curiosity: *A Theatrical Fable*

Director and playwright: Elizabeth Hess
Composer: Lucas Syed
Choreographer: Katie Palmer

Set and costume designer: Barbara Begley
Additional collaborators: Jenna Dioguardi, Brad Raimondo, Colleen
   Toole
Ensemble: Cherrye Davis, Price Garrison, Vanessa Koppel, Javier Perez,
   Katie Palmer, Katie Polin, Danielle Sacks, Lucas Syed

Perfect Curiosity is a multi-disciplinary theatrical fable. Text, movement
and music combine to tell the story of migrating souls, including two sisters, Perfect and Curiosity, who navigate the slippery terrain of a cold, yet
incestuous household.

The piece was written with the intention of investigating an interior
landscape using heightened language. The central theme is psychic incest,
and I wanted to show this crime in a primitive and provocative way without making any overt commentary.

In our initial rehearsal we read through the text and combed through
images and related articles. The collaborators and ensemble offered questions and considerations about the nature and shape of the fable. This
was our only table work, and without concern for immediate answers, the
ensemble got "on its feet" and started to explore the world of the fable
from the opening moment of "Once upon a time …"

This first exploration was based on conjuring up these migrating souls,
who were returning to the same time and place from a shared past. The
actors asked themselves why they were here now. Why had they material-
ized? What did they want urgently? What did they need from each other?
Who was the audience?

The actors began to circle the space, trying to formulate their needs.
They were confused and lost, but I realized that rather than push for a
result, I simply needed to recognize that this was their truth. They were
in a liminal space in which were vulnerable and alone in an over-
whelming unknown. They discovered a genuine need to reach out to the
audience for acknowledgement, while wrestling with other souls to mold
a version of their old, shared "reality" that would affirm or alleviate their
distress.

The text, like many fabulist tales, was spoken in the third person and
the past tense, but all events needed to unfold with urgent necessity. It was
paramount to re-awaken buried psychic contents in an immediate and tangible way. Even though the work was text-driven, movement and sound
were woven into its fabric, becoming inseparable and necessary to the
characters' search for meaning and transformation into distinct characters.

Early on in the story Curiosity, one of the sisters, enters this world. Her birth is messy and labored, causing the death of the Mother. In the exploration around this event, the costume designer had made a red skirt that was pulled out from the Mother's underclothes and became the bloody birth canal from which Curiosity emerged. The primal screams that accompanied this moment were enhanced by the ungainly costume pieces the actors had to cope with as they played midwife to Curiosity, who eventually appeared out from under the Mother's chair. The choreographer, who preferred to think of her role as that of a movement specialist, took this "raw material" and gave it shape. It not only retained its awkwardness but, by becoming streamlined, was now full of urgency. We discovered later in the story—as we did with many movement sequences and gestures—that we wanted to repeat this motif. This time it was with the Father just before his death, when Curiosity finally sees him as the balled-up mess of raw need that he once projected on to her as a helpless newborn.

Music, likewise, was embedded organically into the piece through repeated themes, rather than being "through-composed." Soundscapes appeared whenever characters moved away from reasoned thought and gave way to revelatory feelings through recitatives, arias, extended voice technique or ensemble chorales.

There is a furnace that comes to life during the fable, terrifying the one sister, Perfect, and entrancing the other, Curiosity. Migrating souls engage in an exploration with *Sprechstimme*, (the interplay of speaking and singing), humanizing and distorting its sparks, roaring fire and dying embers. As the fable develops, the furnace transforms into a godmother who is central to Curiosity's psychic survival. The composer wrote a ballad full of sputters and syncopation to underline their lively dialogue, which the choreographer contrasted with a synchronized dance to illuminate this fantastical yet healing vision.

Text was the entry point for the work—and was written before the rehearsal process commenced—but ideas about movement and music were also mapped out in advance. Re-writes often reflected discoveries made about the fable during explorations, as did new choreographic and compositional elements, many of which were generated in the moment. My overall sense of the process was one of breaking things open and re-assembling them only later as necessary.

The ensemble (which included the composer and choreographer) all played characters who embodied archetypes, but were also living, breathing beings in search of individual authenticity. Explorations allowed the ensemble to discover surprising truths about their characters, through instinctive and imaginative leaps that arose organically and intuitively. In the process the members of the ensemble developed an abiding trust in each other, becoming increasingly free to reveal character traits that were ugly or exquisite, brutal or tender in unexpected ways. Throughout the explorations, and the workshop that followed, the members of the ensemble listened and responded to each other in a multi-dimensional way, allowing their choices to be informed by the interplay of temperament and tone, breath and bone, psyche and soul.

NOTES

1. Jerzy Grotowski, *Towards a Poor Theater*, New York: Routledge, 2002, p. 21.
2. Steven Dietz, "On Directing: A Modest Proposal," *American Theater Magazine*, March 2007, Vol.24 Issue 3, p. 54.
3. Theodor Lipps, Chapter 9, "Art as a Catharsis," in *The Psychology of Art* by Lev Vygotsky, trans. Scripta Technica, Inc., Cambridge, Massachusetts, MIT Press, 1971.
4. Arthur Miller, *The Crucible*, New York: Bantam Books, 1959.

CHART: STATES OF BEING

Behavioral *Soul/sentience*	Physiological *Body/soma*	Psychological *Mind/psyche*
Primal	Root	Survival
Organic	Sacral	Connection
Willful	Navel	Power
Humanoid	Heart	Love
Psychic	Throat	Communication
Mythic	Third Eye	Awareness
Cosmic	Crown	Destiny

© The Author(s) 2016
E. Hess, *Acting and Being*, DOI 10.1057/978-1-349-95106-2

BIBLIOGRAPHY

Agnes, Michael. 2002. Editor in chief. *Webster's New World Dictionary*. New York: Hungry Minds, Inc..

Albee, Edward. 2008. *The Goat, or Who is Sylvia?* In *The Collected Plays of Edward Albee, Volume 3 1978–2003*, 598, Sc 2. New York: Overlook Duckworth, Peter Mayer Publishers, Inc.

Aristotle. 1961. *Aristotle's Poetics, XXII*, 104. Trans. SH Butcher. New York: Hill and Wang.

Beckett, Samuel. 1954. *Waiting For Godot*, 29, Act 1. New York: Grove Press, Inc.

Berry, Cicely. 1973. *Voice And The Actor*, 19. London: Harrap & Co, Ltd.

Biedermann, Hans. 1994. *Dictionary of Symbolism*, 159. Trans. James Hulbert. New York: Meridian, The Penguin Group.

Brecht, Bertolt. 1962. In *Baal*, ed. Eric Bentley, 81–82. New York: Grove Press.

Brook, Peter. 1995. *The Open Door, The Golden Fish*, 98. New York: Theatre Communications Group, Inc.

Brooks, Rodney. 2007. *Flesh and Machines* in *The Real Transformers* by Robin Marantz Henig. *New York Times Magazine*. 07/29/2007.

Chekhov, Michael. 1991. *On The Technique of Acting*, 60. New York: HarperCollins Publishers.

Chekhov, Anton. 1992. *Chekhov for the Stage*, 2. Trans. Milton Ehre. Evanston: Northwestern University Press.

———. 1999a. *The Seagull* in *The Plays of Anton Chekhov*, 159, Act 4. Trans. Paul Schmidt. New York: Harper Perennial.

———. 1999b. *Uncle Vanya* in *The Plays of Anton Chekhov*, 229, Act 2. Trans. Paul Schmidt. New York: Harper Perennial.

de Waal, Frans. 2006. *Our Inner Ape*. New York: Riverhead Books.

Dietz, Steven. 2007. On Directing: A Modest Proposal, 54. *American Theater Magazine*, Vol 24, Issue 3.

© The Author(s) 2016
E. Hess, *Acting and Being*, DOI 10.1057/978-1-349-95106-2

Friel, Brian. 1994. *Molly Sweeney.* New York: Dramatists Play Service, Inc.

Genet, Jean. 1962. *The Maids,* 80–81. Trans. Bernard Frechtman, Revised. New York: Grove Press, Inc.

Grotowski, Jerzy. 2002. *Towards a Poor Theater,* 21, 57. New York: Routledge.

Guskin, Harold. 2003. *How To Stop Acting,* 66–67. New York: Faber & Faber, Inc.

Haidt, Jonathan. 2013. *The Righteous Mind: Why Good People Are Divided by Politics and Religion.* New York: Pantheon Books.

Hall, Peter. 2004. *Shakespeare's Advice To The Players,* 4, 8. London: Oberon Books.

Hamilton, Edith. 1999. *Mythology,* 17. New York: Warner Books.

Hesse, Herman. 1963. *Steppenwolf,* 41–42. Trans. Basil Creighton. New York: Picador.

Holt, Jim. 2011. Review of *Thinking, Fast and Slow,* by Daniel Kahneman. *New York Times Book Review.* 11/27/2011.

Hutson, Matthew. 2012. *In Defense of Superstition. New York Times Article.* 04/06/2012.

Ibsen, Henrik. 1961. *Hedda Gabler And Other Plays,* 345, Act 3. Trans. Una Ellis-Fermor. Middlesex: Penguin Classics.

Jung, Carl. 1957. *The Undiscovered Self,* 61. New York: A Mentor Book, New American Library.

Kafka, Franz. 1996. *Metamorphoses,* 3 Trans. and edited by Stanley Corngold, New York: Norton Critical Editions, 1996.

LaBute, Neil. 2001. *The shape of things,* 122. London: Faber & Faber Limited.

Le Doux, Joseph. 1998. *The Emotional Brain* in *Mapping The Mind,* by Rita Carter, 98. London: University of California Press.

Lecoq, Jaques. 2006. *Theater of Movement and Gesture.* ed. David Bradby, 89–91. New York: Routledge.

Lipps, Theodor, Chapter 9, "Art as a Catharsis" in *The Psychology of Art* by Lev Vygotsky, trans. Scripta Technica, Inc. Cambridge, Massachusetts, MIT Press, 1971.

Lorca, Federico Garcia. 1996. *Blood Wedding,* Version by Ted Hughes, 60. New York: Faber & Faber, Inc.

McDonough, Martin. 2003. *The Pillowman,* 51, Act 3. New York: Dramatists Play Service, Inc.

McNally, Terrence. 1994. *A Perfect Ganesha.* New York: Dramatists Play Service. Inc, p. 7.

Miller, Arthur. 1959. *The Crucible,* 130, Act 4. New York: Bantam Books,.

Neal, David, and Chartand, Tanya. 2011. *Embodied Emotion Perception.* Sage Journals, Social Psychological and Personality Science 2(6).

O'Neill, Eugene. 1968. *Long Day's Journey Into Night,* 93, Act 2, sc 2. New Haven: Yale University Press.

Plath, Sylvia. 1971. *Crossing The Water, Transitional Poems, Two Sisters of Persephone*, 46. New York: Harper Perennial.

Racine, Jean. 1961. *Three Plays of Racine; Phaedra, Andromache and Britannicus*, 107, Act 4, lines 1350–1354. Trans. George Dillon. Chicago: The University of Chicago Press.

Rilke, Rainer Maria. 2011. *Letters To Young Poet, Letter 4*, 46. Trans. Mark Harman. Cambridge, MA: Harvard University Press.

Rivera, Jose. 1999. *Marisol*, 18, Act 1, sc 4. Revised. New York: Dramatists Play Service Inc.

Rumi. 2001. *Thinking and the Heart's Mystical Way*, in *The Soul of Rumi*, 75. Trans. Coleman Barks. San Francisco: HarperSanFrancisco.

Schnitzler, Arthur. 1982. *La Ronde*, Adapted by John Barton from a trans. Sue Davies, 56, Sc 9. New York: Penguin Books.

Shakespeare, William. 1958. *Hamlet*, 111, Act 3, Sc 1, line 56. New York: Dell Publishing Co., Inc.

———. 1960. *Richard III*, 12, Act 1, sc 2, lines 138–141. New York: Washington Square Press.

———. 1963. *Macbeth*, 46, Act 1, sc 3, lines 137–142. New York: Signet Classic .

———. 1993. *A Midsummer Night's Dream*, 31, Act 2, sc 1, lines 1–13. London: Everyman by J. M. Dent. .

———. 2002. *Romeo and Juliet*, 170, Act 3, sc2, lines 21–25. Reprinted. London: Arden Shakespeare.

Shaw, Bernard. 2003. *Pygmalion*, 80, Act 4. New York: Penguin Classics.

Sontag, Susan. 1966. *Against Interpretation: And Other Essays, Part 9*, 13. New York: Farrar, Straus and Giroux.

Stanislavski, Constantin. 1989. *An Actor Prepares*, 70. New York: Routledge.

Stanislavski, Constantin,1984. *The Stanislavski System, xvi*, by Sonia Moore, foreward by Joshua Logan, 2nd revised ed., New York: Penguin Books.

Sterner, Jerry. 1989. *Other People's Money*, 78, Act 2. New York: Samuel French, Inc.

Taymor, Julie. 2009. Music: You Have To A Pull Few Strings To Create These New Opera Stars. *New York Times*: 11/19/2006.

Ulanov, Ann & Barry. 1987. *The Witch and the Clown*, 192. Wilmette: Chiron Publications.

Wangh, Steven. 2000. *Acrobat of the Heart*, 217. New York: Vintage Books.

Weiss, Peter. 1993. *Marat/Sade*, English version by Geoffrey Skelton, Verse adaptation by Adrian Mitchell, 37, Act 1, sc 15. Woodstock: Dramatic Publishing.

Wellman, Mac. 1994. *Whirligig*, 143. Baltimore: The John Hopkins University Press.

Williams, Tennessee. 1945. *The Glass Menagerie*, 63, 67, Act 2, sc 8. New York: Dramatists Play Service Inc.

Zimmerman, Mary. 2002. *Metamorphoses*, 23. Evanston: Northwestern University Press.

INDEX

© The Author(s) 2016
E. Hess, *Acting and Being*, DOI 10.1057/978-1-349-95106-2

Lipps, Theodor, 211, 224n3
Art as a Catharsis, 211, 224n3
The London Academy of Dramatic Art
(LAMDA), vi, 2, 17, 184
Lorca, Federico Garcia, 101, 110n14
Blood Wedding, 101, 110n14
love. *See also* universal themes
Chekhov explorations, 202
explorations, 162
Shakespeare exploration, 203
state of being, 13, 59–61, 225

M
magic
emulation, 15
nature of, 10, 70
transformation, 6
McDonagh, Martin
The Lieutenant of Inishmore, 200,
204, 207n5
The Pillowman, 45, 50n6
McNally, Terrence, 108, 110n17
A Perfect Ganesha, 108, 110n17
memory/association, 151
guided exploration, 119
metaphor
explorations in, 9, 33, 70, 71
inter-relatedness, 6, 39
nature of, 17, 33, 70
Miller, Arthur, 62, 67n8, 201, 217,
218, 224n4
The Crucible, 62, 67n8, 201, 217,
218, 224n4
movement landscapes. *See also*
explorations, orientation
approach, 113
breaking patterns, 48, 127, 149
foundation, 33, 34, 113
membrane, 41, 126, 134
mirror opposites, 46, 127, 145
rubber band, 42, 126, 137, 138

sculpture, 39, 126, 131
tree, 37, 126, 127
wind instrument, 44, 127, 141
myth, 6–10, 51, 52, 70
mythic, 8, 13, 16, 27, 28, 93, 105–6,
158. *See also* essence
state of being, 13, 27–9, 225

N
navel. *See also* energy center
explorations, 41, 134–7
state of being, 13, 41–2, 225

O
O'Keeffe, Georgia, 97
Music, Pink and Blue No. 2, 98
O'Neill, Eugene, 47, 50n7, 70
Long Day's Journey Into Night,
47, 50n7
objects. *See also* behavioral
explorations; senses, guided
explorations
blindfold (guided exploration),
42, 119
CD/iPod (guided exploration), 121
exploration, 71, 86
hand sanitizer, 98
incense (guided exploration), 38,
119
mirror, 46, 106
overcoat (guided exploration), 44
pitch pipe, 104
play dough, 87, 96
ring, 108
salt (guided exploration), 40
stone (guided exploration), 49
string, 102
talisman (guided exploration),
121, 176
water bottle, 100

The manufacturer's authorised representative in the EU is Springer
Nature Customer Service Centre GmbH, Europaplatz 3, 69115 Heidelberg,
Germany. If you have any concerns regarding our products, please
contact ProductSafety@springernature.com

Printed and bound by CPI Group (UK) Ltd, Croydon, CR0 4YY
23/04/2026
02095595-0003